PROFESSIONAL CAPITAL

Transforming Teaching in Every School

ANDY HARGREAVES
MICHAEL FULLAN

Teachers College
Columbia University
New York and London

ONTARIO
PRINCIPALS'
COUNCIL
Exemplary Leadership in Public Education

Toronto, Ontario
Canada
www.principals.ca

Published simultaneously by Teachers College Press, 1234 Amsterdam Avenue, New York, NY 10027, and by the Ontario Principals' Council, 180 Dundas St. W, 25th Floor, Toronto, ON M5G 1Z8, Canada

Library of Congress Cataloging-in-Publication Data

Hargreaves, Andy.
    Professional capital : transforming teaching in every school / Andy Hargreaves, Michael Fullan.
        p.   cm.
    Includes bibliographical references and index.
    ISBN 978-0-8077-5332-3 (pbk. : alk. paper)
    ISBN 978-0-8077-5333-0 (hardcover : alk. paper)
        1. Teachers—In-service training—United States.   2. Effective teaching—United States.   3. Teachers—Professional relationships—United States.
    4. School improvement programs—United States.   I. Fullan, Michael.
    II. Title.
    LB1731.H268 2012
    370.71'1—dc23   2011051529

ISBN 978-0-8077-5332-3 (paperback)
ISBN 978-0-8077-5333-0 (hardcover)

Printed on acid-free paper
Manufactured in the United States of America

19 18 17 16 15 14 13 12   8 7 6 5 4 3 2 1

Advance Praise for *Professional Capital*

"Transforming education is one of the signature challenges of our times. *Professional Capital* sets out exactly and undeniably why the only way to do it is to honor and improve the profession of teaching. Written by two of the sharpest educational thinkers in the world, *Professional Capital* is an incisive critique of the failing reform movements in many countries and a powerful manifesto for the only strategy that can and does work. This book should revolutionize how policymakers and practitioners alike think and act in education. The price of failure is more than they or our children can afford."

—*Sir Ken Robinson*, educator, author

"A must-read! Brimming with insights and action ideas, Hargreaves and Fullan lay out a clear and cogent plan to transform American public education, community by community. *Professional Capital* is a finely written and urgent argument for real change in how we do our business."

—*Dan Domenech*, Executive Director,
American Association of School Administrators

"This important book makes it clear that teaching stands at a crossroads between policy decisions that will help create a great profession for all teachers or ones that will make teaching robotic and unexciting—hurting student learning for years to come. Hargreaves and Fullan urge us not to stand aside or to wait. It is time, they say, for the teaching profession to be led by, for, and with teachers and for others to join in concerted action to support that transformation."

—*Dennis Van Roekel*, President,
National Education Association

"I love the focus on professional capital and decisional capital. Hargreaves and Fullan give us a deep, practical understanding of ways to improve our schools and our school systems. This is new, exciting thinking."

—*Steve Munby*, Chief Executive,
National College for School Leadership

"Michael Fullan and Andy Hargreaves' latest book shows that transforming our public school system isn't magic: It comes from supporting all educators to 'teach like a pro.' The best performing education systems focus on improving the entire profession, not just lauding the highest performers and lopping off the lowest. Hargreaves and Fullan have, once again, amassed the evidence to challenge our thinking and better our practice—from the teachers' lounge, to the union hall, to state and national policy tables. Their concept of 'professional capital' can help redefine and refocus efforts at all levels to build and maximize teaching capacity and improve results for students."

—*Randi Weingarten*, President,
American Federation of Teachers

"The teaching profession is at a crossroads. Grounded in global knowledge and experience, *Professional Capital* provides brilliant insight into what the next generation of teaching should look like. This book is a must-read for anybody thinking of teaching in the 21st century."

—*Pasi Sahlberg*, Director General,
CIMO at the Finnish Ministry of Education

"This is a really terrific book. It's balanced, thoughtful, yet also passionate. Remarkable in its reconciling divergent positions in sensible ways. Among the best things Hargreaves and Fullan have done—which is no small compliment, I assure you!"

—*Ben Levin*, Professor and Canada Research
Chair in Education Leadership and Policy,
OISE/University of Toronto

"Anyone, anywhere who has anything to do with schools and the world of education will want to read, reflect, and react to the content of this book . . . a real treasure trove of riveting and informed insight into what really matters in teaching and learning. A powerful duo with a powerful challenge to the world of education. *Professional Capital* cries out for informed action—for the good of *all* children and their teachers."

—*Christopher Harrison*, President,
National Association of Head Teachers, England

To our first graduate teachers and mentors—

> *Dennis Warwick of Leeds University,*
> *Peter Woods of The Open University,*
> *David Hargreaves of Oxford University,*
> *Jan Loubser of The University of Toronto,*
> *Matt Miles of New York, and*
> *Per Dalin of Norway.*

They generously invested in our own professional capital.
We have done our best to give them a decent return.

An investment in knowledge always pays the best interest.

—*Benjamin Franklin*

Contents

Preface

WE SET OUT to write a revised edition of *What's Worth Fighting For in Your School,* a book we first put together more than 20 years ago.[1] We then discovered a whole new world that caused us to radically rethink what is now worth fighting for. The result, for us, is a fundamental repositioning of the future of the teaching profession. In this book, we equip teachers and those who work with them with insights, ideas, and actions that will dramatically improve their effectiveness, which in turn will improve societies and generations to come.

Our book is not about slices of alternatives and slivers of hope in a few classrooms or schools, here or there. It's not about how to procure or prepare a few young and enthusiastic new teachers to lift everyone's spirits. Nor is it about moving leaders along a pipeline of preparation to replace the ones who will retire. And it's not even about creating a parallel system of new charter schools and their international look-alikes that promise to break free from local district bureaucracies. Rather, our book is about a collective transformation of public education achieved by all teachers and leaders in every school. And it's about how to secure this through a new strategy that harnesses the commitments and capabilities of the many: the power of *professional capital.*

In our original book, we highlighted and honored the passions and purposes of teaching—the things that are easily overlooked in standards statements and improvement plans but that give teaching its vibrancy and keep calling people to the work, despite everything. We said that teachers must be treated with dignity, as people who have lives and careers, not just as performers who must produce results. And we urged teachers and administrators to break down the walls of classroom isolation and convert teaching into a more collaborative and collegial profession—not just because this is

professionally supportive but because
it also improves student learning and
achievement.

> ◆❯ . . . people care about the
> quality of teaching. And this is
> putting teachers and teaching
> at the forefront of change.

We have returned to these core
themes in this book and updated them
so they apply to and address a new edu-
cational world of professional learning communities, evidence-informed
decision-making, and large-scale reform. Ultimately, though, we have ended
up critiquing and challenging the entire nature and future of the teaching
profession. This is because we believe we are facing the greatest challenge to
the teaching profession that has occurred in more than half a century.

Teaching is at a crossroads: a crossroads at the top of the world. Never
before have teachers, teaching, and the future of teaching had such elevated
importance. There is widespread agreement now that of all the factors inside
the school that affect children's learning and achievement, the most important is the teacher—not standards, assessments, resources, or even the
school's leadership, but the quality of the teacher. Teachers really matter. And
the good news is that there is now a sense of great urgency in politics, in the
teaching profession, and also among the public about the need to get more
high-quality teachers. More and more people care about the quality of teaching. And this is putting teachers and teaching at the forefront of change.

But alongside the urgency, or perhaps even because of it, there is a lot of
argument and more than a little aggravation about what high-quality teaching looks like and what's the best way to get it and keep it. The crossroads
are shrouded in a fog of misunderstandings about teachers and teaching,
and if we take the wrong road forward, precipices are looming on many
sides.

1. One road is just a flat-out assault on teachers' pensions and security. It comes out of the global financial collapse and the expectation that the public sector and its large teaching force should pay
   the price. In England, one government minister has proclaimed
   that excellence will occur in the public sector only when there is
   "some real discipline and some fear" of job losses.[2] In the United
   States, other commentators have come out against teacher compensation being "heavily weighted towards retirement benefits,"[3] arguing (without any real data) that younger teachers want more money

sooner at the expense of security later on. There's no evidence that less security will increase teacher quality, though, or that, after a global economic meltdown, young people even want such a trade-off. This is a bad road to follow.

2. A second (and related) false road is a monetary one. In the United States, state departments of education have committees stacked with economists who are coming up with formulas to pay teachers according to their individual performance—especially in relation to their students' test scores. They have to do this to comply with the Race to the Top grants that the federal government has given them. The idea is not restricted to the United States. This strategy has no historical precedent of success, it flies in the face of psychological research indicating that financial reward only improves performance in areas of low-level skill, not in complex jobs like teaching, and it creates perverse incentives for expert teachers to avoid difficult students or challenging classes that might depress their test scores.[4] At best, performance-related pay will motivate a few teachers while alienating others and neglecting the majority. It's a political fix that will lead to professional folly, and we should steer well clear of it.

3. A third (and also related) false road is just to make teaching simpler: to diminish teachers' judgment and professionalism so that less-qualified people can do it. Narrow the curriculum, turn to technology, prescribe and pace the instruction, teach to the test, reduce literacy to short comprehension passages rather than rich engagements with absorbing texts, and you start to standardize instruction, ignore cultural and linguistic diversity, treat teachers as mere delivery agents for government policies, and constrain teachers' capacity to respond to their students' varying needs. If this is the kind of teaching you want, it needn't take so long to prepare people to do it—so out go long periods of preparation and Master's degrees, and in come (cheaper) alternate routes to certification and compressed training schemes. These "alternate" approaches are not used by any of the highest performing economies, however. Dumb down teaching, and you will dumb down learning and fall further behind the most competitive educational systems and economies. That cannot be the right road either.

There must be better ways forward than these. Woody Allen was joking when he advised that "More than any other time in history, mankind faces a crossroads. One path leads to despair and utter hopelessness; the other, to total extinction. Let us pray we have the wisdom to choose correctly." Current efforts to reform the teaching profession are in danger of turning this joke into a reality!

In the face of all these threats, teachers and their organizations are right to defend their profession—sticking up for their hard-earned pensions, resisting bureaucratic standardization, and opposing systems and leaders who try to impose required after-school meetings focused on implementing their own or their superiors' agendas that masquerade as professional development. But sometimes this rightful resistance can turn into a 1970s-style defensive nostalgia for a time when professional autonomy was equated with individual classroom autonomy, when the judgment of the teacher seemed to be unquestioningly respected and always prevailed. In teaching, as in medicine, we cannot improve the quality of the profession by retreating to a four-decades-old version of it.

This book tries to bring clarity and power to the teacher quality problem and its solution. How can the teaching profession become a force for continuous change that benefits all individuals and society as a whole?

Ever since one of the teachers' federations in Ontario came to us in the late 1980s with the concept of *What's Worth Fighting For*, we have been on this quest individually and together. In those early days, the federation asked for something that was "deeply insightful" and contained solid and doable "guidelines for action." Now we need something even more. With teaching at the crossroads of the future, we must figure out with urgency and clarity how everyone can rally together for the good of all our children and the next generation of our society.

To teach like a professional or teach *like a pro,* as they say in the language of sports, is a personal commitment to rigorous training, continuous learning, collegial feedback, respect for evidence, responsiveness to parents, striving for excellence, and going far beyond the requirements of any written contract. But teaching like a pro, day in, day out, cannot be sustained unless all your colleagues teach like pros too. Whether you are alone in your classroom or working in a team, teaching like a pro means that the confidence, competence, and critical feedback you get from your colleagues is always with you. This book argues that teaching like a pro is a collective and transparent responsibility—one in which governments and teacher unions or federations must set aside their differences and start to lead the way.

Of course, teams can fall prey to what Irving Janis famously called "groupthink," where the group comes to have an unwavering mind of its own, and individual members go along with it unquestioningly.[5] Psychiatrist Wilfred Bion found that groupthink manifests itself in three forms of behavior that impair the group's capacity to problem-solve and grow: dependency (looking for leaders to lead the way), fight–flight (attack or avoidance), and pairing (spinning off into subgroups).[6] Groupthink occurs when system administrators use cynical and even corrupt methods to raise test scores because "everyone's doing it," or when collegial norms allow sarcastic or other unprofessional behaviors of a teacher toward his or her students to go unchallenged.

Teams and cross-school clusters can also be hijacked to force through top-down agendas. They can become oppressive and contrived. This book is about how to create collective professional responsibility without the effort degenerating into either pervasive groupthink or contrived collegiality. It's a book that uncovers what it is like to be a teacher and explores what the ups and downs of teaching look and feel like. It begins with the *being* and *doing* of teaching and builds from there to explore how to reconstruct and *reculture* the profession as a whole. It is about the radical betterment of the profession for the good of society and for the good of teachers themselves.

Our message is that teachers and teacher leaders, along with system leaders who want to build an effective and highly charged profession, need to seize this crucial moment, confront the core problems, present and develop clear alternatives, and turn those alternatives into an energizing reality. It is time to change the game.

The core of our case is founded on a new concept that we hope and believe can change how we all think about teaching, the quality of teaching, and how to create that quality. We call this *professional capital*—the systematic development and integration of three kinds of capital—human, social, and decisional—into the teaching profession.

Instead of taking false roads and blind alleys, we need to head in a radically new direction. Professional capital is about collective responsibility, not individual autonomy; about scientific evidence as well as personal judgment; about being open to one's clients rather than standing on a pedestal above them; and ultimately about being tough on those colleagues who, after every effort and encouragement, fall short of their professional mission and let their peers as well as their students down. This book defines and fleshes out the essence of professional capital. Just as importantly, it shows how to develop professional capital, how to circulate it, and how to reinvest it so that you can help create a dynamic new profession that will benefit every school in the nation, whatever your country.

> ◆ This book defines and fleshes out the essence of professional capital . . . how to develop professional capital, how to circulate it, and how to reinvest it so that you can help create a dynamic new profession that will benefit every school in the nation, whatever your country.

We are not just talking about having a *good* system. Professional capital, by definition, means having and building a system that will be truly *great*. When McKinsey & Company found that advanced systems relied more and more on peers as the source of innovation and deep improvement,[7] they were saying just that—you can only get great by having an outstanding teaching profession. Professional capital pushes the limits of what teachers will be able to achieve for every child.

If we think about teaching in terms of the creation and circulation, and the investment and reinvestment, of professional capital, this will transform how we understand the teaching profession and how to change it. Professional capital, we believe, can lift the fog of misunderstandings about teaching and point out the road ahead that can be productive for all of us. Our job is to set out the evidence, articulate the idea, and indicate the direction. The resulting actions must eventually occur everywhere, but the most important ones for you and your colleagues must necessarily begin with you.

In the end, nobody can give you professional capital. It's an investment, not a donation, handout, or gift. Governments can create good or bad climates for investment in professional capital, of course, by praising teachers or attacking them, increasing resources for schools or slashing their budgets, and trusting that teachers will usually do their best or micromanaging everything in case they don't. The political responsibilities here are immense. Political leaders must expect, encourage, push for, and invest in professional capital. But first and foremost, individually and collectively, professional capital is something that must be acquired, spread, and reinvested by teachers themselves—individually and together. Nobody's going to be prepared to invest in anyone unless they are willing to invest in themselves. This is by far the best place, and indeed the first place, to begin.

Building professional capital is therefore an opportunity and responsibility for all of us—from supporting and working with the teacher in the class next door, to transforming an entire system. Whole system change, we have learned, is not a kind of magic. It involves and absolutely requires individual and collective acts of investment in an inspirational vision and a coherent set of actions that build everyone's capability and keep everyone learning as they continue to move forward. Our goal in *Professional Capital* is to push, pull, and nudge the individual, the group, and the system—making the development of professional capital a common quest that improves learning and achievement everywhere. Let's begin this critical journey of transformation.

Acknowledgments

WE ARE extremely grateful to Claudia Cuttress, Maureen Hughes, and Karen Lam for supporting us so well through the complex editorial stages of completing this book. Steve Cardwell, J.-C. Couture, Chris Harrison, Ben Levin, Mona Mourshed, Justo Robles, Carol Rolheiser, Pasi Sahlberg, Dennis Shirley, and Marla Ucelli gave us detailed feedback on our earlier draft and were all successful in keeping the title and the big idea of professional capital in this book secret. They knew we would have to kill them if they didn't—but we are grateful all the same!

Our publishers, Carole Saltz and the staff at Teachers College Press, have shown more patience than we had a right to expect, and more faith than we perhaps deserved as we kept promising that the wait would be worth it. And once we delivered, they did a great job in positioning the book in the political and professional action agenda. They are a truly astonishing team!

Our wives and children have also not only supported our work in general but provided candid feedback on this text in particular. Thanks so much to Pauline, Lucy, and Stuart Hargreaves, and to Wendy, Conor, Bailey, Josh, Maureen, and Chris Fullan—our own nest eggs of human, social, and spiritual capital in a complex world.

Our very last acknowledgment is, strangely, to each other. Writing this book together has affirmed for both of us that more important even than learning to agree is the principle of agreeing to learn, as a prime professional value.

Andy Hargreaves
Michael Fullan
February 2012

◈ **CHAPTER ONE** ◈

A Capital Idea

Capital *adj*: relating to or being assets that add to long-term net worth   —*Merriam-Webster dictionary*

CAPITAL RELATES to one's own or a group's worth, particularly concerning assets that can be leveraged to accomplish desired goals. We already know about business and financial capital. We understand that you have to make an investment if you want a return, that if you want growth, you can't just squirrel away your assets but instead you need to put them to work. Capital must circulate if assets are going to grow. And governments are crucial in creating the conditions and the levels of confidence that can stimulate or discourage capital investment. Of course, we're not talking only about financial capital—we're talking about how we invest in people and get returns from those investments too.

People have written about and argued in favor of developing many different kinds of capital. Financial capital is the obvious one. But cultural capital, spiritual capital, "natural" capital, and even "erotic" capital all have their proponents as well. This book is about *professional capital*. It takes the basic and powerful idea of capital and articulates its importance for professional work, professional capacity, and professional effectiveness—particularly in the teaching profession.

TWO KINDS OF CAPITAL

People don't really disagree about the importance of getting and keeping good teachers and good teaching. However, two schools of thought about

1

different kinds of capital are driving entire nations in diametrically oppo-site directions on this front.

Business Capital

In the first view, what kinds of teachers we need and how best to get them are driven by ideas about *business capital*. Here, following the collapse of worldwide property and financial markets, the primary purpose of educa-tion is to serve as a big new market for investment in technology, curricu-lum and testing materials, and schools themselves as for-profit enterprises. In the estimates of some multinational moguls, this is a massive $500 billion market.[1]

When education is organized to get quick returns on business invest-ment, and to increase immediate returns by lowering that investment, it favors a teaching force that is young, flexible, temporary, inexpensive to train at the beginning, un-pensioned at the end (except by teachers' own self-investment), and replaceable wherever possible by technology. Finding and keeping good teachers then becomes about seeking out and deploying (but not really developing or investing in) *existing human capital*—hunting for talented individuals, working them hard, and moving them on when they get restless or become spent. This is the human widget image of the profession.

The *business capital* strategy toward teaching is advocated aggressively in the United States and is gaining ground in places like the United Kingdom and several countries in Europe. Yet, as we will see later, none of the most successful school systems around the world go anywhere near this approach in building one of their most valuable societal assets. In Finland, South Korea, and Singapore, teachers are nation builders, top leaders say. They are indispensable national assets.

Professional Capital

A second view—our own—promotes what we call *professional capital*. This strategy has already been adopted by the highest performing economies and educational systems in the world. Countries and communities that invest in *professional capital* recognize that educational spending is a long-term investment in developing human capital from early childhood to adult life, to reap rewards of economic productivity and social cohesion in the next generation. A big part of this investment is in high-quality teachers and teaching. In this view, getting good teaching for all learners requires teachers to be highly committed, thoroughly prepared, continuously developed, properly paid, well networked with each other to maximize their own improvement, and able to make effective judgments using all their capabilities and experience.

Professional capital is itself made up of three other kinds of capital—human, social, and decisional. A lot has been written about the first kind—*human capital.* Alan Odden's book on *The Strategic Management of Human Capital in Education* defines human capital as "talent" and describes how to get more of it, develop it, and sustain it.[2] Strangely, though, as we will show, you can't get much human capital by just focusing on the capital of individuals. Capital has to be circulated and shared. Groups, teams, and communities are far more powerful than individuals when it comes to developing human capital.

Human capital therefore must be complemented by and even organized in terms of what is called *social capital.* Like human capital, the idea and strategy of social capital, as we will explain later, also has a distinguished history. The important point for now concerns the contributions of human and social capital, respectively. Carrie Leana, a business professor at the University of Pittsburgh, points out the well-known finding that patterns of interaction among teachers and between teachers and administrators that are focused on student learning make a large and measurable difference in student achievement and sustained improvement. She calls this *social capital,* which she contrasts with *individual capital* that is based on the belief in the power of individuals to change the system. By contrast, Leana shows that the group is far more powerful than the individual. You need individuals, of course, but the system won't change, indeed individuals won't change in large numbers, unless development becomes a persistent collective enterprise.

Leana has been closely examining the relationship between human and social capital. She and her team followed over 1,000 fourth- and fifth-grade teachers in a representative sample of 130 elementary schools across New York City. The human capital measures included individual teacher qualifications, experience, and ability to teach. Social capital was measured in terms of the frequency and focus of conversations and interactions with peers that centered on instruction, and was based on feelings of trust and closeness between teachers.

Leana also obtained the mathematics scores of the students of these teachers at the beginning of the year and compared them to the gains by year-end. She found that teachers with high social capital increased their students' mathematics scores by 5.7% more than teachers with lower social capital scores. Teachers who were both more able (high human capital), and had stronger ties with their peers (high social capital) prompted the biggest gains in mathematics achievement. She also found that low-ability teachers perform as well as teachers of average ability "*if* they have strong social capital in their school."[3] In short, high social capital and high human capital must be combined.

Because it is necessary to have both high human and high social capital, the question remains: How can we develop both of them? Here is the answer: If you concentrate your efforts on increasing individual talent, you will have a devil of a job producing greater social capital. There is just no mechanism or motivation to bring all that talent together. The reverse is not true. High social capital does generate increased human capital. Individuals get confidence, learning, and feedback from having the right kind of people and the right kinds of interactions and relationships around them.

Consider what happens when a talented individual enters a school low on social capital. Although it is possible to make a difference through heroic effort, eventually the overwhelming likelihood is that the person will leave or burn out in the process. We set out considerable evidence later on to back up this observation. Now consider the reverse: A teacher who is low on human capital and has poor initial confidence or undeveloped skills enters a highly collaborative school. Chances are high that this teacher will be socialized into greater teamwork and receive the assistance, support, ideas, and feedback to help him or her improve. This is dramatically powerful when you stop and think about it. Imagine that you would become a better teacher just by joining the staff of a different and better school.

Everything we say about individual human capital versus collaborative social capital applies not only to teachers but also to schools. A few unusually innovative schools or ones that beat the odds here or there through the brilliance of individual teachers, the charismatic leadership of their principals, and the endless self-sacrifice of everyone may perform far beyond expectations for a few years. But efforts to turn around individual schools by finding the right individual leaders, or by replacing all the bad individual teachers with good ones, or by parachuting in an outside intervention team are doomed to achieve temporary gains at best. The gains almost always disappear after the intervention teams pull out, once the key leaders leave, or when the overworked and isolated staff finally run out of steam. If we need much more social capital within our schools—colleague to colleague, peer to peer—we need this just as much across and between our schools. Professional capital as human capital plus social capital is therefore a personal thing, a within-school thing, and a whole-system thing. In the end, professional capital must become a system quality and a system commitment if it is to develop school systems further.

There is more. *Professional capital* also has a third essential element. We will unpack this later, but think of professional capital as the product of *human capital,* and *social capital,* and *decisional capital.* Making decisions in complex situations is what professionalism is all about. The pros do this all the time. They come to have competence, judgment, insight, inspiration, and the capacity for improvisation as they strive for exceptional performance. They do this when no one is looking, and they do it through and with their colleagues and the team. They exercise their judgments and decisions with collective responsibility, openness to feedback, and willing transparency. They are not afraid to make mistakes as long as they learn from them. They have pride in their work. They are respected by peers and by the public for knowing what they are doing. They strive to outdo themselves and each other in a spirit of making greater individual and collective contributions.

When the vast majority of teachers come to exemplify the power of professional capital, they become smart and talented, committed and collegial, thoughtful and wise. Their moral purpose is expressed in their relentless, expert-driven pursuit of serving their students and their communities, and in learning, always learning, how to do that better. Those few colleagues who persistently fall short of the mark, even after extensive assistance and support, will eventually not be tolerated by their peers because they let their profession and their students down by not teaching like pros!

THE WRONG STRATEGIES

People can only teach like pros when they want and know how to do so— when they have the right knowledge and background, the colleagues around them who will keep them performing at their peak, and the time and experience that underpin the ability to make wise judgments and decisions that

are at the heart of all professionals'
actions. Instead, in the United States,
at least, there is large-scale evidence
that 40% of K–12 teachers are currently "disheartened" with their job,
hardly an expression of dynamic professional capital driving the nation's
next generations forward![4]

> ◆❯ ...fear, force, and financial
> short-sightedness won't get you a
> high-quality teaching profession
> brimming with human, social,
> and decisional capital!

The United States and England—neither of them impressive performers
on the Organization for Economic Cooperation and Development's (OECD)
highly respected international tests of student achievement, where they lan-
guish somewhere between 17th and 31st, depending on the subject being
tested—have recently drawn most of their teachers from the lower reaches
of the university graduating cohort, not the highest ones (not much *human
capital* there); and they pump more and more wasted resources (or short-
term *business capital*) into schemes like Teach for America, Teach First, and
other kinds of alternate certifications that cram the preparation of teachers
into just a few short weeks and see many of their qualified teachers leaving
after only a few years in the job.[5] These schemes sometimes attract outstanding *individuals,* but they will never change the *system.* If you make a
low investment, you won't get much of a return. These short-term strategies driven by *business capital* deprive younger teachers of the time to
develop the *social capital* of working with long-term professional communities in the school or with the wider communities served by their schools.
They are given insufficient opportunities to develop the practice and experience over many years that underpin the *decisional capital* of wise professional judgment.

In response, there's no use producing a study or two showing that the
results for alternately certified teachers are no worse than the average for the
existing teaching force—because the point is that in the United States and
the United Kingdom, this average, coming, as it does, from the lower ranks
of university graduation, is already far too low.[6] And the "capital punishment" approach taken by too many policy makers of bashing the teaching
profession, killing off its unions, and blaming public schools in impoverished communities for their outcomes is not going to raise this average
either. We need teachers and teaching to be the best and to be drawn from
the best—as in the world's highest performing systems—not just cheap
enough or good enough to get by! Later on we will show that attracting tal-

ented and committed teachers *and* establishing cultures for them to work in teams must go together. There are no silver bullets here, but there are silver linings if you do both in concert.

Nor will defensive teacher unionism do anything to advance the cause of teaching like a pro unless unions and federations can follow their most avant-garde leaders to share or even lead the responsibility for turning around low-performing schools (as the California Teachers' Association has done), work in partnership with their governments on teacher-driven innovation and inquiry (as is the case with teacher federations in Alberta and Ontario in Canada), or implement creative and courageous processes of peer-driven performance review that raise the standards of the profession (as in more than a dozen jurisdictions in the United States).[7]

Thus, fear, force, and financial short-sightedness won't get you a high-quality teaching profession brimming with human, social, and decisional capital! So what will?

THE RIGHT ANSWERS

We wrote this book to lay out a fresh approach to changing education and strengthening professional effectiveness that includes both the vision and a coherent set of actions to enact and sustain that vision. The ideas are based on a deeper understanding of teachers and teaching—of what it means to teach like a pro. Not only do we think the idea is accurate and attractive, but we also believe the action agenda is clear. People are motivated by good ideas tied to action; they are energized even more by pursuing action with others; they are spurred on still further by learning from their mistakes; and they are ultimately propelled by actions that make an impact—what we call "moral imperative realized."[8]

But, as an educator, you can't make progress unless you start the journey in the first place, unless you take the first steps yourself. These first steps are the hardest. Dangers, risks, opposition, and disappointment all lie in wait. But professional capital can be both your armor and your sword. It can cut through the misunderstandings and misrepresentations of teaching. It can protect you against attacks on your profession. If you bring others with you, your strength and influence will multiply—especially if you include a few skeptics and even some naysayers along the way. Be determined that it can be done, by all of you together, and you will not be defeated in your quest.

In *Join the Club: How Peer Pressure Can Transform the World,* Pulitzer Prize–winning author Tina Rosenberg shows how small groups have banded together using each other as peers to work against smoking in one state in the United States, against AIDS in Africa, and against a brutal dictatorship in Eastern Europe.[9] In each case, it was peers, fighting against all odds, who joined together to bring about a social revolution. Their power came from the need for individuals to belong to something greater than themselves and to do something that would transform society for the better.

Their greatest accomplishment was not overpowering their external adversaries, but holding the group together during the difficult initial stages, through peer support and peer pressure. People care greatly about the respect of their peers. What Rosenberg uncovers is how these fragile groups ended up "persuading people [basically each other] to take action that is crucial to their long-term well-being but appears unpleasant, dangerous, or psychologically difficult today."[10] Rosenberg calls it "the social cure."

Social media today carry additional potential for enhancing professional capital, but these media also have their pitfalls. For every Arab Spring there is a "London riot." Technology may have a role in the development of social capital, but the "social cure" is ultimately and perhaps primarily about people and their values, not about technological innovation as the source of inspiration.

Mary Parker Follett, a community developer, writer, and business consultant, knew this over 100 years ago when she showed how *power with* is the source of new breakthroughs, as distinct from *power over.*[11] The husband and wife team of Joe Blase and Jo Blase, experts on micro-politics in education, are the most virulent critics of principals who exercise *power over* their teachers and who silence them by playing off teachers against each other, handing out undesirable rooms and assignments to their critics, reneging on promotions they promised in exchange for their teachers' compliance, and so on.[12] Yet the Blases are equally ardent advocates for principals and teachers to engage in *power with* each other to support energizing changes that benefit their students and the lives of teachers as well. Margaret Mead memorably observed: "Never doubt that a small group of thoughtful, committed citizens can change the world."[13] Mead did not say that *individuals* working alone could change the world. She said that the *group* (albeit in the minority in the beginning) is the key to change—and with professional capital as its armor and political capital as its ally, this group can become very powerful indeed.

Still, there are some mammoth obstacles that can divert group action into unproductive directions. When groups feel mistreated, they can become dysfunctional—whether they are at the top or at the bottom. These tendencies are captured in Briskin and colleagues' *The Power of Collective Wisdom and the Trap of Collective Folly.*[14]

Collective folly occurs when "protecting us" is pursued by "attacking them." Briskin and colleagues show that when highly polarized groups face each other, "motives are often suspect, (and) any interaction can quickly become an opportunity for attack, one side seeking to bolster its positions and undermine the credibility of the other."[15] The authors later observe how "new ideas are often viewed as heretical, and few things are more subversive than the possibility that we can learn to respect each other, find ways to work out our differences, and deepen our capacity for wisdom."[16] This "tragedy of polarized groups" is all too evident in political battles over the future of the teaching profession in places like the United Kingdom and the United States.

The movement from *power over* to *power with* is still a struggle. But it is a struggle for a greater social good, not for self-interest or supremacy. It is a struggle that should not be a win–lose battle, but that will still require initial positive pushes and pulls from small groups at both the bottom and the top—pushes and pulls that you can be part of and that you might even start. Rosenberg's social cure is found in how small groups at any level and all levels of society exercise power with each other for a greater social good. The development of *professional capital* is a quest for such a new "social cure" for what ails and assails the teaching profession, and what ails society as a whole. In the following chapters, in pursuit of this quest, we endeavor to articulate an inspiring vision of the future for the teaching profession, along with a coherent set of actions to get there. These are, we think, capital ideas!

CHAPTER TWO

Competing Views of Teaching

TEACHING IS a glorious profession, but it has been wilting badly over the past 30 years in the United States. With the decline of public funding across the world, it will be increasingly imperiled almost everywhere else too.

Today, the daily agonies trump the occasional ecstasies for far too many teachers and their students. The passion for learning and teaching, the pleasure of being lost in a compelling story, the awe and excitement of participating in great drama or producing original art, the engrossing study of pond life and engaging with the wonders of nature, the time to be consoled over a lost friendship—all these things that make classrooms wondrous and stay with children for the rest of their lives have been superseded in many places by the push for higher test scores, the obsession with numerical achievement data, and the narrow concentration on bulldozing through the basics at the price of everything else.

PINPOINTING THE PROBLEMS

Achievement matters and so does evidence, but the relentlessly serious pursuit of increases in the basic comprehension skills that can be demonstrated on standardized tests should never overshadow what gives teaching its mystery and majesty—what brings children joyfully into classrooms, what introduces them to interests that will absorb them for the rest of their lives, and what lifts them back up when their lives have taken a tumble. The view that what schools should be about are performance, scores, and results to excess has lost sight of all the other things that characterize teaching, that teachers bring to their work, and that keep them and their children motivated. This does not mean that evidence-based strategies are unimportant. On the contrary, we will see later that thoughtful use of such strategies is essential to achieving broad and deep learning goals and is an integral part of professional capital. It is not the employment of evidence that is the problem today, but the obsessions with numerical data, technological gadgetry, and narrow test-driven goals instead of and above everything else, that are dysfunctional.

And all of these problems are magnified many times over when system leaders at the top deplete or strip away assets from the teachers who must carry out the work at the bottom. The new obstacles present debilitating dilemmas:

- How can you embrace new technology when even your most fundamental textbooks are decades old?
- How are you supposed to improve your literacy practice when cutbacks have reduced the number of literacy coaches to one for every 30 schools?
- What messages are you getting about the value of your own professional development when the only professional learning community time is low-cost meetings to implement laid-on agendas?
- Can you really still track and care effectively for your students as a high school teacher when almost all of the counselors have been removed from high schools, as has happened in the state of California?
- Can you truly support the range of students with special educational needs in your class when your classroom assistants have been stripped away from you, as has been happening in Ireland?
- And where is the justice of accountability and performance-based pay when teachers who challenge or disagree with their principals, for the best professional reasons, are sometimes set up for failure by being assigned to fresh grades they are not trained for, with brand new preparation requirements each time, year after year, in classrooms that are falling apart?

But if governments and administrators overlook or overrule the complex, creative, and compassionate realities of what makes excellent teaching, neither are teachers and their organizations always stepping up to the plate with clear alternatives. They are usually right to resist the attacks of their business-driven opponents, but in doing so, they sometimes become their own worst enemies. The issue here is not one of repeating the hackneyed argument about removing poor or bad teachers from the profession. Finland does not obsess about this. Indeed it concentrates on creating a culture and a system that stimulates and supports a teaching profession where practically everyone is very capable.[1] We need to pay attention to incompetence and to incalcitrance toward the quest for improvement where it exists, but we should not treat these things as the most important or most neglected challenges for the profession. The bigger challenges are more sinister and more subtle.

Teachers' organizations and cultures rightly oppose performance-based pay related to test scores. Yet very often, the profession resists acknowledging that anyone is better than anyone else.

- How often have we heard Teachers of the Year say that the first thing that happened to them after they received their award was that they were then ostracized by their existing colleagues?
- How often do schools sink into a saccharine celebration of shared successes instead of clearly recognizing that some teachers perform at a level superior to others, and that less-outstanding colleagues could benefit from their help?
- Why can't more countries develop the different career paths and rewards for teachers that include a Master Teacher category, like Singapore,[2] where you are rewarded and recognized more for your consistent practical excellence (not test score performance) than for extra seniority or administrative responsibility (as has usually become the case with similar schemes in other countries)?[3]

If some energetic or innovative teachers are rewarded for their efforts by being awarded professional development opportunities to present at national or international conferences or to partner with schools overseas, do they get admiration from their colleagues or envy? Teachers may not like how mandated meetings or professional community time are taken up with poring over spreadsheets to find the quick fixes that can push up performance results, but the answer is not to dig in to their classrooms, just do their own thing, and demand that they be left alone. When teachers see colleagues doing harm to their students—for instance by assessing their work arbitrarily or unfairly, by meting out excessive punishments to their students, or by failing to prepare their lessons conscientiously—do they intervene and challenge this behavior as a concerned colleague, or do they pass the buck to the principal after the behavior has escalated and at a time when it has really become too late?[4] And where do the unions or federations stand on rewards, recognition, different levels of proficiency, and challenging shortfalls in professional classroom conduct as a collective responsibility?

Governments and administrators have a lot of work to do in coming to grips with the realities of teaching. In many countries, the transformation of the teaching profession and of professional conduct is clearly also a challenge for the profession itself. To change all this, we really do have to understand teaching and teachers more fully and more fairly—and this is the subject of this chapter and the next.

Good learning comes from good teaching. More and better learning and greater achievement for everyone require being able to find and keep more good teachers. Nobody seriously argues that we should fill our schools with low-quality, unmotivated teachers who don't like children, don't know their material, and can't get it across! So let's concentrate our efforts not on bigger budgets, smaller classes, changing the curriculum, or altering the size of schools—but on procuring and producing the best teachers we can get. It's as simple as that—isn't it?

TWO VISIONS OF TEACHING

In Chapter 1 we introduced two kinds of capital—business capital and professional capital—and described the approach those favoring each view took toward changing teaching. These are two very different images of what teaching as a profession can be. The first image is tantamount to a systematic and pervasive attack on the profession itself. The business capital image feeds on and fuels outworn stereotypes of teachers and teaching—and we address these in Chapter 3. The second image builds the individual and collective capital of the profession to become ever more effective in its charge to improve learning and achievement for all students, develop their well-being and character, and close the gap between those from advantaged and those from disadvantaged social backgrounds.

The *business capital* view of teaching assumes that:

- Good teaching may be emotionally demanding, but it is technically simple.
- Good teaching is a quick study requiring only moderate intellectual ability.
- Good teaching is hard at first, but with dedication can be mastered readily.
- Good teaching should be driven by hard performance data about what works and where best to target one's efforts.
- Good teaching comes down to enthusiasm, hard work, raw talent, and measurable results.
- Good teaching is often replaceable by online instruction.

The *professional capital* view of teaching assumes, by contrast, that:

- Good teaching is technically sophisticated and difficult.
- Good teaching requires high levels of education and long periods of training.
- Good teaching is perfected through continuous improvement.
- Good teaching involves wise judgment informed by evidence and experience.
- Good teaching is a collective accomplishment and responsibility.
- Good teaching maximizes, mediates, and moderates online instruction.

Note that neither of these positions—*business capital* nor *professional capital*—defends a system where older and more experienced teachers get the easiest classes, where job allocations are made according to seniority and not suitability, where professional learning is an individual option rather than a collective responsibility, and where contracts are anachronistically defined in terms of classroom contact time. Neither position supports a world where the many-headed Hydra of system bureaucracies squares off against the one-eyed Cyclops of old-style unionism to block innovation and let poor performance persist. So let's not defend the indefensible, but get on to grittier terrain instead.

The Misplaced Focus on Individual-Teacher Quality

The most abused educational research finding these days is this: "*the quality of the teacher is the single most important determinant in the learning of the student.*" This finding was first presented by an agricultural economist— William Sanders—who made some remarkable claims about the impact of individual teacher quality on student achievement.[5] Using value-added evidence that took two hypothetical students starting equally at the 50th percentile of performance, Sanders and Rivers demonstrated what happens when Student A receives 3 years of learning from a high-quality teacher (top 20%), while Student B experiences 3 years with a low-performing teacher (bottom 20%). At the end of the 3 years, Student A performs at the 90th percentile, while Student B is at the 37th percentile. One has gained ground substantially; the other has actually gone backward—and the two now differ by 53 percentile points.

If this evidence seems outdated, in 2010 the *Los Angeles Times* shook the teacher quality debate with another explosive set of findings. Reporters gained access to 7 years of value-added test performance data for 6,000 third-through fifth-grade teachers in English and mathematics in the Los Angeles Unified Public School District—one of the poorest performing districts in the United States. They passed the data to expert economists, who came up with an even more remarkable finding. There were differences of up to 41% in value-added performance between teachers of the same kinds of children *in the very same school*! Reporters even identified the poorest performing culprits by name, heaping shame and scorn upon them.[6]

With such shocking and seemingly self-evident findings, politicians and pundits have not been slow to reload their guns with silver bullets. Under-standably, people have little sympathy for the bottom 20% of teachers, who are so clearly letting their students down. What about those top 20%, succeeding against the odds? Surely they deserve to be rewarded based on their students' value-added test score gains! Get tough on those at the bottom and reward those at the top! Ditch the expensive old slackers cruising into retirement on tenure and benefits and replace them with young and eager tyros ready to make schools rock! That's pretty much the answer in the United States these days. It seems obvious, doesn't it—until we look at what America's competitors are doing! These competitors know that the main point is not the effect of the individual teacher, for better or worse, here and there, that counts, but rather how you maximize the cumulative effect of many, many teachers over time for each and every student. Students do very well because they have a *series* of very good teachers—not by chance, but by design. In other words, you have to transform the *entire profession*—not just the bottom 20% and top 20%, but the whole 100%. There is no getting around that hard fact! And continuously improving the 100% is indeed what the top-performing countries do. Their students experience high-quality teachers year after year.

Sharpening the Focus on the Quality of the Profession

Focusing on individual teacher quality reminds us of the old joke about the person looking under the streetlamp for the keys he lost, even though he dropped them in the shadows. The person preferred to look where the light happened to be, not where the act of searching would prove harder but would more likely enable him to find what he was looking for. The keys to teacher quality are not to be found where the light is most obvious or where some prominent figures may choose to shine it. We must look harder for these keys, but the result will reward our search.

High-performing countries—Finland, Singapore, South Korea, and Canada, which make up the four leading nations on the OECD's Programme for International Student Assessment (PISA) tests of student achievement—typically draw their teachers from the top 30% of the university graduating class, while the United States and other lower performing countries such as England (both positioned way down in the low teens to twenties percent on the PISA rankings) at best recruit mostly from the bottom 40%.[7] Put another way, 100% of teachers in Finland, for example, come from the top 30% of graduates, while in the United States only 23% are from the top third (and just 14% in high-poverty schools). Just as crucially, the top nations invest in better working conditions on the job—a clear and commonly held sense of purpose and direction, opportunity to work with good colleagues, professional development to increase skills, new leadership roles, access to technology and good data, and so on. In short, both initial attraction to the profession and continued learning on the job with others combine to systematically foster, strengthen, and maintain professional capital.

Teaching is an attractive profession in all high-performing countries. Teachers are praised and prized for what they do. They are seen as the builders of their nations. Starting salaries for teachers in Singapore, for example, compare favorably with the salaries of engineers and other professionals so that teaching can attract the best of the best—even and especially in mathematics and science. Finnish teachers have such high status that teaching is one of the top two preferred occupations for a future spouse—right up there with medicine and higher than business or law![8] In stark con-

> ◆> Teaching is an attractive profession in all high-performing countries. Teachers are praised and prized for what they do. They are seen as the builders of their nations.

trast, in the United States, teachers and teacher unions are constantly vilified by politicians and in the media. They are portrayed as being a blight, not a blessing. Teachers are the new bankers—soft targets for all of society's complaints.

Then there's the matter of working conditions. In Canada, with the exception of a few schools in remote aboriginal communities, you can go to the most isolated rural backwaters or into the country's toughest urban neighborhoods and find well-resourced schools staffed by knowledgeable, competent, and highly qualified teachers.[9] In Finland, whatever the socio-economic status of a school's students, all schools are good to the extent that the nation has the narrowest achievement gaps in the world. In Singapore, where no schools are rundown or shabby, teachers regard it as an honor to be asked to move to a school or a track that serves a challenging cohort of students. The reassignment is seen as recognition of their professional quality and a test of their commitment and their skills.

There's something else about these high-performing nations. Their private school systems are either very tiny or virtually nonexistent. Almost all of the public is invested in their nation's public schools and in the quality of the teachers who work there. By comparison, many U.S. urban schools are disgracefully dilapidated, woefully lacking in technology and other resources, and little more than sinkholes for poor minorities. Affluent and even not-so-affluent white families have long since abandoned these schools for schools in the plusher suburbs or in the privileged independent sector. With no resources and no support, it's no wonder many of the best teachers won't go to urban schools!

We're not inventing these claims or even depending on second-hand sources. One or both of us has worked with or studied these high-performing systems directly. Along with influential international organizations like McKinsey & Company and OECD, what we've learned is that the successful countries don't only prize academic qualities in their teachers; they also focus on "suitability to teach" in initial selection, on rigorous pre-service development, and on support on the job. These high-performing systems deliberately develop professional capital in their teaching force. And in every case, almost all of the public is invested in having high-quality teachers serving practically all of the children who are their nation's future.

FLAWS IN THE U.S. STRATEGY

If you think through the current strategy in the United States—reward the top; get tough on the bottom—you will realize that it cannot possibly work. For one thing, it can affect 40% of the teaching profession at most, missing the middle 60%—a huge percentage! For another thing, where are all the new teachers suddenly going to come from, and how prepared for the tough assignments that await them will they be? Schemes like Teach for America (TfA) or Teach First in the United Kingdom, which are now extending into Australia, New Zealand, and China, might well fulfill their founders' vision of giving future corporate and political leaders a taste of teaching for 2 or 3 years at the start of their careers—so that they might become informed and influential advocates for public education a generation from now (although even if they do become influential eventually, what kinds of reforms will they advocate, given that their experiences have likely been to prop up what they see as schools with teachers inferior to themselves?). In some U.S. inner cities, conditions and support for teachers are so poor that many schools could not even operate without TfA. But even if you triple or quadruple the number of teachers trained this way, it is but a pinprick on the teacher supply problem today—especially when only 60% of these teachers remain after 2 years and only 15% remain in low-income schools after 4 years.[10]

Don't get us wrong. We welcome the fact that TfA and Teach First can draw high-quality entrants into the profession and that they are working on improving their teacher retention rates, so that the longer their teachers stay, the better they can become. And, depending on how they go about it, they can make a contribution to improving collective capacity. But in the end, these strategies can never be a systemic solution. They give false hope that they can transform the profession as a whole.

Rewarding the Individual

Then there's the fact that merit pay in teaching has a century-old track record of failure. Time and again, attempts to pay teachers based on their students' test scores as a way to improve practice just haven't worked.[11] More than this, as business psychology guru Daniel Pink points out, merit pay doesn't even work in the corporate world except in the simplest and most standardized of jobs.[12] With work that requires sophisticated levels of judgment and skill, merit pay has *no* positive effect on performance. Indeed, it actually makes performance *worse* by distracting people from their core purpose with short-term rewards. So either merit pay will make the best teachers worse, or teaching will have to be turned into standardized, simplified, and scripted operations so the reward system can have a positive effect. This second option is, of course, what many U.S. systems have actually been doing—reducing teaching to a set of basic skills such that what teachers have to do is laid out in step-by-step, rigidly paced manuals under tight regimes of strict compliance. It is hard to see how this system, which works only for narrowly conceived goals, will cope in the face of the challenging new Common Core State Standards endorsed by almost all U.S. states.

Relying on Standardized Measurement

When narrowly conceived high-stakes testing becomes the drill, cheating inevitably creeps in and sometimes runs riot. In 2011, the *New York Times* wrote a lead article with the title "Systematic Cheating Is Found in Atlanta's School System."[13] The article reported how a state investigation had uncovered blatant cheating (inflating or downright altering test results) in 44 schools involving at least 178 teachers and principals. The system was held together by "a culture of fear, intimidation and retaliation in the district, which led to a conspiracy of silence." We are not talking here about individual dishonesty but about a systemic problem of epidemic proportions. The degradation of professional capital could not sink much lower unless it involved the direct abuse of children.

In the face of solutions that haven't worked, some people's answer is simply to push these solutions harder. Perhaps we just need better measurement, they say. Hundreds of millions of dollars are being poured into developing measurement systems that might be helpful for some purposes, but that will never drive up standards or quality in teaching.

- ◆ What use is even the best measurement system if the overwhelmed principal doesn't know the teachers it is being applied to, or is never to be seen in classrooms, or is the fifth principal the school has had in 2 years?

- What use to you as a teacher is a measurement system administered by someone you don't know, don't respect, or don't even like?
- How motivated will you be by an evaluation system that rates what your Word Wall looks like, whether you are at the decreed point in the Literacy Teachers' Manual, or whether you have posted the lesson's standards on the board—but doesn't account for how you inspire your students, whether you can detect specific learning disabilities, or how you've helped a distraught child deal with a bereavement?
- And will the best teachers come into teaching if video cameras will be forever monitoring their performance, as some multi-billion-dollar foundations are now proposing?

Beyond a minimum level, it's not the metrics that drive most people, but the work itself—whether it inspires you, what it feels like, what it's for, and how you and your colleagues become energized by striving to solve difficult learning problems. Change the culture and develop professional capital, and good appraisal systems flourish; throw a good appraisal system into a negative culture, and you get nothing but further alienation.

More sophisticated metrics and measurement systems can enable good performance in teaching to be recognized, reinforced, and refined; but they can never drive it in the right direction. Beyond the many critiques and all the quibbles about the accuracy and validity of value-added assessments, and beyond the unsettling findings that perceived quality in teacher performance varies wildly according to what measure is chosen, or even, for the same teacher, from one class to another and one year to the next—judging teachers according to their individual performance has one more fatal flaw.[14]

Ignoring the School Environment

Teaching, like any other profession, doesn't come down only to individual skill or will. It's also profoundly affected by the environment—by the culture of the workplace where the job is carried out. If the teaching in a school is all over the place, we shouldn't so much be asking questions about the abilities or commitments of individual teachers. We should be wondering what is wrong with the school. Just because there is one outstanding pioneer in a school where everyone else has settled for an easier existence, doesn't mean that by will and effort alone, all or most of them in that school can be pioneers as well—not unless we do something about the school as a whole.

This is true in just about any line of work. When you walk into a fine restaurant, you don't expect the maître d' to ignore you, the sommelier to be indifferent to your preferences, and the waiter to be downright rude. You don't expect an airline crew member to be courteous or cranky depending on which particular individual you get. If one hairdresser in a salon makes you look like a fashion model, while next time a colleague turns you into a scary clown, there's something wrong with the salon. In any good airline, restaurant, salon, or school, you should expect quality and consistency that is personalized for you. If you have no way of predicting how different people in an organization will deal with you, something is profoundly amiss with that organization. And rewarding the good people, while removing or intervening with the poor ones, will not give you greater consistency or turn the whole organization around. You need the group working on this solution—the very professional capital we advocate in this book.

Like a hotel or a car rental service, you can tell what a school is going to be like the moment you walk in. Is the office staff kind and courteous or do they make you feel like a stranger? Do students welcome and acknowledge you or push you out of the way? Are classroom doors shut, walls bare, and children grimly concentrating on the next passage in their textbook? Or are classrooms buzzing hives of activity with actively engaged children immersed in challenging learning, effortlessly using appropriate technology to demonstrate their knowledge, and sad when the lesson has to come to an end? This is called culture—and in schools and other organizations, it's everything.[15] Culture shapes the experience you are likely to have when you fly with a high- or low-performing airline just as much as when you enter a school! At its best, culture doesn't give you a good teacher here and a weaker teacher there, but many strong and capable teachers working passionately together, under visionary leadership, so all of their students succeed. And not just in a few schools, but in all schools across the system.

In our work on whole system reform and "beyond expectations" in which we have studied and documented large-scale and impressive success, we have not been interested in a heroic teacher here and there, or a great school or district, hit or miss.[16] What's worth fighting for in teaching is to change every classroom and every school for the better—to come as close as possible to 100% of teachers, schools, districts, and governments being not just good enough but very good or great in their cumulative impact. But only a few countries and systems are going about this in the right way.

The teacher is indeed the key. But this doesn't mean we should focus on getting and rewarding better *individual* teachers. The highest performing systems in the world have good teachers all right, but they have them in numbers. High-performing systems have virtually all of their teachers on the move. It's a school thing, a professional thing, and a system thing. The only solutions that will work on any scale are those that mobilize the teaching force as a whole—including strategies where teachers push and support each other.

CONCLUSION

Teaching like a pro is about undertaking difficult, inspiring work; constantly trying to improve practice; and working with all the collective might and ingenuity of professional colleagues to do so. This means three things that are at the heart of this book:

1. *Teaching like a pro* means continuously inquiring into and improving one's own teaching. It means constantly developing and reinvesting in professional capital. All teachers need to become not just good, but excellent at teaching. Driving up standards, narrowing achievement gaps, engaging young minds amid all the distractions that now surround them, and preparing young people to live successfully and cohesively in the 21st century are all higher order requirements that call for the highest quality of teaching. Mere proficiency or passing will no longer serve as the yardstick for success. Teachers and teaching will need to keep on improving for everyone, all the time. Constant inquiry and continuous individual and collective development are essential to professional success.

2. *Teaching like a pro* means planning teaching, improving teaching, and often doing teaching not as an isolated individual but as part of a high-performing team. It means developing shared professional capital within an organization and community. All successful organizations in all walks of life, including business, sports, and schools, build effective teams as a core part of performance. Again, we are relying not just on second-hand sources here. We have studied high performance in different sectors first hand—in ice hockey, soccer, rugby, retail, e-commerce, and automobile manufacturing, as well as in schools, school districts, and government departments. We have studied, been part of, seen, and felt up-close the power of team building, team performance, and team spirit for ourselves. Professionals understand the power of the team, promote the devel-

opment of the team, and become integral parts of the team themselves. *Teaching like a pro* is not about yet more individual accountability, but about powerful collective responsibility.

3. *Teaching like a pro* means being part and parcel of the wider teaching profession and contributing to its development. To grow, professional capital must circulate freely, energetically, and openly. This means rethinking how teachers work with, support, and also challenge their colleagues. It means recasting teacher unions not only to become sources of outraged opposition to negative, imposed changes that narrow learning, harm students, and create burnout among classroom teachers, but also to become active and inspirational agents of changes that serve students, especially the most disadvantaged, improve quality among the teaching force, and put teachers in the vanguard of large-scale change. Contrary to their negative press, some unions and federations have already been taking the lead here—working in close partnerships with their governments in Alberta, Ontario, and Finland to improve teacher learning and innovation; or successfully challenging their governments, as in California when the government failed to provide the financial support that gives the most disadvantaged students proper opportunities to learn. Free circulation of professional capital also means that schools need to become less isolated from each other and that insecure districts and even principals should not be allowed to restrict or micromanage the professional learning and assistance that teachers can access from outside their own school or district.

In short, *teaching like a pro* is about improving as an *individual,* raising the performance of the *team,* and increasing quality across the *whole profession.* It is about developing, circulating, and reinvesting professional capital. Together, these things define what's worth fighting for as a teacher and in teaching.

But to change anything, we must first know what it is that we are changing. We must go much deeper into what that thing currently is. In the next chapter, therefore, we delve into the nature of teaching—beyond the nostalgic memories and stereotypes that many people hold of it. We can't change anything if, in reality, we are unclear about the starting point. It's time to expose the stereotypes and move beyond them to develop something more constructive together—a development that will profoundly increase the efficacy of the profession as a whole.

CHAPTER THREE

Stereotypes of Teaching

WHAT IS TEACHING?

What is teaching? Most of us think we know. After all, we were taught by teachers. We remember our best teachers vividly—how they inspired us, made us believe in ourselves, or set us on a better path. Our worst teachers can still make us shudder with laughter or fear. Their hopeless and hapless actions added little to our education. We don't remember all of our teachers, but we do remember the best and the worst of them.

So it's not surprising we have strong opinions about teachers and what teachers do. Teachers were a big part of our lives, and many made a big impression on us—sometimes in a good way, but not always. These memories and feelings profoundly influence people's views about teaching today and what they want from it—to benefit their own children and to justify the taxes they pay for the children of other people. They affect how people vote and the reforms that politicians feel they have to pitch to them to stay in office. They also have an impact on those in high office who often design policies that try to recreate their own school days, if they loved them, or right the wrongs that past teachers inflicted on them, if they didn't.

But the memories are selective. They recall what may have been true 10 or 15 years ago, at best, not what is the case now. They are seen through a child's eyes—memories of watching the teacher teaching, but not grading, preparing, or meeting. And emotional memories only recapture the most intense experiences—ones that were utterly inspiring or unforgettably awful. Our memories miss the majority and the complexity of what teaching is or can be. No wonder so many teachers feel mistreated and misunderstood.

Memories of teaching, then, often become stereotypes of teaching that profoundly influence how people want to change teaching and teachers.

Among these stereotypes of teaching (and also of other lines of work, such as business or medicine, which people compare teaching against) are the ideas that teaching is (or should be):

- *A precious gift* possessed by a few "born" teachers. So, as soon as you can, you recruit the ones who already seem to have the "natural" leadership skills to do the job and you give them the briefest preparation so as not to deter them from joining the profession with long and costly training programs. Charter schools and Teach for America in the United States, or Teach First in the United Kingdom, operate off this theory of action. Attract young and enthusiastic, academically smart, and naturally gifted teachers to schools and neighborhoods that will bring out their talents, they say; then work them really hard. That's the answer.
- *A practical craft* of implicit know-how that can only be learned over thousands of hours of practice through experience by trial and error. With the mentorship of a skilled and gifted master and countless hours of repetition and refinement, it is practice that makes perfect, not ivory-tower research. Experience counts; theory doesn't. Long-in-the-tooth veteran teachers sometimes hold to this vindication of their own hard-earned wisdom. "Wait until you've been teaching as long as I have!" they say. Policy makers may also claim that the practical school of hard knocks is superior to the "progressive" politics and intellectual self-indulgence of university-based teacher education programs. Get rid of these programs, they urge. Let's give beginning teachers something more real instead.
- *A laundry list of simple techniques* that can be prescribed and even paced so that minimally trained and modestly paid teachers can perform them satisfactorily. Books with upbeat titles such as *Teach Like a Champion* turn complex ideas into quickly learned tricks of the trade with catchy headings such as 4Ms, The Hook, and Binder Control.[1] Interestingly, you don't see handbooks such as *Heal Like a Champion* or *Litigate Like a Champion* in other professions! Several widely adopted literacy programs also provide minute-by-minute scripts of exactly what the teacher has to do or say to get the kind of student achievement that drives up test scores. All you need for effective teaching here are detailed teacher-proof instructions, hard work and compliance (euphemistically called "fidelity") from teachers

in delivering the lessons, relentless oversight to ensure that they do, and pay-by-results schemes to reward the most successful among them and eliminate those who are not up to the job. Teaching like a pro is also different from teaching like a champion when it comes to the unit of change. Champions battle alone on behalf of their people. Pros, however, are more effective in achieving their worthy ends because they do this not just individually and heroically but also and especially with the force of the team.

- *A precise science,* like medicine, grounded in hard quantitative evidence and clinical trials of what works with most people, most of the time. Proponents of evidence-based education say that what matters most is what is scientifically proven to be effective for student achievement, not what is merely fun for children or feels good for teachers. Their solution is to identify the practices that have the highest yield for student achievement—such as three-part lessons, mind-mapping of ideas, or forecasting the plots in assigned books— then to require teachers to use them, with training and coaching support from experts in these practices. Other professionals keep up to date with evidence-based practices instead of hanging on to ones they have always liked or become accustomed to. Why shouldn't teachers?

- *A data-driven enterprise,* like business, where Key Performance Indicators (KPIs) at every level, from the individual product to the entire enterprise, drive up standards, eliminate waste, and reduce defects to almost zero. Derived from the principles of World Class Manufacturing, data-driven instruction and intervention promise to track the performance (especially on test scores) of every nation, school, teacher, and student. Through frequent cycles of evaluation with every student, they set out, in real time, to identify where the weaknesses and shortcomings are—who is ahead and who is behind. Individually and together, teachers can then review spreadsheets of tested achievement among and with their students to make just-in-time interventions that will rectify underperformance with particular students, categories of students (e.g., boys, Hispanic learners, children with behavioral disabilities, and so on), subject departments, or classes. Setting measurable targets and benchmarking standards against the best teacher, school, or country are designed to prompt improvement among the rest. Collecting real-time data, talking about data, and acting on data are, in this view, the granular ingredients of relentless improvement—achieving improvement one item at a time. It seems to work in business, so why shouldn't it work in schools?

- *An ineffable art* of sublime, yet mysterious practice. The late Seymour Sarason argued that teaching is a kind of performance art.[2] It is part gift, part craft—dramatic, engaging, passionate, and all-consuming. In the film *Dead Poets Society,* students feel moved to stand on their desks to declare their power to shape their own destinies.[3] In the BBC's *The Choir,* an inspirational young choirmaster turns a group of groaning secondary school students who are barely able to stay in tune and whose own music teacher believes are incapable of singing into impressive performers at the international world choir championships (he even achieves similar results with track-suited physical education teachers!).[4] In this view, the art of teaching (and learning) can't be captured in quantifiable outputs or measurable test scores. Its results are to be seen in how the learning looks and feels, in the exhibitions and performances that arise from it, and in the kinds of people that learners eventually become. Remove the shackles of scripts, scores, and spreadsheets, and set teachers free to be their creative and inspirational best. Isn't that what the heart of teaching is about?

- *A sacred calling* of service and sacrifice to a community and its greater good. Those who regard teaching primarily as a sacred vocation or a missionary commitment put a premium on teachers' piety and their care for the community they serve. Teachers who subscribe to an ethic of sacrifice should have little desire for material reward, or so it's felt. Their emotional, spiritual, and social contribution should guide their effort. A number of faith-based schools and systems put a high premium on these moral commitments and personal sacrifices in teaching. The caring ethic is also abundant in the teaching of vulnerable populations such as minorities, the poor, the very young, and those who have special needs. Duty and sacrifice presumably should be able to overcome any circumstances and all odds. Mother Teresa did it. So did Nelson Mandela. Heroic and outstanding teachers and principals still do. Poor pay, limited materials, and harrowing conditions are no reason to fail. There need be no excuses. In the vocational view, good teaching is about doing good works. Recruiting dedicated teachers with the right dispositions, then reminding or even haranguing them about their duty and loyalty, also ensures they do good work. Poor results are just failures of effort and dedication. Work harder, give more, don't gripe about the conditions or the pay—isn't that what teachers should do?

In his 1932 classic, *The Sociology of Teaching,* Willard Waller pointed to just one prevailing stereotype of teachers and teaching. In this ungenerous caricature, teachers developed a false and forced kind of dignity because their classrooms were in a "state of perilous equilib-

> ◆〉 . . . teaching isn't one-dimensional. It's a lot less simple than most people think.

rium"[5] and they had to learn to get "on and off their high horse rapidly."[6] Spending years asking questions to which they already knew the answer, teachers came to make "a sad and serious business of learning,"[7] and the decisive moment in their career was when they finally grasped that all that truly mattered was the opinion of other teachers. Little wonder that, in Waller's time, many regarded teaching as a job for "unsalable men and unmarriageable women"![8]

Waller acknowledged that this stereotype, like all stereotypes, was an exaggeration. Yet there was also more than a grain of truth in it, he said. Indeed, he based quite a lot of it on himself! Nor is the stereotype a complete anachronism. Too many young teachers are still beaten down for being too enthusiastic. In the United States, many teachers' contracts still widely prohibit involvement in shared professional development outside the scheduled school day. And when the financial services sector shakes out, where do its unemployed go? Into teaching! After all, teaching is still something you can fall back on until things pick up, isn't it?

Today, though, there's not one stereotype, but many. All are part truth, part fiction. They come from many standpoints. And they overlap and intertwine. Choose the case you want to make about teachers and teaching, and you can find the stereotype to support it. Be practical, care more, give generously, fulfill your natural gift, respect the evidence, express yourself, track everything with data, follow your heart, get with the program—all of these preferred approaches to improving teacher quality come from popular and interlocking stereotypes about the job.

Because they *are* based on one-sided stereotypes, it's easy to overstate such solutions.

- Caring is an admirable ethic, but caring teachers can easily overprotect children and fail to challenge them. More than this, in the face of relentless and debilitating odds, some of the most caring teachers can turn into moral martyrs, disillusioned cynics, or cheerless workaholics.
- Checklists of procedures and techniques might work for simple things like liability procedures for school trips, or ensuring you don't operate on the wrong leg in surgery, but checklists won't help you motivate many poor minority students to study Macbeth, or enable you to treat the complex conditions of a patient in elder care or a student with multiple learning disabilities.
- KPIs can draw attention to things that are easily measured, like blood cell counts, customer satisfaction levels, or achievement test scores, but they can also be a distraction from things that aren't easily measured, such as patients' feelings about death, students' phobias about mathematics, or how to inspire boys to be passionate about singing or reading.
- Expressing yourself in teaching and being driven by your passions can be a very good thing, but it can also lead to self-indulgent narcissism that gives teachers pleasure and entertains their classes but doesn't necessarily secure effective results.
- Independent evidence is important in teaching, as in any other profession, but the role of evidence can be exaggerated, failing to acknowledge the role that experience and intuition also play in decision making, usually in combination with external evidence, but sometimes in ways that challenge it.

So teaching isn't one-dimensional. It's a lot less simple than most people think. More than this, teaching isn't just an art, a craft, a science, or a sacred vocation—or even a mixture of all these things. Teaching is also a job, a line of work. Depending on how the job is designed, if you do the same kinds of things day in, day out, year after year, eventually they start to rub off on you.

TEACHING AS WORK

What do you think one of the most satisfying careers is? In the United Kingdom, year after year, it's hairdressing![9] If you're a hairdresser, every day, in just an hour or two, several times over, you take something that is unkempt and turn it into something that looks fantastic. You work in a stylish atmosphere, and you get to chat and have caring, physical contact with your clients. At the end, satisfied customers tell you they love how you have transformed them—and they leave you a big tip! And those who aren't happy know there's no point in complaining. They just don't come back! Good conditions, great relationships, quick results, and no complaints—you can't really beat that for a living, can you?

So what about the job of teaching? Let's go back to Waller, His particular picture of teaching might be dated, but he was right when he said that all occupations make their mark on the people who engage in them. "What does teaching do to teachers?"[10] he asked. What mark does the job leave on them?

Teachers aren't just completely free individuals. They are creatures of circumstance, products of their working environment. Today, there's not just one way to teach. What it feels like to be a teacher and do the job every day varies. It depends on what you want to achieve in it, whether you are capable of meeting your own and other people's expectations, how your job is designed, what your contacts and relationships with colleagues are like, and what sorts of conditions you work in. How the work of teaching is shaped determines the kinds of teachers employed and how they eventually turn out.

Public schools don't have conditions that can rival plush corner offices or stylish salons. Conditions for teachers are pretty ordinary at best, and in many U.S. urban schools they are often wretchedly poor. Teachers might have admirable goals and expectations for themselves—to make a difference in children's lives, perhaps, or to inspire them to take up a new field of study—but they are constantly assailed with other people's goals and expectations too—to raise test scores, appease pushy parents, keep to the basics, turn everything around in a year or less, or implement the latest pet programs. If teachers are lucky, they will have excellent leaders who support them. Less fortunate ones will have leaders who are incompetent, indifferent, controlling, or corrupt; leaders who pay more attention to the mandates of their superiors than to the needs of their teachers and students; or revolving-door leaders who get fired or move on whenever the going gets too tough. And the results in classrooms are frustratingly elusive, because it takes ages for teachers to see the fruits of their efforts, or the results just feel irrelevant, because test scores don't seem to measure what teachers are trying to accomplish. If you want to change teachers, you have to change the job that teachers do and then bring in good and well-prepared people to do it.

Unlike hairdressing, teaching is usually performed in imperfect conditions, in the face of conflicting expectations and demands. It's more like triage near the front line of battle than the clinically controlled environment of an operating theater in a teaching hospital. Of course, a few heroic teachers can triumph over any obstacle and beat all odds by dedicating their entire lives to the children they serve. Although their colleagues may be seething with jealousy, the media have a field day with teachers like these. We should be grateful for these few heroes, but like "born" teachers and leaders, we can't run an entire system off them. Even the best teachers and their leaders typically have to operate in, adapt to, and negotiate circumstances more like the ones described below:

1. *New York State, late 1990s.* Teacher after teacher described the effects of the new high-stakes testing environment on their classes. One teacher's class used to be "based on the literature and theories about how people learn—multiple intelligences and cooperative learning." But then the high-stakes tests arrived. The teacher switched to "overheads and class notes." "After a week or so, a couple of the kids said, 'Are you going to teach like this the rest of the year?'" "Unfortunately," their teacher responded, "I'm probably going to have to. I've seen the tests and it's content, content, content. There's no way I could allow you to go and sit for this exam knowing that I have not used the book the district has given us." Yet the tested state curriculum was less rigorous and relevant than this teacher's previous approach. It was "more content-driven, a lot more dates, vocabulary, identification, rather than probing critical-thinking questions." The teacher declared, "Kids, I'm not any happier than you are about this, but I could not live with myself knowing that I did not teach you in a way that would prepare you to jump through that hoop. I couldn't do it personally or professionally."[11]

2. *Ontario, Canada, 2009.* Seven years ago, a suburban elementary school was in the doldrums. Now it's dancing on the ceiling. Results in literacy have risen steadily. The achievements are real. There are no sudden spikes in scores as a result of teaching to the test or other quick-fix trickery. Teachers and students have been transformed. All

the teachers care about all the students, not just those in their class or grade. They look at each child's progress that's posted on the data wall for all to see. Everyone's energies are passionately and relentlessly focused on moving these students along and lifting them up, one at a time, every week. Teachers don't just feel responsible for children in their own class or grade. Grade 1 teachers, for example, share responsibility for how students are doing in Grade 6, because those students used to be in Grade 1. Special education teachers work alongside other teachers in regular classes. They help all students who need it, not just those who have been formally identified. This stimulates intense conversations about learning and how to improve it. With the right teachers and leadership, regular tests and assessments can enliven discussions about children's learning instead of prompting cynical reactions like teaching to the test.

Everyone has worked hard, no one more than the principal. She really drove the improvement. She took the school and the staff somewhere, everyone says. She believed and now everyone else believes that children's social backgrounds should not prejudice their ability to achieve. She got all the staff focused on taking collective responsibility for every student, in discussion after discussion, meeting after meeting. She took a real interest in what was happening in classes and got to know every child personally. Armed with the knowledge that this would be her last job before retirement, she courageously fought the district to secure the technology resources that would enable special education students to succeed. And with this technological support, students with learning disabilities developed the confidence to read and write more, and they finally started to demonstrate what they could accomplish.

All this has taken incredible effort. Teachers sometimes feel on the edge of exhaustion, but they are immensely proud of what they have achieved. They wouldn't want to take any of it back. Yet when asked if they have lost anything as a result of this drive to increase literacy achievement, they worry that the curriculum has become too narrow. Children and teachers have little time to focus on things they are truly passionate about, they say. The school needs to get some of that back, everyone pleads. And this is in a "good" system, not a narrow, high-stakes one! So, good literacy scores are not enough. The school and the system need to move beyond these into higher order skills that engage and motivate students into habits of life-long learning. How are they supposed to do this?[12]

3. *Northern England, 2008–2009.* Grange Secondary School seemed to have the answer. The "flagship" school of its town when it was established in the 1960s, Grange Secondary had fallen "into the doldrums" by the 1980s and 1990s. Only 15% of its students were achieving the threshold standard of 5 grades A–C in their General Certificate of Secondary Education (GCSE) examinations. The school passed its 1996 external inspection only by the skin of its teeth. "The facilities looked grotty," one senior leader reflected. "In the press, we were muck. The kids didn't have very high expectations of succeeding and we had quite a high staff turnover."

The emergence and arrival of new leadership slowly started to turn the school around. Many of the turnaround strategies were familiar: settling down behavior, taking personal responsibility as leaders for some of the most difficult students, inspiring the staff, and engaging the community. But the school also adopted an unexpected and counterintuitive approach to underachievement. It didn't just urge teachers to work harder in tracking, monitoring, and managing individual students' progress so they would perform more strongly in the basics in the existing curriculum. After many hours observing in classrooms, Grange's teachers and leaders came to understand that the standard secondary school curriculum did not recognize how the school's predominantly Bangladeshi students learned best. To "make rapid progress," it was felt, "the school had to allow the children to do more of what they're good at and more of what they enjoyed."

The school tested students on their learning styles and found they were "very visual, very kinesthetic." Grange Secondary therefore made a bold move to get the curriculum to fit the students by moving it strongly toward visual arts. Eventually, the school became one of the top two out of 30 Visual Arts Colleges in the country and received a range of national awards. With a wider variety of courses in art now on offer, and after adopting more visual and kinesthetic teaching methods in all subjects, students "were leaving with a higher number of GCSE passes" and a stronger sense of pride in their accomplishments. Teachers started to feel that the curriculum really was "designed for" and "fits the needs of [the] pupils." Results "zoomed" from 15% achieving 5 GCSE grades A–C in the 1990s to over 70% in 2008. Although it was situated in the poorest 1% of communities in the country, on value-added or growth measures of improvement, Grange was among the top 2% of schools nationally. Inspection reports also became increasingly favorable, remarking that the school had made "very good" improvement since the 1996 inspection and also had "some outstanding features" by 2006.

Imagine being a teacher or leader at Grange, then, when the following happens to you. In May 2008, the government set new "floor targets" for secondary schools, where at least 30% of students were expected to achieve 5+ GCSE grades A*–C, including mathematics and English (the target had not previously specified these two subjects as requirements). More than 600 schools were listed as failing to meet these targets and were notified they would be subject to intervention and possible replacement by new Academies if they did not meet the targets within 1 year. Despite its 10-year improvement trajectory on previous official criteria, its increasingly favorable inspection reports, and its collection of honors and awards, Grange's positioning below these newly defined floor targets placed it on the list.

Graeme Hollinshead was head teacher of Grange Secondary in 2008. He had worked at the school all of his career. His reputation for successful turnaround had led him to be appointed as a national consultant to advise other schools on how to improve. He appeared in the national press, on public radio, and on the BBC because Grange now had the largest disparity in performance rankings of all schools in the country between the previous and the newly introduced criteria. The *Times* Educational Supplement described Hollinshead as "indignant about a statistical exercise which led to hundreds of schools being branded as failing." "Is this a high-performing specialist school or a failing school? Make your judgment," he declared. "Every head I know would say Grange is a high-performing school. Who has got it wrong?" Grange Secondary achieved stellar turnaround success using creativity and curriculum relevance that also produced increased measurable performance by one set of rules, but was then branded as a failure when the rules were changed in the middle of the school year. It has now been turned into an Academy![13]

You may want to keep your teaching creative and challenging, but if you don't teach to the test and narrow your teaching, you feel you will be letting your students down by not helping them to pass. By contrast, you may be enthusiastic about the assessment and testing process and see real benefits for students' achievement, but you still feel you are sacrificing those price-less elements of learning and teaching that really engage teachers' and stu-dents' passions. Or you work out a way for everyone to have their cake and eat it too, innovatively fitting the learning to the children in a way that also gets impressive test results—only to see those far beyond your school change all the criteria for success, then close down the cake shop when you don't meet them. There seems to be no pleasing people. You're damned if you do and damned if you don't! This has been going on for a long time, but it seems to be getting worse, particularly in the United States, which is why we seek a far better road forward.

TEACHING TODAY

If you open the newspapers, or listen in on teachers' gossip, you would think teachers' problems and dilemmas were relatively new. Fingers are pointed at megalomaniac politicians, recalcitrant unions, spineless leadership, quick-fix policies, and gridlocked local bureaucracies. But when we wrote our earlier book on *What's Worth Fighting For* more than two decades ago, many of the problems facing teachers and teaching were not all that different from those that schools and teachers have to deal with today. We see "continuities" good and bad; we see "intensification" of negative pressure; we see "failed solutions" through the desperate spraying of silver bullets; and we see "new opportunities," most of which contain the seeds of professional capital.

Continuities

Twenty years ago, teachers felt the job was expanding incessantly, that there were too many things to deal with, and that so much was expected of them.[14] There was "so much social worker involved in the job; so many behavioral and social problems sitting in your classroom that have to be dealt with long before you teach." More and more special education students were now in regular classes. There were many different abilities, yet teachers were "always being told" they were "constantly responsible for all the chil-dren." Teachers felt frazzled. They "always seemed to be on the tear"!

Accountability was increasing and endless. Teachers felt caught in a pin-cer movement between parents on one side and bureaucrats on the other.

: "more demanding" about "what kind of program their
, how it's being delivered, how the test was marked that
olitical and administrative initiatives, meanwhile, seemed
herent, and faddish.

anything, many teachers, especially the more experienced
ones, it   had no voice. Nobody seemed to be listening to them. A
teaching couple with 45 years' experience between them complained,
"nobody has ever asked our opinion about anything. . . . They just go ahead
and proclaim and we have to follow."

Teachers felt overloaded, pulled in different directions, and never lis-
tened to. They often also felt isolated, unsupported, and left to their own
devices to manage on their own. Teachers in portable classrooms couldn't
even leave their classes to go to the toilet. In winter, at recess or break-time,
by the time they had got the children's snowsuits on and off, they had no
time left for themselves. "Nobody comes. Nobody goes. So you become
your own little body of people," one of them remarked. As a result, teachers
became "absorbed in [their] own stuff." What other teachers were doing
didn't concern them. "There's so much to do in my own class," one of them
said. "I spend all my time thinking about that."

Overload, isolation, increasing expectations, contradictory demands,
and no real forum for ordinary teachers to make themselves heard—these
seem to be the continuing companions of teaching and of the work that
teachers do. In teaching, you will always have to balance the needs of the
one against the needs of the many; parents will always pressure you to pay
special attention to their prize possession, while you have to consider the
needs of all the children in your class. In teaching, you will perpetually feel
you never have enough time to cover all the history standards, prepare a
flawless display of students' work, grade all your papers properly, listen long
enough to a distraught child, or give a struggling new colleague all the help
he or she needs. The day is never over. The job never ends. There's always
more work to be done. And everyone wants a piece of you. Only in retirement will the moment arrive when you can say you have too much time.

Luckily, most of the *joys* of teaching are timeless too. The moment a
child is first able to read; the parent critic who turns into your staunchest
advocate; the second-hand present wrapped in newspaper that the poorest
child in your class brings for your birthday gift; the immigrant youth you
taught who is the first in his or her family to go to college; the light bulb that
goes on when a child finally learns something, or when you grasp how to

teach it; your returning graduates who show you what a difference you made in their lives; the laughter on a school trip when your students see other sides of your personality; the passions for learning you have ignited; the human legacies you have left—these are the ever-present joys of teaching that have, in spite of everything, brought teachers into the profession, kept them in it, and gotten them out of bed every morning, for decades. The challenge in teaching and among those who want to change teaching is to treasure and preserve the joys and find ways to manage the frustrations.

Intensification

But not everything in teaching stays the same. Some of the problems and challenges have continued, but now they are more intense, more pervasive, and more severe. In the 1990s in England, parts of Canada, and much of Australia, there was a coordinated assault by governments and the media on public school teachers and teaching. In the United States, in 2011, the teacher-bashing season persists.[15]

In the 1990s, resources became scarce and public education was a prime candidate for cutbacks. Voters and taxpayers were getting older and didn't see what the schools were doing anymore because their own children had grown up and left. In an age of globalization, politicians were losing their grip on their own national economies and immigration policies, but they could at least promise to turn around schools by changing and controlling their captive population of teachers.

Schools received fewer resources. Class sizes often grew. Teachers had to spend more time in the classroom and less time with each other. Professional development time was cut. The curriculum was standardized and sometimes even prescribed in excruciating detail. Testing increased and spread. Schools were publicly ranked in tables of crude performance measures that shamed the wayward and the laggards, who were seemingly letting down children in the poorest communities.

Outside inspections and top-down interventions were swift and punitive. There would be no excuses. Failure would not be an option. No matter how poor the community, lack of improvement would never be tolerated. If you failed to improve, parents would be given other alternatives. Failing schools would be closed down, then reconstituted. The strong would survive and the weak would be tossed to the side. Bad old teachers would be replaced with young and energetic ones. Weak leaders would be replaced with strong ones. Underperforming schools would lose their children to higher performing ones, or to new academies, or to competing charter schools, or to private education that tax breaks would make more affordable.

Some felt the system was broken. Others seemed hell-bent on breaking it. But in either case, teachers were presented as being more part of the problem than the solution. Old teachers had gone soft, overprotected by the security of their pensions. Teacher unions defended the status quo, resisted more flexible contracts, and became the enemies of progress. Teachers didn't work hard enough or long enough. Compared with other occupations, the days were short and the holidays were inexcusably long. Closure, competition, and intervention would be the answers. If teachers didn't improve, they would have to get out of the kitchen. If they couldn't take the heat, they would have to make way for young and hungry replacements. Meanwhile, an equally aging cohort of education professors, who had been too long out of the classroom or never even been in it, filled new teachers with dangerous ideologies, muddled practices, and irrelevant theories. The teaching that resulted, critics claimed, was a trendy mishmash of vaguely progressive but undemanding practice. Children were failing, teachers were responsible, and teacher education wasn't helping.

Most of the results of this strategy proved disastrous for the commitment of teachers and the quality of teaching. Our work on teachers and leaders in the United States and Ontario in this period set out compelling data from which modern U.S. reformers might learn. In the 1990s, the standardized curriculum was less responsive to culturally diverse learners, there was less creativity, there was demoralization, there was less collegiality, and there was an exodus from the profession. Overall, there was simply less pleasure in teaching. In the words of one teacher, "There just seems to be so much focus on meeting standards set from the outside that I don't think we get to spend as much time thinking about what we're going to be doing in the classroom and enjoying it." All this did little or nothing to improve the quality of teaching and learning. Some of the best teachers became alienated and left, while the poorer teachers just struggled.

So, on the one hand in the 1990s, and still in the United States today, reforms that have been at best misguided and at worst malicious took the joy out of teaching and learning, drove many teachers (sometimes the brightest and most enthusiastic ones) out of the profession, destroyed classroom creativity, and reduced teachers' capacity to respond to diversity.

But it's more than governments and bureaucrats that are the problem. Teachers and their unions are far from blameless too, according to Charles

Payne, who has dedicated most of his career to working in and being a community organizer and researcher for some of America's toughest public schools in Chicago and elsewhere. He is not afraid to attack the corrupt politics and inept bureaucracies of America's urban public school systems—books sitting in warehouses that never get to the classrooms where they are needed; windows that take an eternity of form filling and administrative approval before they can be fixed; principals who embezzle resources or deal drugs to their own students; and schools generally pushed and pulled through endless, lurching shifts in direction because they are held hostage to the political fortunes of electioneering mayors and transient superintendents.[16]

In the nightmare scenario of American urban education that Payne so shockingly depicts, he doesn't spare teacher unions from his withering assessments either. When it comes to organized teachers and entrenched bureaucracies, he wishes a curse on both their houses. Payne spells out example after example of egregious union acts that have impeded positive change and development, many of them in Chicago. Unionized teachers in late 1980s Chicago, for example, took "11 sick days a year, nearly double the national average, with most people being afflicted on either Monday or Friday."[17] Much later, a more traditional union leader elected in 2004 turned back the union's engagement in professional development because, she claimed, funds had been "funneled to this educational wing of the union at the expense of direct services to the members." She also denied that the union should help turn around failing schools on the grounds that "it's not the union's responsibility to run Chicago Public Schools."[18]

So you can understand where U.S. educational reformers are coming from. The district bureaucracies are inflexible. The unions have seemed entrenched. An aging teaching profession appears set in its ways, overprotected by its contracts, and unwilling to change. Parents want things to go back to the way they remember them. Isn't it time to stop the downward spiral, to try something else, no matter how draconian? Desperate times call for desperate measures!

Failed Solutions

In the United States, the desperate measures are like a shrinking bag of silver bullets. Each silver bullet is based on one of the flawed or partial stereotypes of teaching discussed earlier. Many of these silver bullets are missing their target, most of them are duds, and the chamber of quick-fire school reform is almost empty.

1. One silver bullet went to closing down all the bad schools, but the students who were dispersed and displaced from these schools ended up in others that were just as weak. That's what happened to U.S. Secretary of Education Arne Duncan's strategy in Chicago, when he tried to shut down all of its underperforming schools. Ninety percent of the students just ended up in other underperforming schools, now far from their homes, where they were more likely to be picked on by alien gangs.[19]

2. Another bullet was fired at bringing smart and inexpensive young teachers into urban schools, as in Teach for America or Teach First in England, but within 3–5 years, two-thirds of them move on (somewhat fewer in England), leaving little legacy or stability behind them.[20] And there aren't enough of these young "born teachers" to staff an entire national school system anyway. You can change some schools for a while with this strategy, but you can't change all or even most schools in the long run.

3. The third bullet took a shot at replacing principals when they got poor results, but their poverty-stricken schools then just ended up with more and more short-term, unstable leadership in a frenetic carousel of leadership succession that compounded all the problems of these schools even further.[21]

4. Relentless timelines for yearly improvement in test scores were a target for one of the remaining potshots, but insisting on continuous improvement in everything all the time doesn't match even best corporate practice, where sustainable growth rates don't go up every quarter and are much more uneven than that. By the middle of 2011, the U.S. federal strategy to keep pushing tested performance upward so that 100% of students would be successful by 2014 had become so unsustainable that state after state simply refused to comply with the policy.[22]

5. Charter schools in the United States or Academies in England are one of the shiniest silver bullets of all, and some of them are very good, but the evidence on whether they are better than public schools in general is at best uncertain. While you can change some lives with a few exceptional charter schools, you can't change a nation with tens of thousands of them that can no longer skim the best students and teachers from the top, that leave out students with the most challenging disabilities, or that have no systems to support students when they get into trouble.[23]

6. So we're down to the last silver bullet. The target is teachers, especially those feckless time-servers who are messing up kids' lives. The silver bullet is performance-based evaluation

> ◈> Silver bullets make for slick political promises. But they almost always concentrate on the wrong things.

based on measurements of student growth—precision weaponry, with laserlike accuracy that can reward the best teachers and rid urban schools of the worst teaching and the worst teachers, who perpetuate low standards and failure. Ready. Aim. They're fired! What could be simpler or fairer than that?[24]

Silver bullets make for slick political promises. But they almost always concentrate on the wrong things. Big structural changes don't address the people who experience them. Getting rid of all the wrong people—principals, teachers, and students—and replacing them with the right people just turns reform into what Doug Reeves calls the "neutron bomb strategy of educational change," where you eliminate all the existing people and only the buildings are left standing.[25] Paranoid political minds also split professionals into good guys and bad guys, heroes and villains. Organizational success and failure are reduced to the moral success or failure of individuals—how dedicated they are and how much time and effort they put in.

In short, too many current U.S. policy strategies are based on a foundation of *wrong drivers* and *flawed fallacies*.[26] Each of us has written about these wrong drivers or flawed fallacies in whole system reform. Drivers are policies and strategies that you count on to successfully drive the reform forward. The four wrong drivers of policy are negative accountability, individualistic solutions, fascination with technology, and piecemeal or fragmented solutions. The five fallacies of misdirected educational change are excessive speed, standardization, substitution of bad people with good ones, overreliance on a narrow range of performance metrics, and win–lose inter-school competition.

There are better alternatives, which we will discuss in the rest of this book:

- Professional capacity building
- Collective responsibility, teamwork, and collaboration
- Moral commitment and inspiration
- More rather than less professional discretion

- ◆ Personally engaging curriculum and pedagogy with technology as its accelerator
- ◆ Better and broader performance metrics
- ◆ School-to-school assistance rather than punitive intervention from on high
- ◆ Systemic policies that are coherent and cohesive

These measures produce more transparency and responsibility on the ground than the more blatant and punitive attacks on the system. They transform *the hearts, minds, and culture* of the profession *and* spread the impact across the whole range of institutions where it does its work.

If you want to change teaching, you have to understand it, and very often appreciate it. You have to understand the teachers who are responsible for the teaching—what motivates them and makes them tick. And you have to understand how to find not just a few young teachers for a few years, but how to keep the best of them until they reach their peak, how to circulate professional capital from one generation to the next, and how to recognize and re-energize the older teachers we already have. This means looking at how to get teachers to work together within their schools, across whole systems, and throughout the entire profession—because great teachers usually work in great schools.

It is time for school reformers to stop shooting off wasted silver bullets. All they are firing is blanks. Better ways forward already exist—although all of them can recoil on you.

New Opportunities and Challenges

In the opening years of the 21st century, the tide is turning toward teachers again. There are promising examples of new developments that invest in the collective efficacy of the profession—that build *professional capital*—but they are still very much in the minority in the United States, and not thoroughly developed elsewhere.

On the positive side, in very many countries, there is more recognition and more support for teachers. People realize, and research clearly demonstrates, that the most significant in-school factor affecting student achievement is the quality of teaching.[27] New generations are entering teaching, and new possibilities come with them. And many teachers are not so isolated now. They have more opportunities to learn from their colleagues.

Outside the United States, many educational policy makers have been working with the profession, not against it (though this tide may change in the wake of the global recession). The public is becoming more and more confident about what teachers are achieving. There is more evidence, more data, and more transparency. Teachers are no longer flying by the seat of their pants, and parents know more about what their children, and in turn their teachers, are doing.

There are fresh opportunities in teaching and in the improvement of teaching, yet there are also fresh threats that accompany them. There is no nirvana in educational change. Every solution brings a new batch of problems. But over time, the impact improves, and so does the quality of the problems. What are some of these new opportunities and their accompanying new problems?

- *Older generations in teaching are giving way to younger replacements* who bring fresh enthusiasm, energy, and flexibility to the profession. But these younger replacements are often thrown in at the deep end, many do not or cannot stay long enough, they have few professional elders left to show them the ropes, and burnout is an ever-present threat.
- *There is more human resource support for teachers* these days. Teachers are no longer on their own, and when they struggle, there are mentors and coaches to help them. But when programs are mandated inflexibly, coaches can quickly turn into compliance officers, and mentors into tormentors.
- *Experienced teachers are being used as mentors, as group leaders,* and in other related roles in which they build new relationships with the new wave of teachers (we are reminded of the African saying, "every time an old person dies, a library burns"), but too often the sage criticisms of top-down leadership and quick-fix systems made by experienced teachers are dismissed as alienated grumblings of high-priced old curmudgeons.
- *There is more interactive professionalism* among teachers. Teachers are less isolated from each other. More and more of them find learning, support, conversation, and other interaction in networks and professional learning communities. But interactive professionalism can turn into hyperactive professionalism as teachers are thrown into hurried meetings to devise quick-fix solutions that will lead to

instantaneous gains in student achievement results. And cultures of collaboration can degenerate into contrived collegiality—where teachers have to collaborate on agendas they are given, for purposes that belong to someone else, in ways that others decide.

- *There are better and more readily available data* about student progress, and clearer evidence about what works. Data can inform improvement, guide instruction, and prompt earlier intervention so no child is allowed to fall behind. But data can replace professional judgment instead of enhancing it, directing teachers' efforts only toward the tested basics, and driving them to distraction.

- *We know more about other high-performing countries* and jurisdictions such as Finland, Alberta, and Ontario and how they achieve strong results with superbly qualified, well-trained, and effectively supported teachers. At the same time, we tend to dismiss them too quickly when their politics don't fit our own ideology. Conversely, we tend to cherry-pick bits of their policies, such as *all teachers having to possess Master's degrees,* in ways that bear no resemblance to how those factors operate in the places from which we are copying them.

- *We are paying more attention to leadership and leadership development* but still putting too much faith in leaders as heroic individual saviors, rather than in communities of leaders who work together effectively and build on each other's work over time.

Everywhere we see pockets of groups of educators achieving success on some level. Leaving aside individual school achievement (because it will never add up to system change), we know of many school districts where committed collaboration and sustained inquiry are getting results for all students. There are some in the United States and United Kingdom, many in Alberta and Ontario, and entire nations of them in Singapore and Finland, where partnerships between governments and teachers, ministries of education, and school districts have created high-quality systems.[28] These are shining examples of professional capital *par excellence.* Elsewhere, though, the examples are infrequent and inchoate—thin and thinly spread versions of what will be needed in the future. But at least they are a start.

CONCLUSION

Teaching will always have its abiding joys and frustrations. But compared to the situation 20 years ago, after years of upheaval and turmoil that persists and is intensifying in the United States, teaching in many parts

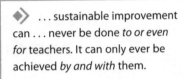

> ... sustainable improvement can ... never be done *to or even for* teachers. It can only ever be achieved *by and with* them.

of the world has started to come out of the shadows again. We know that, to change teaching, we must truly understand it and the people who do it—rather than forcing through simplistic solutions based on or justified by one-sided stereotypes of what the job entails. When the classroom door is closed, the teacher will always remain in charge. Where students are concerned, the teacher will always be more powerful than the principal, the president, or the prime minister. Successful and sustainable improvement can therefore never be done *to or even for* teachers. It can only ever be achieved *by and with* them.

We are at a new crossroads in educational reform, let us remember, and the solutions can go either way—getting tougher on teachers, or figuring out how to realistically develop a profession that becomes more inspiring, tough, and challenging in itself. This still requires leadership, but it is the kind of leadership that reconciles and integrates external accountability with personal and collective professional responsibility. It is the leadership that focuses on developing teachers' *professional capital*—as individuals, as teams, and as a profession.

If we want to improve teaching and teachers, we must therefore improve the conditions of teaching that shape them, as well as the cultures and communities of which they are a part. We must invest in developing teachers' capabilities and give them time to sharpen these capabilities to a high standard. It's no good just hunting for a few more hidden gems for teaching—people who might possess unseen talents or who have been hiding in other walks of life. We must develop more *professional capital* among the vast majority of teachers. This is what the rest of our book is about.

CHAPTER FOUR

Investing in Capability and Commitment

SO WHAT EXACTLY does it mean to *teach like a pro*? There are five Cs of *professional capital* that enable the teaching force to become highly effective: (1) capability (or expertise), (2) commitment, (3) career, (4) culture, and (5) contexts or conditions of teaching. When these ingredients are right—that's when you teach like a pro. Weaken any one of them and the others will suffer. And when they really work together, almost all teachers are able to fire on all cylinders. This chapter deals with the first three; later in the book we explore the final two.

EVIDENCE AND EXPERIENCE

You might be the most dedicated and passionate teacher in the world, you might be good on your feet and able to improvise brilliantly, you might have a natural empathy for young people and be very responsive to their needs—but in the end, if you don't know the difference between good and bad teaching, if you aren't aware of the strategies that succeed with students and haven't learned how to use them, if you do things that are fun but that don't really get students to learn more, then you will sell your students short. Even with the best of intentions, even if you seem like a "natural" as a teacher, unless you deliberately learn how to get better so you can teach the students of today for the world of tomorrow, you will not be teaching like a pro. You will be just an enthusiastic amateur.

Evidence in Excess

So is more and better evidence the answer? It can be, but not completely. For half a century, researchers claimed they had discovered the secrets of effective teaching. Mainly, though, these came down to a few strategies of whole-class teaching—the use of wait time in questioning techniques, coverage of material, pacing of content, and so on. Also, other than reading the teacher's manual, there were no real ideas about how to put these findings into practice.[1]

With the resurgence of the evidence-based teaching movement since the 1990s, data now drive more and more classroom decision making. The knowledge base of effective learning and teaching with more than just whole-class methods has grown considerably. There is more for teachers to work with now than just their philosophies and preferences.

In his work on underperforming schools, Richard Elmore has observed that teacher collaborations often focus on passion and enthusiasm for teaching rather than evidence about what students are actually learning.[2] Some teachers, it seems, would rather drool over each other's dioramas (these are a teacher's words, not ours) than ask hard questions about what is or isn't effective.

So having more research-based evidence and paying attention to that evidence is a good thing. But the case can also be overstated.[3] Here's why:

- *Evidence-based decisions can be tainted with self-interest*—when they are tied to publishers' textbooks or to programs associated with their founders and promoters, for instance.
- *Cast-iron evidence can get rusty later on.* The highly acclaimed literacy gains made by New York District 2 in the 1990s, for example, were later criticized by Diane Ravitch for being at least partly a result of the rising status and affluence of students' incoming families whose children started attending the schools, rather than solely due to the teaching strategies that were introduced at the time.[4]
- *Evidence-based principles are used very selectively* and sometimes politically. For instance, there is extensive evidence in favor of mixed ability rather than tracked (streamed) classes, and in favor of immigrant second language students being given early instruction in their own language—but many politicians find these too hard to sell to their public.

- *Evidence isn't always self-evident.* What's balanced literacy to one person isn't the same to another. And though tracking might in general be harmful to students, if you allocate some of your best teachers to lower tracks (as does high-performing Singapore), rather than putting inexperienced or more poorly qualified teachers there (as in the United States), the results can turn out differently.

- *Evidence on what to change isn't the same as evidence on how to change.* This is Change 101. Research-based practices might get good results in small-group experiments, well-funded pilot projects, or innovative schools. But when they are mandated for all schools with less support, and fewer resources, and with whole classes rather than smaller groups, they sometimes can't be implemented even by the schools that invented them.[5]

- *Positive initiatives based on evidence in one area can inflict collateral damage on* programs and teaching in other areas. Excessive attention to the evidence of what produces test score gains in literacy and mathematics can leave little time for teaching and learning in other important areas such as humanities and the arts. Evidence that leads to incremental *improvement* in knowledge that is easily tested may undermine the *innovation* that is essential for 21st-century learning.[6]

- *People can cook the data* when stakes are high and loaded with perverse incentives, resulting in gaming the system and systemic cheating, as we saw in Atlanta, which is just the tip of a sinister iceberg.[7]

- *Evidence-based teaching is only somewhat like evidence-based medicine.* An evidence-based teacher is less like a clinically precise surgeon than like a family care physician or a general practitioner (as they are called in Canada and the United Kingdom). And even surgery and clinical trials aren't all that precise. As Caroline Riehl points out in her comparative study of educational and medical research, they are "really just a probability."[8]

- *Evidence comes from experience as well as research.* Indeed, research often picks up and tries to generalize practices that begin with real teachers in real schools.

So the appeal to advances in research-based evidence about teaching and learning might seem like a field of dreams for improving professional practice. But the field is more like a minefield. So-called evidence can be unclear, ambiguous, compromised, out of date, indecipherable, contested, or just plain wrong. This is not a reason to fall back on intuition or personal preference as the sole basis for teaching. We just need to be a bit more humble and careful about what we are claiming. Teachers with professional capital are not driven by data or overly dependent on measurable evidence—but they do inquire into, identify, and adapt the best ways for moving forward, making intelligent, critical, and reflective use of measurable evidence and considered experience alike. And they are committed to knowing and showing what impact they have on their students, and to fulfilling their responsibility for making this transparent to the public they serve.

Joining Research to Practice

There is a place where research and practice *do* meet. Now that classrooms have become less privatized, and new strategies have not only gotten "behind the classroom door," but have also opened the "walls of schools" to working with each other, we have a golden opportunity to sort out good from bad practice.

The dilemma involves avoiding too much prescription of pedagogy on the one hand versus laissez-faire autonomy on the other. The era of individual classroom autonomy in the 1960s and 1970s is sometimes looked upon nostalgically as the golden age of teaching.[9] In reality, though, while it represented the freedom to be creative and brilliantly effective for some teachers, it was also a license to be ineffective (and not even know it) among others. As the student population grew more diverse and more complex, individual classroom autonomy became a liability.

The English tried to solve this problem through their focus on literacy and numeracy during Tony Blair's first term in 1997 by developing a system of "informed prescription."[10] The center mandated new instructional practices that it believed had a solid evidence base behind them. This did some good in the short run by tightening up a loose system and adding new practices to all teachers' repertoires (although this might have been just as achievable with equivalent amounts of new resources and a less autocratic improvement approach). But it ultimately failed to form a foundation of continuous improvement, because new teachers never developed the ability to create new practice themselves.[11] By eliminating teachers' license to design and perhaps even misuse their own ideas individually, the adoption of excessive prescription also undermined teachers' collective capacity and responsibility to design and develop, inquire into, and implement good classroom practice together. Compare this to high-performing Finland, where, within broad guidelines, teachers routinely create curriculum and pedagogy together as an integral part of their collective professional responsibility.[12]

Like all professional practice, teaching cannot be politically and administratively prescribed line by line. The best chefs don't rely literally on cookbooks. As co-authors and colleagues, we recognize that we each have different strengths and weaknesses in our work and in other areas of our lives. One of us is a reasonably good cook; the other definitely isn't. Reading a new recipe for goulash many years ago when making the family dinner, one of us read the line in the text "salt, two tablespoons." Unfortunately, salt was one ingredient, and two tablespoons of something else that was described on the next line of the recipe was the next. The recipe absolutely wasn't meant to have two tablespoons of salt! The meal was inedible. And classroom practices are just as unpalatable when they are prescribed down to every last sentence in the manual.

In 2003, when Ontario began its own pursuit of literacy and numeracy reform, it took a proactive middle ground between prescription and individual autonomy. The goal was to pursue and consolidate effective instructional practices—many of which were already "out there" in this or that school—and spread them, all the while testing their effectiveness and searching for new practices wherever they could be found in research and practice around the world. This is what one of us has called "precision, and innovation."[13] Effective practices such as providing feedback to students cannot spread just by describing them or advocating for their use. They have to be seen, observed, experienced, interpreted, inquired into, tried out, and so on.

Best Practice and Next Practice

What is needed is a profession that constantly and collectively builds its knowledge base and corresponding expertise, where practices and their impact are transparently tested, developed, circulated, and adapted. There needs to be a continuous amalgamation of precision and innovation, as well as inquiry, improvisation, and experimentation. The sorting process involves one's own and other teachers' practice informed by the research base and interpreted together. And there needs to be a mix of committing to *best prac-*

tice (existing practices that already
have a good degree of widely agreed
effectiveness) and having the freedom, space, and resources to create
next practice (innovative approaches

 Professional capital is about communities of teachers using best and next practices together.

that often begin with teachers themselves and that will sometimes turn out
to be the best practices of the future).[14] Best practice without next practice
just drives teachers through implementing and fine-tuning what already
exists. Next practice without best practice has no way of sorting out the
strong emerging ideas from the weak ones. Professional capital is about
communities of teachers using best and next practices together.

What this means is that while it can be helpful for a school district to
come up with an alphabetized list of 26 memorably titled practices of differentiated instruction, for example, this should never be treated as just one
more menu of fun strategies for teachers to try out when they are bored
with their other practices or feel like a change. But these practices can be
selected when they are right for this moment, for these outcomes, with these
students—decisions that are best made as a community of teachers and
other leaders in a grade level, a school, or a group of schools, not as a bunch
of autonomous individuals working by themselves. Research in any field can
be dangerous if you are not a thinking professional, and if you and your colleagues are not deliberating on what is working or not, and what should
come next. And it can be drastically diminished if professionals are not provided with that thinking time to inquire into and improve their own expertise—if they are given scarcely any time, or if almost all of the time is eaten
up with implementing external policies. Teachers in Finland spend less time
in the classroom each week than teachers in any other developed country.
They have time to inquire into what they are doing. The opposite is true in
the United States—being a teacher means spending almost all your time just
teaching and teaching without time to reflect on and refine that teaching.[15]

It turns out that the best practice does actually have a compelling evidence base of a particular kind. One of the most trusted sources of knowledge in educational and medical research is called meta-analyses. These are
comprehensive and careful reviews that draw conclusions from many studies, not just one, about the balance of evidence on chosen issues. For many
years, New Zealand was committed to evidence-based improvement. It com-
missioned highly regarded scholars to undertake state-of-the-art reviews of
many studies for areas such as subject area teaching, educational leadership,

professional learning, and effective instruction; then it used these to guide change. John Hattie, now at the University of Melbourne, led the review of studies of teaching and learning from across the world.[16] He delved into over 800 meta-analyses spanning a 15-year period relating to the influences on achievement of school-aged children (in effect he did a meta-analysis of hundreds of meta-analyses). He drew conclusions about the classroom practices that had significant effect sizes on student outcomes. The top teaching practices with the biggest effect sizes included:

- Reciprocal teaching (teachers enabling students to learn and use self-learning)
- Feedback (specific response to student work)
- Teaching students self-verbalization or self-questioning
- Meta-cognition strategies (awareness and knowledge of one's own thinking)
- Problem-solving teaching

Hattie concludes, "these top methods rely on the influence of peers, feedback, transparent learning intentions and success criteria . . . using various strategies, attending to both surface and deep knowing."[17]

It's important to know which practices have the biggest positive effects, but a list like this has little value by itself unless you are working with a group of other professionals sharpening the operational meaning of the items on it, and determining how and when to use these different strategies with one's own students. Hattie points to this more richly contextualized meaning through six signposts:[18]

1. Teachers are among the most powerful sources of influence on learning.
2. Teachers need to be directive, influential, caring, and actively engaged in the passion of teaching and learning.
3. Teachers need to be aware of what each and every child is thinking and knowing, to construct meaningful experiences in light of this knowledge.
4. Teachers need to know *the learning intentions* and success criteria of their lessons, know *how well they are attaining* these criteria for all students, and know *where to go next* in light of the gap.

5. Teachers need to move from single ideas to multiple ideas . . . such that learners are able to construct and reconstruct knowledge and ideas whatever specific method is being used at one time.
6. School leaders and teachers need to create [learning] environments where error is welcomed as a learning opportunity and where discarding incorrect knowledge and understanding is welcomed.

In *Visible Learning Inside: Maximizing Student Achievement,* Hattie takes these ideas further. He organizes his advice around the teaching and learning unit of the lesson: preparing the lesson, starting it, the learning phase, the feedback phase, and the end of the lesson. "What is most important," says Hattie, "is that teaching is visible to the student, and that learning is visible to the teacher. The more the student becomes the teacher and the more the teacher becomes the learner then the more successful the outcomes."[19] How different this is from the days when only the teacher knew what the point of the lesson was, when the students didn't know what they would be graded on until after they got their grades, or when the teacher only grasped the students' level of insight after an entire final assignment had been completed. And how much this shift in teaching is like the transformation in medical practice—where the best practice takes the patient transparently through the steps of diagnosis and makes the patient's own awareness of his or her changing body and symptoms a key and open part of that diagnosis. So, making teaching and learning reciprocally visible is more than a cliché—it is sophisticated practice in any professional sphere.

Recall that the 800 meta-analyses covered the world, with a high predominance of research from the United States. This means, for example, that Hattie draws heavily on Bob Marzano's research over a decade that confirms many of these findings in the best of U.S. classrooms.[20] Effective practices, in other words, are out there; they are just not as widespread as they should be, nor are there clear strategies to make them so.

But even with this evidence, shrewd professionals should still remain cautious and questioning about all of the information they use. The good thing about these meta-analyses of effective teaching practice is that they go back 15 years and more. This is, of course, also the bad thing about them. The unit of the lesson that Hattie adopts as the standard currency of teaching and schooling is more than a century old. Yet, lessons have never been the only unit of teaching and they will likely become less and less the unit of teaching in the future. What about the nature field trip, the drama production, the afternoon integrated social studies project, the ongoing student-led engagements in cooperative group work, the scientific investigation of pollution in the

> ◆〉 Professional expertise is not just about having the evidence or being aware of it. It's also about knowing how to judge the evidence and knowing what to do with it.

local river, the learning of assistive technologies among learning disabled students, or the use of Twitter and other cell-phone technology as a real-time classroom feedback device as opposed to feedback being something that is confined to a single time slot or lesson phase? And then, even if we stay within the framework of lessons, what about the far less linear dance performance, the teaching of music or art, or the magical start to an upcoming literary theme such as the experience of loss or being treated as an outsider, where the teacher purposely decides *not* to disclose the purpose of the lesson at the beginning in order to maximize the impact of surprise later on? If we are saying that it is outdated to base teachers' contracts on class sizes, using the class as the unit of calculation, then we have to acknowledge that among administrators and researchers, the lesson may be and should be becoming equally outdated as the unit of teaching and learning too.

Look at tried-and-tested best practice by all means, but don't use it blindly to reinforce or repeat past practice that may be moving beyond its sell-by date. Don't allow the perpetuation of certain kinds of *best* practice to eclipse the constant pursuit of *next* practice in subjects other than literacy, mathematics, and science, or in formats of learning other than the century-old lesson. In other words, let's deliberately have more learning, fewer lessons—just as we now have less surgery that tears open the body in favor of microsurgery instead. And most of all *do* keep looking at the evidence and judging the evidence, remaining open to what it teaches, but *do also* stay professionally shrewd and watchful about the limitations of that evidence.

Expert teachers are always consolidating what they know to be effective, testing it, and continuously adding to it. It's not just the evidence, but what you do with it, how you evaluate it here and now, and how you connect it to other evidence, including the evidence of your own collective experience, that matters. You can't mandate evidence-based programs in lockstep fashion. Professional expertise is not just about having the evidence or being aware of it. It's also about knowing how to judge the evidence and knowing what to do with it.

CAPABILITY

When you get the expertise issue right, the consequences are far-reaching. What you get is *capability,* the first of the five Cs that define teaching like a pro. Capability is more than mere competence. The dictionary definition of competence refers to having "requisite or adequate ability." Capability is more than this. To be capable means "to have attributes required for performance or accomplishment."[21] Capabilities set higher bars for performance than simple competencies. They are about accomplishment, not just adequacy. They are about capital as a generative asset.

Capabilities—skills and qualities that lead to accomplishment—build confidence. When you know you are truly capable of performing better, and when you have the knowledge and skill to reach your students and develop their own capabilities far beyond what anyone first expected, then this is invigorating. Culinary skills make you feel more capable as a cook. A wider repertoire of well-founded classroom strategies makes you feel more capable as a teacher. And when this produces results in the form of delicious dishes or successful learning, it is self-reinforcing—leading to a hunger for more learning, stronger commitment, and professional fulfillment. Winning streaks work in sports, and they work as upward spirals of confidence and success in schools too.[22]

In case this all sounds a bit abstract, let's look at some examples. What do you do when teachers in a high-poverty school believe their children can't learn? Show them that they can. And do so in a way that includes the teacher as part of the solution, equipped with new experiences that enable him or her to *realize* success of a kind that hadn't been thought possible. Take these two cases from longer descriptions developed by our colleague Mary Jean Gallagher in Ontario and research team member Katherine Ghent in England, respectively:[23]

Ontario, 2009. Elementary teachers met every two weeks with their colleagues to review progress of students in order to set and try to meet learning outcomes for these students over six weekly cycles. Many students' performance at the end of the cycle far exceeded their teachers' predictions. One Grade 4 teacher testified how she "came to these PD sessions because my principal sent me." At the first session, she said, "I knew I should not have come. I looked at examples of Grade 4 student work from other teachers and I felt really badly. I had been teaching for years and knew my students could never produce such high quality writing. I did my best, though, to follow the process, feeling sick at heart for my kids. As the cycle progressed my classroom soared. Every one of my kids (who had been at Level 2) has produced writing at the high end of Level 3, some at Level 4. For 25 years of teaching I have set our goals too low. How many more of my students could have reached so much higher if only I had known I could take them there?"

Sometimes, teachers like the one above have to be steered into new practices before they will change their beliefs. But sometimes it's more complicated than that:[24]

Limeside, 2000. In June 2000, Limeside Primary School, on a deprived council estate in the North of England, was classified by the English inspection service, Ofsted, as needing to go into "Special Measures." Less than a third of the children were reaching proficiency on standardized achievement tests and many children were leaving school "not able to read." "It really hurt," the head teacher recalled. The school was "a slum school that nobody wanted to go to, in a slum estate that nobody wanted to live in. . . . There were no real expectations for the children. It was kind of, 'Well they're Limeside children, so what can you expect?'"

Over the years, the school turned around with many familiar strategies such as establishing a calm climate with a positive behavior strategy, setting a common vision, relentlessly tracking children's progress, and changing teachers' roles and responsibilities. The great leap forward, though, was developing higher expectations for success and the teaching and learning strategies to match them. These days, in the words of a teaching assistant, "Limeside gives them the confidence to achieve."

The challenges don't get any easier. Many children entering the school are barely toilet trained, and staff spend the first weeks "literally mopping up." Language skills and social skills are "off the scale in terms of being very low," but within 3 years the children perform well above the national norm.

Some of Limeside's strategies came from research, some from experience. Both kinds of evidence matter. But it's the success that matters most of all. Philosophy sessions enabled children to discuss things in an open forum. The head teacher introduced meditation each morning to settle children and staff into the day. Children are also explicitly taught prior learning, learning styles, and meta-cognition. Wall displays show jigsaw puzzle pieces with the key thinking skills and activities within them. Children are able to follow the framework, looking at prior knowledge, identifying the task, working together, and trying to find the best way of solving the problems, then teaching somebody else when they've managed it. Limeside is a place where John Hattie's list of successful practices comes alive in action.

The school bought wizard hats and cloaks and anybody who has shown they are a wizard learner in mastering the key thinking skills is dressed up in assembly to receive their certificate. "The wizard learner is a real event and this wizard is able to ask questions. He's able to work with somebody else. He's able to do lots of home learning. He's able to know what to do when you don't know what to do." The consequence is confidence, accomplishment, and more confidence for children and teachers alike. "It's a major high when you see a child that has struggled and struggled but persevered and has shown that 'I am going to do this' and they walk up on that stage at the end of so many weeks and they get there and what they say is, 'I've turned a corner, I can do it and not only can I do it but I can show somebody else how to do it.' That's a real high when you see that."

These two examples start in different places. One begins with a teacher's required attendance at a professional development event and an uncomfortable confrontation with what other teachers have achieved with similar students. It's like a cold shower. The other is driven more by an inspiring vision, collective determination, and innovative teaching and learning strategies. It's more like a hot Jacuzzi.

Politicians and administrators, and those who work a lot with them, might prefer the first example. It vindicates a kind of imposed change—that you must push or force teachers to alter their practice before they will change their beliefs (although if you look closely, it is also *peers* who put pressure on their colleagues to start looking at and using the most effective practices).

Professionals, especially teachers, might be more drawn to the second example. It validates inclusion, inspiration, and innovation—the idea that inspiring people and drawing them into change must precede the action of bringing change about. These alternatives prompt many pointless arguments about how to make change happen. But the reality is that both of them are true. It's the cycle and synergy that matters—new expertise, emotional high, more expertise, greater highs, leaders and peers mixing it up, and so on. Or you can start with the emotional high of an inspiring vision before accessing new expertise. Like a Finnish sauna, the sequence of hot sweats and cold wake-up calls stimulates the greatest professional invigoration of all.

The truth is that whatever the route, teachers must experience the moral passion and depth of learning and achievement in their own classrooms and schools. To go back to Hattie's work—it's not so much about using a list of techniques, but about having a lust for success. Some teachers with a passion for teaching and success are thwarted by bad working conditions or by poor leadership—in effect, waking up daily with moral purpose they cannot use. Others may have been missing some of the expertise or may have had insufficient or misplaced professional passion, but they can rise to the occasion when inspired and supported—when the positive pressure and support to do good kicks in. When this pressure and support is embodied in one's peers, it is an irresistible force for most people. For the few remaining immovable objects who cannot or will not respond when all the circumstances start to push and support them, it's probably time to leave.

We can draw two conclusions. First, in teaching, impassioned commitments and moral causes are just pious posturing unless they come with experiences of success. Teachers soar not just when they want success but when they also know *how* to get it, and when they know it's achievable. Second, expertise alone is equally inadequate without the desire and the drive of teachers' purpose and passion. Knowing what to do and how to do it is of little value if you don't care about what you do or whom you're doing it for, if you're told to do things you don't agree with, if you no longer have any say in what you do, or if you're exhausted by doing too much of it for too long.

Capability and commitment have to come together at every level. Teachers in Finland, for example, have incredible qualifications and expertise (5 years of rigorous training including understanding children's learning through cognitive science and undertaking inquiry and research) plus extended periods of school practice. Yet when they enter teaching, they are also screened for whether they are suited to working with young people.

Their classes are small enough for them to really know all their children well—in elementary school, being with them for more than 1 year where possible.[25] Rigor and relationships, expertise and engagement—all of these things matter. Let's look at the commitment part of this combination in more detail.

COMMITMENT

Teacher quality and capability clearly matter for students' learning. But the big question is: What matters most in creating teacher quality? In *Teachers Matter* and their follow-up book on *The Lives of Teachers,* Chris Day and his colleagues have undertaken one of the most systematic studies ever of factors determining teacher quality and effectiveness.[26] Surveying and interviewing 300 teachers in 100 schools over a 3-year period about their professional and personal lives as well as their sense of their own effectiveness, and connecting the findings to sophisticated measures of value-added achievement among their students, Day's research team has unearthed some fascinating findings.

Like the economists who calibrate teacher performance, these researchers demonstrate that there is more variation in effectiveness among teachers within schools than between schools. It's what explains this difference that's the critical point. The economists' implicit theory seems to be that the more effective teachers are simply better, work harder, or are more conscientious and therefore deserve to be rewarded for their efforts. By contrast, Day and his colleagues link effectiveness to teachers' commitments in their work—commitments to children, to the work itself and becoming more capable in it, and to serving others with dedication and effort.

All of this still begs the key question: How do you sustain and renew teachers' commitments to their work over time? For the value-added economists, it's monetary incentives and rewards. For Day's team—and they are not alone—the evidence points to other factors:

- *Career stage.* The highest levels of effectiveness occur around 8–23 years in the job. So if strategies for improving teacher quality bring in enthusiastic young people for 3–5 years and then see a lot of them move on, there will be a failure to maximize any return on investment of money and time because the young teachers leave years before they have achieved peak performance.

- *Leadership,* More than three-quarters of teachers who demonstrated sustained commitment said that good leadership helped them sustain their commitment over time. These teachers mentioned the importance of leaders having a "clear vision,"[27] treating them "like an adult,"[28] being committed to and visible about the school, being open and approachable, trusting teachers, and demonstrating personal care for people. On the flip side, among the quarter of teachers whose commitment was declining, 58% said that poor leadership was a key factor. These leaders didn't "appreciate what teachers were doing,"[29] made teachers feel "unsupported"[30] and "picked on,"[31] left them feeling "on their own,"[32] and pushed out staff, who "left under a cloud,"[33] So, better leaders produce better teachers. Why penalize a teacher financially for having a bad leader?

- *Colleagues.* Teachers who can sustain their commitment notice when they are surrounded by excellent colleagues. In the study by Day and his associates, 63% of teachers with sustained commitment felt colleagues were crucial. Primary or elementary teachers especially valued teamwork, someone to talk to when things went wrong, and a feeling that everyone was pulling in the same direction. Of course, a few teachers can still be resilient and maintain commitment in the absence of collegial support—they can be eccentric outliers, heroic iconoclasts, and courageous lone warriors in the face of indifference and adversity. And we should always be thankful for them. But in general, you get more good teachers by having more great colleagues who are able and willing to work together for the same cause. Conversely, apathetic or cynical colleagues can erode your own commitment. Indeed, people who might make good teachers sometimes don't go into teaching because they don't think they will have quality colleagues. We say more about this later.

- *Workload and policy.* This was the biggest issue for teachers experiencing declining commitment—affecting almost 60% of them. We're sorry to have to tell political leaders that teachers (in fact, people in general) don't usually gush with praise over successful policies. But they do notice when policies are awful or annoying. They complain about the "massive workload"[34] that "eats away at your life,"[35] about excessive paperwork, about policies that are "very prescriptive,"[36] and about training that is overwhelmingly directed toward government initiatives—making teachers lose focus because they have no time for their own professional learning and reflection.

High-performing countries on international tests provide their teachers with strong support and give them a lot of (though not limitless) professional discretion rather than subjecting then to dumbed-down mandates and pre-scriptions.[37] In Finland, it's creating curriculum together as colleagues, district by district. In Singapore, it's having "white space" to develop your own integrated curriculum projects. In Alberta, it's 90% of schools and their teachers receiving government funding to design their own innovations within the frame of existing priorities.

Meanwhile, what should countries like the United States and England do when they have been mediocre performers on international tests in spite of imposing years of high-stakes testing and pervasive prescription? On the one hand, they need to reduce the excessive emphasis on testing (as England has recently done, with Alberta now following suit); and on the other hand, they need to create an alternative system such as Finland's testing by confidential samples, where the use of diagnostic evidence is integral to day-to-day improvement as well as to maintaining public accountability.

Commitment is an emotional state as well as a moral value. It is purpose plus drive and direction. It has consistent effects on perceived and actual effectiveness in relation to student achievement. For most teachers, commitment is not just a personal virtue but something that is profoundly affected by what happens at work and what happens in their life. Day and his colleagues' work shows that over time, your commitment is likely to be sustained or to decline depending on what's happening in:

1. Your *personal life* (health, relationships, dependents, and so on)
2. Your *professional life* (experiences of learning, support, or progression—or of intrusive policies and top-down training)
3. Y*our school* (supportive or unsupportive leadership, and strong or weak collegiality)

If all three areas line up positively, or even two of them do, then your commitment and effectiveness are likely to be strong. If all three are weak—your personal life is beset with problems, you are not progressing professionally, and the school environment is toxic—then your commitment and effectiveness are likely to plunge into decline. Three strikes and you're out! Teachers can usually cope with one strike if they have sufficient support elsewhere in their lives. They can outlast a poor principal if they feel supported by their colleagues or by their partner at home. They can endure a personal breakup or bereavement if colleagues and their principal are understanding and supportive rather than making them feel guilty for being absent. They can withstand insensitive or badly implemented policies if principals and colleagues know how to twist them to suit the focus of their school. Overall, Day and his colleagues conclude:

> For commitment to flourish and for teachers to be resilient and effective, they need a strong and enduring sense of efficacy—the ability to handle new situations confidently, believing that they will make a difference—and they need to work in external and internal environments which are less bureaucratically managerial, less reliant on crude measures [that] sap rather than build morale. They need to work in schools in which leadership is supportive, clear, strong and passionately committed to maintaining the quality of their commitment.[38]

The research of Day's team and of many other studies highlights how the expertise argument can be overstated. When expertise is imposed and elevated as the only answer to improving teaching, it promotes and perpetuates a passive view of the teacher, who is seen as empty, deficient, and lacking in skills—needing to be filled up and fixed up with new techniques and strategies. It develops things *for* teachers, not *by* them or *with* them. It takes responsibility for concentrating curriculum development away from teachers, in the district or government office—unlike what is done in high-performing countries such as Finland and now Singapore, where highly qualified teachers design much of the curriculum and a lot of innovation together. Riding roughshod over teachers' purposes and undermining their discretionary judgment only leads to resistance and resentment.

Saying that teaching is a matter of moral commitment isn't just a sanctimonious statement or an assertion that any purpose will do. Commitment—a combination of purpose and passion—has a direct effect on *self-efficacy* (teachers' beliefs that they actually can make a difference) and in turn on student achievement. We have known this for over a quarter century, since Pat Ashton and Rod Webb and many others showed that teachers with a lower sense of efficacy produced lower rates of achievement and were more preoccupied with covering prescribed material.[39] Commitment contributes to capability, then.

In the United States and England, between 70% and 75% of teachers see themselves as committed.[40] Not bad—but not brilliant either. You can't build a strong system when more than a quarter of the profession is not committed. And many among the so-called committed would not necessarily be focused on developing professional capital—where ever-increasing capability is deliberately and systematically added to teachers' commitment. There is clearly a lot of work to be done here—not instead of developing teachers' expertise or capability, but alongside it. Capability and commitment are reciprocal in professional capital. They drive each other.

A further clue about where to act and what to do is provided by the research on teachers' careers. We need to understand the socio-psychological dynamics of different stages of a career. And we need to appreciate and cultivate what teachers of all ages have to offer.

CAREER

Teachers are more than performers. Teachers are people too. You can't switch teachers on and off like a computer. You can't understand the teacher or his or her teaching without understanding the person the teacher is. And you can't fundamentally change the teacher without changing the person the teacher is, either. This means that meaningful or lasting change will almost inevitably be slower than nonteachers want it to be. Human growth is not like producing hydroponic tomatoes. It can be nurtured and encouraged, but it cannot be forced.

You can't make a proper judgment about a teacher's performance in isolation if you behave like a clipboard king or queen on a quick classroom visit to fill out a checklist. Dropping in unannounced on a teacher's lesson for an evaluation, a walk-through, or an instructional round, it's easy to take a dim view of the teacher who is administering a routine test, or just having quiet time. But this is a view taken out of context, which judges the teacher against ideal models of instruction rather than against the backdrop of classroom realities. These may include the teacher's health or energy level, his or her need to catch up with one particular student group, or the need to deal with the emotional spillover effects of a previous lesson taught by another teacher or to recover from a confrontation with a troublesome student. You can't judge people if you don't know them or if you don't know what they are doing.

One thing that helps us get to know teachers, or anyone for that matter, is to understand what stage of life and career they are in. When teachers become more and more jaundiced about reform strategies over time, this sometimes has to do with the reforms themselves. But it also has to do with how teachers experience changes and change as they progress through the job. And all this affects their commitment. Some think it comes down to the stage of life teachers are in—how much energy and openness to change they can sustain as they get older. Some think it comes down to career stage—where teachers are in the job, what expertise they have built up, and what responsibilities they have taken on. The most recent research also points to a third factor—the generation teachers belong to and how that whole generation travels through life and work with its own distinctive way of looking at the world.

Building on the landmark study of teachers' lives and careers by U.S. researcher Michael Huberman in Switzerland in the 1980s, Day and his colleagues identified six career/life phases within teaching.[41] Each one of them, they found, has a mixture of teachers who are either sustaining commitment or losing it. No surprises there! But the interesting thing is that although committed teachers outnumber those who are losing commitment in all groups, the proportions vary substantially from one career phase to the next. Here are the six phases:

1. Phase 0–3 years: Commitment: support and challenge
2. Phase 4–7 years: Identity and efficacy in the classroom
3. Phase 8–15 years: Managing changes, growing tensions
4. Phase 16–23 years: Work-life transitions, challenges to motivation and commitment
5. Phase 24–30 years: Challenges to sustaining motivation
6. Phase 31+ years: Sustaining/declining motivation

There are three key phases where these life/career/generational phases have a critical effect on teachers' commitment: the first years in teaching, the final years in the profession, and the middle—about 8–23 years into the job. Let's start at the end.

Ending Up

In teaching, as in life, we are quick to judge those who fail more than those who succeed. When teachers are new to the job, incompetence can, perhaps, be forgiven. They are only learning after all. Experienced teachers, who should have matured with their years in the classroom, get away less lightly. We have graphic labels for teachers like these—"deadwood," "burned out," "time-servers," and "past-it"! But these labels don't really explain these teachers' difficulties. They explain them *away*. They don't invite solutions except ones that remove or give in to the problem altogether. The fault is presumed to be in the teacher, deeply ingrained in that person's personality. There is little point, therefore, in trying to change him or her. Not much you can do about bad teachers, especially bad *old* teachers, except wait for them to leave, retire, or die! Or dispense with them altogether. "If only I could get some new teachers" or "Wait until my new teachers arrive"—these are principals' stock responses to this apparently intractable problem.

Yet have you ever wondered what these 50-something or even 60-something "time-servers" were like when they were 35, or 25? Were they just ticking over then too? Were they *that* cynical? Is it possible that they were once as enthusiastic and idealistic as many of their younger colleagues are now? And if they were, what happened to them in the meantime? Why did they change? Have you ever wondered what it might be like to be one of these people, to be the man or woman behind the mask? "Dead wood" doesn't kill itself. It's usually the product of an infertile environment. To be blunt: schools, systems, and countries end up with the teachers they deserve. It's really a question of how much each society supports and values its teachers, and what it does to build and develop the teaching profession.

The years approaching the end of a teaching career are the most precarious for teacher commitment. In the study by Day and his colleagues, 43% of teachers with 24 years or more of experience were finding it hard to sustain motivation or were feeling trapped. These are big numbers. But they don't mean the decline is inevitable.

A few years ago, one of us examined how age and career stage affects how teachers respond emotionally to educational change.[42] Teachers with more than 20 years of experience described how they were losing energy and transferring some of what remained to their personal lives. They were aware that their "patience may dissipate much quicker,"[43] and they had to remind themselves that they were "tired and it's not the kids' fault."[44] In a classic study by Pat Sikes on *The Life Cycle of the Teacher,* one teacher put it in a nutshell: "The kids are always the same age and you gradually get older and older. And unfortunately too, their capacity for life, their energy remains the same as yours diminishes."[45]

Generationally, these teachers were aware of approaching retirement and of the need to have their contributions recognized before they moved on. They were also more outspoken than many colleagues—using the unsinkable status that comes with upcoming retirement to resist and "be more questioning" of unreasonable, repetitive changes imposed from the outside.

So perhaps this all confirms that if teachers haven't made it into administration or some other role after 20-odd years, it may just be time to get out the big hook and pull them off the stage. There's a lot more to it than this, though. Teachers in this group might be more vociferous about questioning external changes—and let's face it, when they say the training is poor, or they have seen a lot of it before, or it's all a numbers game—they are often right! But if older teachers might get more stressed outside the classroom, they often become more phlegmatic about the universal annoyances of teaching—poor behavior, forgetting equipment, and so on—inside the classroom. They are more accepting, more focused, more serene.

Back in the 1980s, Michael Huberman saw that the older generation of teachers couldn't all be lumped into one category.[46] Some did, of course, fit the stereotype of their critics—they were self-interested, protective of keeping the best students and schedules, resistant to any change that required extra work, and they had sometimes ended up in teaching for the wrong reasons in the first place. These *negative focusers,* as Huberman called them, are the bane of administrators' lives and are regularly and perhaps rightly demonized as expendable baggage or toxic jerks in popular leadership texts. And the profession as well as the system needs to get much tougher on them because otherwise their colleagues who display similar behaviors, but for very dissimilar reasons, get tarred with the same brush.

One of these other subgroups is what Huberman calls the *disenchanted*—people who have invested themselves heavily in two or three major change efforts only to see the rug pulled from under their feet every time because the focus shifted, the resources were withdrawn, or the leaders and champions of change moved on. More performance assessments are not what these teachers need—they just need a reform environment that isn't constantly driven from the outside, overloaded with endless interventions, and afflicted with unstable leadership that turns over like a hyperactive carousel. What these teachers need is to get *re-enchanted,* to be in an inspiring and improving environment, to get back some of the magic, and to know that it will stay. They need principals and colleagues who will excite them, invigorate them, and even provoke them and who will, just as importantly, commit to seeing things through.

A third subgroup is the *positive focusers.* They care about students and their achievement and have learned to avoid the distractions of repetitive reform efforts. They decide to spend their remaining years in the profession by concentrating on their own schools and classrooms, where they believe they can make a difference. They may not be cheerleaders for the next BIG THING, but if they can be convinced that change really will benefit their children's learning, that their leaders know what good learning looks like, that the way they have taught before still has something of value to contribute today, that the achievement data speak to and don't just serve as a substitute for their own real students, and that it isn't all about test scores and someone else's agenda—then the system can expand the *professional capital* that these teachers have already accumulated over the decades.

Finally there's one more subgroup—those who renew their commitments by finding challenge and being challenged throughout their careers. This *renewal* group is at the center of the drive advocated and exemplified by Ann Lieberman, Frank Crowther, Alma Harris, The California Teachers Association, and others to develop powerful teacher leadership that isn't just about taking on administrative responsibilities but also about leading innovation and improvement in schools.[47] Teacher leadership that prompts teacher renewal is about:

- Starting and spreading new projects and not just implementing them
- Finding colleagues who can create something exciting with you together
- Helping struggling peers in your own school and in schools that struggle more than yours
- Receiving resources for change that sometimes go direct to the teacher and not always via the superintendent and then the principal
- Being part of high-level conversations where the teacher can come across as being just as smart and confident as the principal or the policymaker
- Being open to change but not exploitable by fashion
- Managing upward and challenging the system when you have to, so you can help your students
- Grasping that as soon as something is operating like clockwork— then it's probably time to change it!

If these things are done *by* teachers, *for* teachers, and *with* teachers, then most people's teaching career will end in a bang, not a whimper. But so far, the sorts of renewal endeavors outlined above have, with few exceptions, been undertaken largely outside the mainstream of reform, or at best as an appendage to it. Our book, by contrast, is about making professional capital the core of a whole new profession. It is about a transformation of the system that affects all teachers—every one of them.

It will help if the career patterns of teachers provide more built-in opportunities for leadership. In Singapore, for example, when teachers are first hired they become eligible to choose among three possible career ladders: the Master Teacher track; the administrative Leadership track, or the Senior Specialist track (these ladder placements are also reviewed on a continuous basis in conversation with school leaders and Ministry staff). Although we are not advocating global adoption of this particular scheme (because of the dangers of cherry-picking we mentioned earlier), imagine how the psychological mind-set of many teachers might improve across the years if they became engaged in leadership and peer interaction opportunities on a regular basis with the accompanying satisfaction, stimulation, and recognition.

It will also help immensely if the culture and working conditions of teachers change to make renewal a normal part of what the profession does as part of its daily work (see Chapters 5 and 6). Aging teachers should not just think themselves fortunate if they get opportunities for renewal—this should be an expected part of their career path and their working conditions.

Starting Out

In addition to teachers' twilight years, the other point where teachers' commitment and effectiveness are really vulnerable is at the start of the teaching career. Study after study points to the high numbers who leave in these early years—around 30% on average, with the number closer to half in high-poverty situations in the United States.[48] Of course, some go on to other work that deals directly or indirectly with children and learning. The numbers of exits from public school classrooms are still very high, though. They represent an enormously costly revolving door with the students in greatest need getting the teachers with the least experience.

Getting the right people to start with is one way to prevent early exits. Consider the findings of a major report by McKinsey & Company, who asked top-third students in university graduating classes who were not contemplating teaching as a career, how they ranked attributes of the teaching profession compared to the career they planned to pursue.[49] The most important job attributes for top-third graduates (not going into teaching), in order of importance were the quality of coworkers, prestige, a challenging but feasible work environment, and high-quality training. It was these attributes, they surmised, that fell short in the teaching profession. The reference to quality coworkers is really about social capital. Top graduates who rule out teaching as a career imagine that their colleagues will not be intellectually strong. In other words, strengthen professional capital and you will attract better performers, who will strengthen that professional capital still further. It's a virtuous spiral.

Colleagues at Boston College, where one of us works, have tracked a sample of Master's level teacher education graduates into their jobs over 4–5 years and monitored their performance at four different points during that time. On entry, in research terms, teachers were tagged as red, yellow, and green in terms of their effectiveness and commitment to social justice, from low to high. The greens got greener (validating just how much selecting the best people to begin with really matters). The yellows and reds, by contrast, mainly held their initial position—especially as they confronted difficult work environments.[50]

This brings us to the second reason for early exits from teaching—unsupportive working conditions and contexts. Beginning teachers get frustrated when they feel their own effectiveness is declining. Forty percent of teachers in the first 3 years of the job felt like this in the sample of Day and his colleagues. The key difference between those who have good beginnings and those who have painful ones, between those who feel like they are getting better and those who are not, they found, is the quality of the school's culture and its levels of support. This is why our professional capital proposal involves changing the culture—the normative, logistical, and interactional working conditions—of not only the school but of the profession itself (see Chapter 6).

Ever since Howard Becker studied the careers of public school teachers in 1950s Chicago, the story has been unchanged: beginning teachers struggle when they are overwhelmed by the challenges of teaching children in conditions of violence and poverty and where there are few resources and little adult support.[51] Although this is blindingly obvious, it still persists.

More unexpected are the findings of the remarkable study driven by Susan Moore Johnson and the project on The Next Generation of Teachers at Harvard University.[52] Following a sample of about 50 beginning teachers in Massachusetts, Johnson and her team came across three kinds of environments that dramatically affected the experience of these new entrants and whether they would be likely to stay or leave:

1. *Veteran-oriented cultures.* These were mainly made up of very experienced colleagues who dominated the culture of the school. Here, new teachers felt isolated and unsupported, tended to keep their heads down to focus on survival, became cynical, and were among the most likely to leave the profession.
2. *Novice-oriented cultures.* In hard-to-staff urban schools or brand new charter schools, new teachers felt energized by being surrounded by kindred spirits, but soon became exhausted and prone to burnout because of the demands of constant curriculum writing and the absence of more experienced colleagues willing to point out shortcuts and show them the ropes.
3. *Mixed cultures.* Here mentoring for new teachers was not just a relationship with an individual elder, but part of the wider culture where all teachers, young and old, worked together and helped each other.

The secret to higher efficacy and to keeping teachers after the first 3 years is not just making sure that new teachers get individual support, here or there, but that they get to work in well-led, dynamic, strongly supported schools, where there is a belief in student success, a knowledge of how to bring it about, and a willingness and eagerness for everyone on the staff to keep learning and improving—inexperienced and experienced alike. It is, in other words, *the culture of the school* that makes the difference. If you get this right, if you change the new teacher by changing the entire school and profession, then no matter what challenges teachers have to face, a big payback will come through just a few years down the line.

Striding High

The most overlooked group in teaching is teachers in mid-career. Like the middle child in the family, they often feel left out—sandwiched between a large Boomer generation ahead of them and a bulging Echo generation of newcomers right behind. Corrie Stone Johnson (no relation to Susan Moore Johnson) has done some groundbreaking work on this numerically modest and much-maligned group of mid-career Gen Xers.[53]

Johnson is critical of those Boomer generation academics who have themselves been overly critical of the Gen X teachers in mid-career who came along behind them. Boomer critics of Gen X teachers, or "new professionals" as they have sometimes been called, complain that they don't have the same sense of mission, that teaching is not such an all-consuming passion, that Gen X teachers want to make individual differences in children's lives but no longer want to change the world.[54] They accept change too readily, it's said, have nothing else to compare it against, and are reluctant to kick up a fuss. They are a bit more calculative and careerist than their forbears, more interested in their lives as well as their work, and more prepared to accept and even embrace what the Boomer generation more usually detests—prescription, standards, and testing.

Johnson (a Gen Xer herself—and nothing wrong with that) tries to understand her generational peers instead of attacking them. And here are her three big insights: First, they welcome many aspects of standards and prescribed programs that guide their work, (though they don't like them in excess) because they build their capacity. Second, even when the testing and prescription go over the top, though, they are still more phlegmatic about their impact—believing that these constraints don't significantly affect their feelings about their job. Third, Gen Xers can be both highly committed to their work *and* actively considering leaving teaching for something else. Lack of retention isn't for them about lack of commitment. Johnson concludes, "Many if not most teachers in mid-career . . . feel control over their work (and) the changes being asked of them at worst do not negatively impact them, and at best focus and hone their teaching work."[55]

The study one of us did on teachers' life and career stages and their emotional responses to change fits some of these insights.[56] By about 8 years or so in the job, teachers felt more established, competent, and confident about how to deal with students. They had "less frustration" about student misbehavior and discipline. They were "more aware of where [students] were coming from . . . [and] more tolerant of why they didn't get the assignment done." They were "thicker-skinned," "calmer . . . able to laugh," and had developed duck's backs, where "a lot of things slide off." Pragmatic about external change, they were also "willing to try new things" in their own practice.

Teachers in mid-career are confident but not complacent, open but not innocent, questioning without being cranky. And all this matters very much indeed. It matters because, as Day's research team has compellingly shown, almost 80% of teachers who had been in the job for 8–23 years were able to sustain or even increase their high levels of commitment over time. In developing professional capital, this is perhaps the most neglected group in the entire teaching profession. If we get more teachers this far into their careers, we will significantly increase our store of professional capital just by holding on to more teachers until they start performing at their best. Increase what counts as professional capital still further by providing quality professional development throughout these middle years, for example, and the returns among this group especially will be even more impressive.

While all the official attention concentrates on the extremes at either end of the teaching career, as it does on the extremes of teacher performance too, the biggest answer is actually in the middle. Make a big move in the middle, in terms of capability and career stage, and you will generate real forward momentum in the system as a whole. Right now, this omission of the middle is having debilitating consequences for the teaching profession as a whole.

COMMITMENT, CAPABILITY, AND CAREER

All these career patterns and their implications are underscored by research in the United States by Corey Drake.[57] She has undertaken a secondary analysis of data drawn from a stratified random sample of over 500 California elementary teachers, 9 years after the passage of state mathematics reform standards in the 1990s and 1 year after the introduction of assessments related to those standards. Drake was interested in how the career stage that teachers were in affected their willingness and ability to implement the standards. The most significant differences were between teachers with 3 years experience or less and teachers in mid-career, who had spent between 4 and 20 years in the job. Her results underline how youthful enthusiasm is no substitute for hard-earned expertise:

> The least experienced teachers . . . felt very positive about the reforms, although they had the lowest level of understanding of the reforms and felt the least prepared to teach the reforms. Furthermore, despite their support of the reforms, they reported low levels of reform practice and high levels of traditional practice. Thus, it seems that although these teachers were in favor of the idea of reform, they were unable to effectively implement reform practices

due to lack of understanding and lack of preparation. They supported the reform in theory but not in practice.

The midcareer group . . . had relatively high levels of understanding of and familiarity with the reforms and midlevel support for the reforms. They also felt more prepared than did the early career teachers to teach in ways consistent with the reforms. As a result, they reported high levels of reform teaching and lower levels of traditional teaching than those teachers with either less or more experience. They seemed to be able to support the reform standards, at least at a moderate to high level, in both theory and practice.[58]

The more that teachers progressed through mid-career, racking up their hours of experience and professional development, the more capable they became at using the reforms in practice. Indeed, they were "both more willing and more able than any other group to implement the ideas and practices proposed by the reforms."

By late career, though, after 20 years in the job, teachers had less understanding of the reforms than did their mid-career counterparts (though still more than the beginning teachers) and were the least willing of all groups to implement the reforms, having grown suspicious of almost all external reform by this point.

When we bring together Drake's research with the other contributions on teachers' career stages, a compelling pattern emerges in terms of the connection between teachers' capabilities and commitments to change, and the career stage they are in. The patterns are summarized in Figure 4.1.

Top-down reformers often begin from the starting point of the bottom right-hand cell. They assume that all teachers are going to be the same in

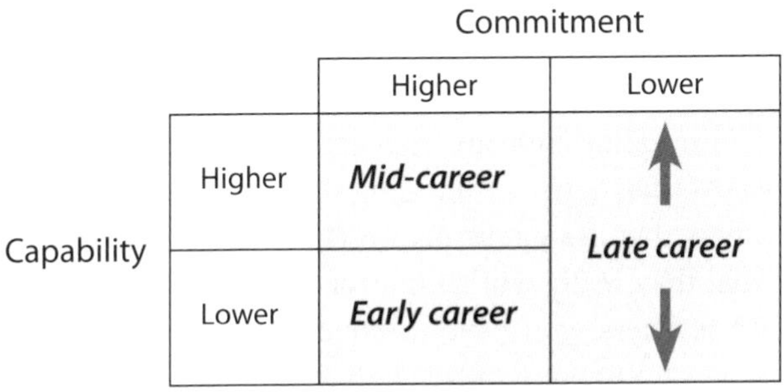

FIGURE 4.1 Relationship Between Career Stage and Capabilities/Commitment

relation to a required reform—neither capable in terms of their skills nor committed in terms of their willingness to give the reform a try. The answer, in this case, is to do what the English did in their National Literacy and Numeracy strategy: impose and prescribe a program for everyone so there is no escape, and add on intensive coaching and training support so teachers can develop the skills they are lacking.[59] This strategy may work in very low-capacity systems like those in some developing countries, but elsewhere it ignores the fact that teachers have different degrees of willingness and capability and it therefore inappropriately imposes a one-size-fits-all model on everyone.

Principals of charter schools or U.K. Academies, along with advocates of alternate certifications and programs like Teach for America, are attracted to teachers in the bottom left-hand corner. These teachers are willing to take on new ideas. They are more flexible, less expensive, and offer little or no resistance to their leaders. Unfortunately, though, their levels of understanding are weak, as are their abilities to put reform ideas into practice. They may be keen but they aren't very capable. In any job, everyone has to start somewhere, of course, but all the data indicate that we really shouldn't be filling schools with young cheerleading teachers who are extremely eager but not yet effective.

By late career, perhaps as a legacy of the 1970s age of individual autonomy when older teachers started their careers, teachers seem to be all over the map in terms of their capabilities. Indeed, Drake's research shows there is more variation in this group than in any other. But whatever their capabilities, like Huberman's late-career teachers, they have become disenchanted with and resistant to external reform by this point. Their capabilities may vary, but their commitment is definitely low. It's no use if teacher federations and unions defend this group *en masse* and celebrate the richness of their long experience, because in some cases that experience has, for whatever reason, turned into a liability rather than an asset. And there's no use defending these teachers' rights to individual classroom autonomy when it permits them to ignore reforms that could actually be of great benefit to their students. At this point, outstanding school and system leadership must convince teachers that these reforms won't be a passing fad like their predecessors and that they really will help teachers to teach their students better. And for those teachers who have reached a point where they just cannot crank themselves up for one more change, constructing a teaching career with other pathways so late-career teachers don't paint themselves into this corner, is also a central priority.

All of these results point to three flawed strategies for changing the teaching profession and its practices:

1. You shouldn't just impose an instructional change uniformly on everyone even with intensive training and coaching, because teachers at different stages have varying commitments and capabilities. One size really doesn't fit all.
2. If you invest all your energy and expenditure in early-career teachers, you will fill schools, especially schools serving the most disadvantaged students, with transient teachers who are keen but just not capable.
3. If you defend the rights of late-career teachers to choose whether to engage with reforms or not, you will be supporting the judgments and choices not just of those who are already capable enough and who don't need to be trained in things they already know, but also the judgments of that sizable number who are not really capable in the proposed reforms at all.

The golden cell, of course, is the top left-hand corner of the diagram. It is the one where teachers are both still open enough to be committed to change if they can be convinced it can be adapted for their students, and where they have developed enough experience and judgment to be capable in using new practices. These teachers are dream teachers—committed and also capable. This is the cell where teachers have reached beyond the 4-year point in their career, and in most cases have progressed further than that. This is when teachers make the most difference, and in the phony war of experience versus youth in teaching, they are the golden group we are overlooking, to everyone's cost. In Drake's words, "policy designers might think about both supporting and leveraging the continuing growth of this group of teachers."[60]

CONCLUSION

If you want to *teach like a pro,* you have to stay long enough, but you needn't stay forever. You need to find your fire and sharpen your knowledge and skills. And, apart from a few brave loners, if you want to teach like a pro, you are going to need a lot of help—from your leaders, your colleagues, and your profession—because what's worth fighting for in teaching cannot be separated from what's worth fighting for in your school and your entire profession—one where all teachers teach like pros, not just you. This is the essence of *professional capital*—capability and commitment that are constantly developed, applied, and refined with colleagues within the school and beyond it.

To sum up, there are three lessons from this chapter about what it means to *teach like a pro*:

1. Recruiting strategies that tolerate and even encourage high numbers of young and inexperienced teachers to move in and out of the job within 3–5 years might keep down short-term costs, but they squander taxpayers' investment. They also sell disadvantaged students short by condemning them to inexperienced and therefore less effective teachers who leave long before they reach their potential. We clearly need to find more strategies to keep teachers on until they reach peak performance in the classroom around 10–20 years into the job. One way to do this is by attracting better qualified and better prepared teachers in the first place. And this is more likely when the working conditions in teaching are supportive, and if political leaders demonstrate more of the respect for teachers that the public then needs to emulate.

2. At the other end of the career, we can't ignore the decline in commitment among many teachers after 20-something years. It's not everyone, but it is a lot. This is not a reason to blame the decline on individual teachers or their unions and federations—whose first duty and reason to exist is, after all, to represent their members. Some of the answer to the corrosion of commitment has to do with better leadership, support, and management of change so that more and more of these elders shift over into Huberman's *renewal* category. Some of the answer may have to do with how to structure the career and career tracks with more definable leadership opportunities, as Singapore does, or by diversifying the teaching job for late-career teachers beyond remaining exclusively and perhaps exhaustingly in the classroom. This will provoke us to look at teacher leadership and the culture of the school in Chapter 6.

3. While the mid-career Gen Xers seem to be a bit more concerned about having the expertise than huge commitment, compared to their Baby Boomer predecessors, it is important that no one con-

cludes that this is the next permanent state of affairs, and builds entire systems around temporary contracts for short-term teachers. There is another generation coming along behind this one, and it will not be like the one before it either.

Teachers need to have expertise and also commitment. It's no use having one side saying teaching should all be about performance and precision, and opponents countering with the case for commitment and passion. And it is not about just finding some harmonious balance between the two. We need capability and commitment in equal intensity—like a hot Jacuzzi and a cold shower that will make teachers (and students) tingle with excitement.

What we have seen from Day and Huberman in this chapter is the career-spanning differences among teachers operating in a profession that by and large has *highly variable professional capital*. What if the profession was altered, as the highest performing countries have done, to build a profession with a strong foundation of individual and collective assets. There would still be differences across the career, but these would turn out to be complementary strengths. This is the new profession we seek to portray and promote.

This takes us to our central concept and strategy of professional capital—what comprises it, and how you invest it, grow it, and circulate it. Imagine how the careers we have portrayed would look if the teaching profession really were to have all the commitments, capabilities, and cultures of professional capital we are advocating? It would transform the psyche and efficacy of the entire profession, as it already has in some of the world's highest performing systems. It is, in other words, time to consider solutions to the problems we have been discussing.

⟡ CHAPTER FIVE ⟡

Professional Capital

NOW WE GET to the very core of our case: *professionalism* and *professional capital.* Teaching isn't easy; it's hard. Like dentistry or architecture, it's not something you can make up as you go along or carry out by following standard procedures. This is not to deny that some parts of the job, like other professions, can be picked up fairly quickly by people with good ability and minimal training. In Australia, one way of providing medical support to remote cattle stations or indigenous communities is to supply families and communities with a large medical chest containing a core supply of instruments, drugs, and diagnostic charts so that, with a bit of radio support from a doctor or nurse at a distance, people can deal with the most likely problems such as snakebites, accidents, or infections by themselves. It works quite well with simple problems or in emergencies, but you wouldn't want to run an entire medical service, or even most of it, like this. The same goes for teaching.

Young teachers with minimal training might be able to maintain order and discipline, teach whole-class methods of question and answer, and raise performance and results in tested literacy and mathematics. This is exactly how a lot of charter schools operate in the United States. They are strict, demanding, whole-class driven, and focus on the basics. But ask these teachers to develop the innovation and creativity needed for 21st-century economies; to teach a range of children simultaneously in smaller groups that engage with their different learning styles (oral, written, digital, manipulative, or visual, for example); or to use diagnostic assessments effectively so that students receive instruction that is tailored just-in-time for them—and these teachers are likely to struggle.

So in teaching, as in medicine, we face a choice. Should isolated rural communities or poor urban ones get a low-cost service that will cover the

> ◆❯ . . . if you want a high-performing school system,
> a competitive economy, and a cohesive society, . . .
> we need the very best, most highly qualified teachers
> who have a deep and broad repertoire of knowledge
> and skill in the schools that *don't* have the luxury of
> screening out children.

basics and work in emergencies—relying on underqualified or minimally qualified people to deal with the most likely diseases in health, or on equally underqualified people to stick to the basics in teaching within under-resourced and crisis-torn communities? Should we condemn children in public schools, and especially in urban schools, to a standardized service of coach-class teaching, while those in private schools and wealthy suburbs are provided with a professional and personalized platinum service instead? Or, like high-performing Finland and Canada, should it be the goal to provide a high-quality professional service in education to everyone alike, irrespective of income or location? Should it really all come down to paying your money (if you can) and taking your choice?

We know where we stand. And if you want a high-performing school system, a competitive economy, and a cohesive society, you will stand with us. We hold the position that teaching today—not 30 or 40 years ago—is complicated, not simple. We are of the view that we need the very best, most highly qualified teachers who have a deep and broad repertoire of knowl-edge and skill in the schools that *don't* have the luxury of screening out children with moderate or severe learning disabilities, that *can't* weed out those with disruptive behavioral problems, or that have to provide an edu-cation to children whose families *don't* know how to join a selection lottery or choose a school for their child, because they are in prison, working two or three shifts, barely scraping by financially, or have spent years on crack cocaine. The most challenging schools don't just need teachers as good as those who work in wealthy suburbs or private academies. They need teach-ers who are better.

We believe that like the top-performing countries, teaching everywhere must therefore be a profession and must constantly improve as a profession. Teaching isn't something to try out before you move on to something else, or to fall back on when there's nothing better. Effective teaching has to be prepared for fully, and practiced repeatedly, but it will take years to perfect until you reach the heights of proficiency.

This chapter looks at what it means to be a profession and to be professional. It explores in depth the new idea of *professional capital*—the capital that teachers need to develop if they are to be at the peak of their effectiveness.

PROFESSIONALS AND PROFESSIONALISM

Normally, when we think of the word *professional,* it calls to mind two things: being professional and being *a* professional. These ideas are connected, but they are not the same.

Being professional is about what you do, how you behave.[1] It's about being impartial and upholding high standards of conduct and performance. Being professional is about quality and character—not getting too personally involved with children, refraining from gossiping about parents, and learning to challenge colleagues' actions without criticizing them as people.

Being *a professional* has more to do with how other people regard you, and how this affects the regard you have for yourself. This is what people are usually referring to when they ask whether teaching is truly a profession or not. Does it have the same status and levels of reward that other professions do? Is the training as long and as rigorous? Do members of the profession have collective autonomy over their own actions, and freedom from excessive outside scrutiny?

Classic definitions of what constitutes being *a profession* point to the following features:[2]

- Specialized knowledge, expertise, and professional language
- Shared standards of practice
- Long and rigorous processes of training and qualification
- A monopoly over the service that is provided
- An ethic of service, even a sense of calling, in relation to clients
- Self-regulation of conduct, discipline, and dismissals
- Autonomy to make informed discretionary judgments
- Working together with other professionals to solve complex cases
- Commitment to continuous learning and professional upgrading

What does this mean for *teaching like a pro*? Are teachers professionals in the ways that practitioners of law and medicine are? Is there an agreed-upon knowledge base? Do teachers get the same respect and support from the public at large as do other professionals? Is teachers' conduct as disciplined and their judgment as well founded? Are they allowed the same degree of autonomy and discretion? We address these questions below.

Status with Quality

Ideally, of course, it's best to *be professional* and be *a professional* at the same time—to have status and autonomy and be trusted and able to make informed judgments effectively. This happens in high-performing systems such as those in Finland that not only get some of the best achievement results in the world but also have the smallest differences between children from better-off and poorer families. Finland is in fashion right now among international organizations and countries looking for exemplars of how to succeed in education. One of us led a team, including Beatriz Pont and Gabor Halász, that undertook the first external international review of Finland's modern educational system and the reasons for its high performance for the Organization for Economic Cooperation and Development (OECD). This is what we found out about the country's teachers:

> Other nations are experimenting with ways of rewarding differential performance within the established teaching profession. Teaching is already an attractive and desired profession in Finland. It has high status in a learner-centered society, where it contributes to the wider social mission of economic prosperity, cultural creativity, and social justice. In a society with high taxation and relatively modest income differentials, teaching is paid quite satisfactorily. Working conditions and resources are supportive, schools are well equipped, and like other professionals, teachers enjoy considerable trust and autonomy. Teaching is highly competitive and attracts high-performing secondary school graduates. Professional entry also requires Master's degrees. Teacher training blends theoretical and practical components, and continuing professional development is becoming more integrated into the collective life and needs of the school.[3]

If you're looking for validation of these findings, then go to the horse's mouth—the Finns themselves. Pasi Sahlberg, former educational reform specialist for the World Bank, and now Director of the Centre for International Mobility in Finland, has written the most comprehensive and insightful account, which only an insider could assemble, of the reasons for his nation's success. In *Finnish Lessons: What Can the World Learn from Educational Change in Finland?* he compares Finland's improvement path to what he calls the Global Educational Reform Movement (or GERM) and its preoccupations with standardization, external accountability, high-stakes testing, and market-driven competition, which are supposed to drive up the performance of schools and teachers.[4] GERM, he points out, characterizes low-performing systems such as those of the United States and England under its previous governments. It restricts teachers' autonomy, subjects teachers to endless intervention, drives them to compete instead of collaborate, and makes the work of teaching so unappealing that it can't attract the best-qualified university graduates to do it. In Finland, however,

> Teachers at all levels of schooling expect that they are given the full range of professional autonomy to practice what they have been educated to do: to plan, teach, diagnose, execute, and evaluate. They also expect to be provided time to accomplish all of these goals in and out of normal classroom duties. Indeed, in Finland, teachers spend relatively less time teaching than their peers in many other countries. For example, in North American schools, teachers are engaged in teaching during the vast majority of their daily working time in school, which leaves little space for any other professional activities.

> Interestingly [in Sahlberg's interviews with primary school teachers about what would make them leave the profession], practically nobody cites their salary as a reason to quit teaching. Instead, many point out that if they were to lose their professional autonomy in schools and their classrooms, their career choice would be called into question. For example, if an external inspection to judge the quality of their work or a merit-based compensation policy influenced by external measures was introduced, many would change their jobs. Many Finnish teachers report that if they encountered similar external pressure through external standardized measuring and test-based accountability, as do their peers in the UK or North America, they would seek other professional challenges. It is, first and foremost, the working conditions and moral professional environment that count as young Finns decide whether they will pursue a teaching career or seek work in another field.[5]

At its best, then, *teaching like a pro* means you get high status *and* high quality. You can have autonomy and respect *and* do a good job at the same time. Indeed, if you are missing one of the two, it may not be long before the other one disappears as well! When you teach like a pro, all your training and all your knowledge, the disciplines you have learned and the thousands of hours you have invested to apply them in practice, bear fruit in the quality of how you teach and in what your students can learn and achieve. Here, the status that teachers get isn't just symbolic. The trust that people have in teachers isn't blind. It's based on something solid: on highly qualified people who have undergone rigorous training that connects theory to practice and who stay many years in the job—people who are constantly perfecting their practice and always inquiring into how to do it better.

Status over Quality

But let's not get carried away. More courses and longer periods of training don't always give us better professionals—in teaching or anywhere else. A period starting in the 1970s saw concerted efforts to raise the status of teaching and to make it into a proper profession.[6] This was a worthy quest, because until the third quarter of the 20th century, teaching was scarcely a profession at all. Most teachers of younger children, especially, trained for 2–3 years in colleges of education that didn't offer degrees. In-service training was limited, and the only thing new teachers found valuable was learning by the apprenticeship model during their "teaching practice" or "practicum," where they watched and copied other teachers who used relatively simple methods of whole-class teaching such as lecturing and question and answer.

Because of their disillusionment with modern teacher preparation programs, many educational reformers in the United States and elsewhere now want to turn the clock back 50 years to this far-from-Golden Age before teaching was anything like a profession—shortening the training, easing the licensing, and having most of the training organized not by universities but by school districts and schools.[7]

This is an overreaction, of course, but there is some substance to what these people are criticizing. Converting college of education certificates into degree programs added more courses and another year on to the training for teachers, but the courses were typically provided on the university campus, separate from the schools. They didn't often join up the dots between theory and practice. In-service courses were the same. Programs were organized more around what professors wanted to teach than what students needed to learn. When new teachers went into schools, they found that the theory didn't fit into the realities of their classrooms. Meanwhile, teachers who did in-service courses at the university on their own, away from their schools, came back to face uncomprehending and uninvolved colleagues who had no wish to discuss or implement anything that had been learned. The quest to *professionalize* teaching by increasing the level of qualifications and lengthening the period of training was not actually improving the *professionalism* of what teachers did in their schools.[8] It was an individualistic approach to improving professional status, not a collective enterprise to develop deep pools of professional capital that would include social capital.

We have seen this ourselves. In the late 1980s, we were both working at the Ontario Institute for Studies in Education in Canada. It had a near monopoly on all the doctoral-level programs in the province. In minuscule print, the Institute's catalogues listed courses with mind-numbing titles such as "Teachers and the Administrative Process" that were the antithesis of user-friendliness. Across the road, the University of Toronto's Faculty of Education, which trained beginning teachers, was still stuck in 1970s patterns of delivery that separated initial teacher education from school improvement, disconnected both of these from academic research, and struggled to link up what was going on in the university to what was happening in schools.

In some countries and universities, it's still like this. A 2011 review of the Norwegian educational system, for example, identifies outdated teacher education programs as needing reform if the country's achievement levels are going to increase.[9] Elsewhere, there is sometimes still a great gulf between high-powered researchers who commandeer the research grants and graduate courses, and teacher preparation programs that are mainly farmed out to lower status (usually female) adjuncts still working in schools. And what is the point of student teachers doing extensive inquiry projects into how to teach the concept of gravity, or into what is the best way to engage second language learners with Shakespeare, when in their heart of hearts they know that the unsympathetic school systems they are entering will give them no time or encouragement to inquire into their practice when they start their regular jobs? In circumstances like these, the promise to upgrade teachers so they will all have Master's degrees is not a magic wand for improvement, if teachers are just going to get more of what they had before.

But in the past 10–15 years, university-based teacher education has changed quite a lot. In Toronto, partly under our leadership as the dean and as a head of a major research and development center, respectively, our institution created major partnerships with five surrounding school districts. These partnerships concentrated student teachers in sites focused for improvement, held both teacher education courses and doctoral classes on school sites (after periods of data collection or school improvement work at those same sites), and invested in professional development provision in cooperative learning or literacy development in ways that connected research and improvement work to teacher education and to the research work of doctoral students.

We were not alone. Very many university education faculties have now established professional development schools that connect theory and practice in this way. When Teach First in the United Kingdom established a university-based summer program for its student teachers, one of the most interesting outcomes was the high ratings that student teachers gave this program for its quality. A 2008 Office for Standards in Education (Ofsted) inspection report on Teach First noted that the instruction participants received at the summer institute was "a particularly successful and innovative feature."[10] And leaders among schools of education in the United States now work closely with local schools and school districts, grounding theory in deep and extended engagements and partnerships with those in practice—an approach that has now been advocated nationally by the leading accrediting agency for teacher education programs.[11] So, if critics of university-based teacher education still have an ax to grind, the ax is now exceedingly rusty.

There is a second reason for the assault on teacher education, however. This comes from a common complaint about all professions—that the push for professionalization can be self-interested and self-serving. Western doctors fight off alternative therapies such as Chinese or chiropractic medicine because they threaten the doctors' monopoly over their service. Lawyers warn people about the risks of managing their own property transactions. Dentists can talk you into having expensive procedures you may not really need. Teachers, like doctors, often have to write reports in impenetrable language that is too mystifying for most laypersons to understand. All professions close ranks very quickly when one of their members is criticized or attacked. No wonder that Irish playwright George Bernard Shaw said, "All professions are conspiracies against the laity."[12]

Making teaching more like the ideal that others have of mainstream professions may not always be the answer, then. It's not professionally worthy if teachers are pushed into accumulating more and more paper qualifications just to meet a career benchmark. It's not professionally admirable when school reports or standards statements are expressed in words that look less and less like ordinary language. And it's not professionally defensible when teachers put themselves on a pedestal above parents and proclaim, as one teacher did in a study that one of us conducted on teachers' emotional relationships with parents, *"I'm the one with the expertise. I'm the one with the degrees. Her job is to be here to help!"*[13]

Status and Quality Reunited

The existence here and there of bad teacher education programs and of questionable attempts to use professional status to promote self-interest is no reason to say there should be little or no teacher education, or that the idea of teaching being a profession should be abandoned altogether. Let's return to the top educational performers. Finland does well because it combines high-quality teachers with high-quality teaching. So does Canada. Let's aim as high as we can to get the best quality and qualifications we can in teaching, rather than lowering our sights and settling for a system where average teachers can deliver conventional outcomes to a satisfactory but less-than-stellar standard! Teachers need to be *professional* and to be *professionals*. This is the way they can exercise excellent professional judgment and discretion with the clients they know best. If they do both and are supported to do both, then we can build the *professional capital* that will increase teachers' capacity to help all students learn and achieve.

Conditions and Quality

Inadequate initial teacher education and poor working conditions go together. Societies that do not care to improve the profession from the beginning continue to disregard it throughout educators' careers. It is on the job where professional capital is realized or not. The McKinsey report *How the World's Most Improved Systems Keep Getting Better* found that as school systems developed greater educator capacity (i.e., as teachers got better), it was *peers* who became the strongest source of innovation.[14] This says an enormous amount about the nature of the teaching profession in these countries. It reveals

- How teachers work together
- How what they do is transparent to each other and to the system as a whole
- How the profession is collectively responsible as well as externally accountable
- How professional knowledge is continually being developed and consolidated

In short, it says that professional capital is being generated, circulated, and reinvested all the time because it is endemic to the culture of the profession and is embedded in the daily work of teachers.

High-quality peer interaction among professionals doesn't evolve from nowhere or emerge by chance. It depends on peers being of high quality to begin with—well prepared and well qualified. Otherwise what peers share may be ignorance instead of knowledge. High-quality peer interaction also depends on

- The conditions for professionals to meet (high-performing countries provide more time for this than low performers)
- Expectations and frameworks of learning and curriculum that are challenging and open enough for teachers to innovate and inquire into their practice together (to have something significant to meet about)
- Ongoing timely data that enable teachers, individually and together, to diagnose student learning needs and tailor their instructional responses accordingly—rather than standardized test scores that give no information about particular students and that are received long after the fact, when they are no longer useful for diagnostic purposes
- Outstanding, stable leadership that can galvanize professionals as a team in pursuit of a greater good (rather than principals or political leaders who come and go through revolving doors of school leadership)
- Opportunities as well as incentives to learn from colleagues in other classrooms, other schools, and even other countries (as in Singapore, for instance) in the quest for ever higher performance

All of this constitutes the climate for investing in professional capital. In poor conditions of high fear and low support, teachers will be unlikely to invest in each other or even in themselves. In confident climates that encourage growth and even a little risk because they provide an essential underpinning of security, the chances of teachers investing in their own development and reaping the rewards of high quality in their practice are considerably greater.

THREE KINDS OF CAPITAL

In the world of business and finance, if you want to get a return, you have to make an investment. And if you want to make an investment, you need to have capital to invest. Whether you are Adam Smith, Karl Marx, or Warren Buffett, the rules are pretty much the same. In this section, we set out the case for *professional capital* that consists of the confluence of three other kinds of capital: human, social, and decisional.[15] It is the presence and product of these three forms of capital that is essential for transforming the teaching profession into a force for the common good.

Professional capital is essential for effective teaching, and it is most essential in the most challenging educational circumstances. We can now express it in a formula (Figure 5.1), where PC is professional capital, HC is human capital, SC is social capital, and DC is decisional capital. Effective teaching for the whole profession is a product of these three kinds of capital amplifying each other. Let's examine this powerful phenomenon more closely.

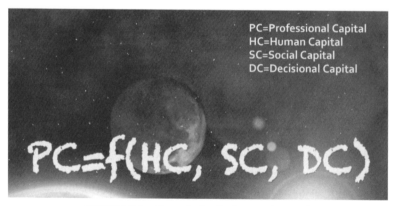

PC=Professional Capital
HC=Human Capital
SC=Social Capital
DC=Decisional Capital

$$PC = f(HC, SC, DC)$$

FIGURE 5.1　Formula for Professional Capital

Human Capital

For a long time, capital was largely viewed as a financial phenomenon that came out of economic production. But in the 1960s, a group of economists pointed to the importance of another kind of capital: *human capital*.[16] This concept referred to the economically valuable knowledge and skills that could be developed in people—especially through education and training. In the *human capital* view of education and economies, investing in people's education and development brings economic returns later on. Indeed, it is now accepted wisdom that the sooner people start their education in early childhood, at home or at school, and the longer their period of schooling, then the more economic returns a nation will get on this investment in its people. Education is a capital investment—and so too is teaching.

Human capital in teaching is about having and developing the requisite knowledge and skills. It is about knowing your subject and knowing how to teach it, knowing children and understanding how they learn, understanding the diverse cultural and family circumstances that your students come from, being familiar with and able to sift and sort the science of successful and innovative practice, and having the emotional capabilities to empathize with diverse groups of children and also adults in and around a school. It is about possessing the passion and the moral commitment to serve all children and to want to keep getting better in how you provide that service. Human capital is about individual talent.

As we said in Chapter 1, you cannot increase human capital just by focusing on it in isolation. Some of the most powerful, underutilized strategies in all of education involve the deliberate use of teamwork—enabling teachers to learn from each other within and across schools—and building cultures and networks of communication, learning, trust, and collaboration around the team as well. If you want to accelerate learning in any endeavor, you concentrate on *the group*. This is *social capital*.

Social Capital

In the 1980s and beyond, the concept of capital and its relationship to education took another metaphorical leap. Economist James Loury first brought *social capital* into the modern limelight in the 1970s.[17] In the late 1980s, sociologist James Coleman put it front and center in his influential analysis of the reasons for high-school dropout and why educational outcomes varied between Catholic schools and regular public schools.[18]

Social capital, Coleman said, exists in the relations among people. It's a resource for them. And like economic and human capital, it contributes to productive activity. "For example, a group within which there is extensive trustworthiness and extensive trust is able to accomplish much more than a comparable group without that trustworthiness and trust."[19] Groups with purpose that are based on trust also learn more. They get better at their work.

Social capital refers to how the quantity and quality of interactions and social relationships among people affects their access to knowledge and information; their senses of expectation, obligation, and trust; and how far they are likely to adhere to the same norms or codes of behavior. In families, social capital "depends both on the physical presence of adults in the family and on the attention given by the adults to the child."[20] In blunter terms, if the lights or the DVD are on, but nobody is physically or psychologically "home," there are going to be grave deficiencies of social capital.

Social capital increases your knowledge—it gives you access to other people's *human capital.* It expands your networks of influence and opportunity. And it develops resilience when you know there are people to go to who can give you advice and be your advocates. In *Bowling Alone,* Robert Putnam famously bemoaned the decline of social capital and community life in modern American society.[21] The decline of public schools in the United States has also weakened social capital in urban communities, as connecting with others in those communities through one's children is a prime way to build relationships with neighbors.

Much more recently, Wilkinson and Pickett, in their intriguingly titled book *The Spirit Level,* show that societies with low levels of trust have higher levels of income inequality.[22] People who are insulated from each other by income, in different neighborhoods or even gated communities, don't trust people they don't know. The same patterns hold between different states in the United States—high-trust states have smaller income disparities than low-trust states.

Social capital is significant in education too. We have already seen how it affects high-school dropout rates. Coleman's Catholic schools did better, he said, because they had a clearer sense of common mission and stronger relationships organized around it. And in their modern classic *Trust in Schools,* Tony Bryk and Beverly Schneider demonstrate that among public schools in Chicago that deal with similar kinds of students, the ones that reach greater achievement levels have higher levels of trust between teachers and students, parents, administrators, and colleagues—levels that precede the gains in achievement.[23] It's not just a correlation—it's cause and effect. Trust and expertise work hand in hand to produce better results.

Unfortunately, the development of social capital as a strategy has not yet caught on in the teaching profession. Alan Odden doesn't mention it at all in his otherwise fine treatment of human capital in education.[24] Ironically, some of his most powerful learning examples involve teachers working together, but he doesn't connect the dots. For us, social capital strategies are one of the cornerstones for transforming the profession. Behavior is shaped by groups much more than by individuals—for better or worse. If you want positive change, then get the group to do the positive things that will achieve it.

People have begun to tap into the ideas of social capital among students and their families—arguing that it is students from disadvantaged homes especially who are often lacking the networks of trust, information, support, and advocacy that can help them succeed.[25] But the concept has not yet been applied to the performance and success of teachers—yet the connections are already there for all to see. Every time you increase the purposeful learning of teachers working together, you get both short-term results and longer term benefits as teachers learn the value of their peers and come to appreciate the worth of constructive disagreement. There are many examples of this. Critical friends networks, for example, give teachers constructive and also challenging feedback with the aid of protocols that create a safe environment in which these conversations can occur. Moderated marking similarly enables teachers to learn from each other with expert facilitation as they examine student work according to standards-based criteria. These expressions of social capital are an asset that keeps on giving. They are a kind of "collective capacity" that can extend to whole-system reform.

The research project by Carrie Leana that we cited in Chapter 1 makes the point about the power of social capital and its relationship to human capital simply but powerfully.[26] Recall that she measured both human capital (the qualities of individual teachers) and social capital (how much teachers worked together) in 130 elementary schools in New York City. She compared mathematics scores of students at the beginning and end of 1 year, and found that the students of teachers who reported higher social capital had a higher increase in mathematics scores, and that even teachers with lower human capital did better if they were in a school with greater social capital. Using our words, business capital is a "wrong driver," social capital a "right driver." Cohesive groups with less individual talent often outperform groups with superstars who don't work as a team. We see it in sports all the time. With professional capital, you get both because the expertise of both individuals and the group develop in concert.

What Leana is getting at, we believe, is a significant part of what we identify as *professional capital*—the resources, investments, and assets that make up, define, and develop a profession and its practice—be this in law, medicine, sports, or education. Her work points to how business capital that wants to lower the investment and strip down assets for temporary, short-term gains is a wrong driver in education, while human capital and especially social capital are the right drivers that keep on growing and giving.

Contrast Leana's findings with the rather perplexing research that claims to show that professional development (PD) does not make much difference in student outcomes. In their large-scale studies, Garet and his colleagues examined the impact of PD in early reading instruction and in middle school math. In both cases, teachers had 8 full days of professional development, and one group had individual coaching between sessions.[27]

Garet and colleagues found some evidence that teachers retained knowledge from the PD experience, but they also discovered that this knowledge did not result in change in practice and that consequently there was no impact on student achievement. Moreover, after 2 years, even the knowledge that teachers had initially acquired no longer remained. This could, of course, be interpreted to mean that PD is simply a wasted investment that could justifiably be cut when resources are scarce. Yet PD has little or no impact when it relies on "individual learning" and does not focus on follow-through support for teams of teachers to learn together. Not all or even most professional development, until now, has been *good* professional development. Working with big ballroom audiences, or conducting training workshops outside of school, or using one-to-one coaching to enforce compliance with imposed programs, has little deep or long-standing impact on teachers' daily practice.

What is crucial is what happens between workshops. Who tries things out? Who supports you? Who gives you feedback? Who picks you up when you make a mistake the first time? Who else can you learn from? How can you take responsibility for change together? The key variable that determines success in any innovation, in other words, is the degree of social capital in the culture of your own school. Learning is the work, and social capital is the fuel. If social capital is weak, everything else is destined for failure.

Decisional Capital

But even human capital and social capital are not enough. There is still something missing. We call it *decisional capital*. The essence of professionalism is the ability to make discretionary judgments. When you put a difficult question to an employee and he asks you to wait until he consults his supervisor, you know that person is not professional because he can't exercise any discretion. If a teacher always has to consult a teacher's manual, or follow the lesson line-by-line in a script, you know that teacher is not a professional either, because he or she doesn't know how to judge or isn't being allowed to.

Judges have to judge even when the evidence isn't conclusive. In fact, if the evidence *were* conclusive, there would be no need for judges at all. Doctors have to judge when they examine a set of symptoms or interpret a brain scan. Teachers have to judge when they treat acting out by one child differently from how they treat another—because they know different things about those children: how they learn, what frustrates them if they have a disability, and so on. You can't be a judge if you can't judge—and you can't be a doctor or a teacher (or at least an effective one) if you can't judge either. The capacity to judge and judge well depends on the ability to make decisions in situations of unavoidable uncertainty when the evidence or the rules aren't categorically clear.

We take the idea of *decisional capital* from case law, though it could come just as easily from any other profession. Decisional law is "the law as determined by reference to the reported decisions of the courts."[28] In Anglo-American legal systems, this is known simply as *common law*. Becoming a lawyer in these systems involves remembering reams of factual information but also understanding how this mass of information relates to and can be interpreted through particular cases. Case law is always developing as cases refer to and move on from each other over time. This kind of law sets out the facts of the case but also describes how judges came to their decision, including the judges who held minority dissenting views.

If you know how to examine a case and have practiced this with hundreds or even thousands of cases, alongside partners, associates, and other counsel, then eventually you know how to judge. *Decisional capital* here is the capital that professionals acquire and accumulate through structured and unstructured experience, practice, and reflection—capital that enables them to make wise judgments in circumstances where there is no fixed rule or piece of incontrovertible evidence to guide them. Decisional capital is enhanced by drawing on the insights and experiences of colleagues in forming judgments over many occasions. In other words, in teaching and other professions, social capital is actually an integral part of decisional capital, as well as an addition to it.

Lawyers qualify for their profession and develop their professional capacity in part by studying lots and lots of cases, first from the textbook and then in the context of practice, in real time. Judith Shulman and others introduced case analysis into teacher education as a way to try to develop the same capacities to act and judge among beginning teachers.[29] Medical students learn the capacity to diagnose and judge in part by accompanying surgeons and other doctors on medical rounds or "walkthroughs" of the hospital, as they view different patients and discuss their symptoms, conditions, and treatment. Attempts to introduce "walkthroughs" or "instructional rounds" into schools—where school leaders and an entourage of teachers or other leaders go from classroom to classroom to witness and then discuss classroom instruction—reflect similar efforts to adapt the study of cases so educators can judge good or bad instruction when they see it.[30]

The transpositions of case methods or medical rounds from law and medicine into education have probably tried to mimic practice in these two giant professions a bit too closely, though. Case analysis won't have lasting effects in teaching if, like inquiry projects, beginning teachers know they can drop it as soon as they start teaching for real. Instructional rounds will lose their power in schools if teachers twist what they do to conform to "correct practice" because they are afraid of their superiors or have their eye on their next performance-related pay packet. Medical and legal techniques of case analysis have perhaps been applied a bit too literally to education, then. But the central principle remains important: you get better at making discretionary judgments when you have lots of practice examining your own and other people's judgments, with your colleagues, case by case.

Practice, deliberately pursued, really does make perfect. In his best-selling book *Outliers*, Canadian writer Malcolm Gladwell brought this simple principle to widespread popular attention. In a chapter on exceptionally high performance, he discussed a classic study that compared amateur and professional pianists:

The amateurs never practiced more than about three hours a week over the course of their childhood, and by the age of twenty they had totaled two thousand hours of practice. The professionals, on the other hand, steadily increased their practice time every year, until by the age of twenty, they had reached ten thousand hours.[31]

Ten thousand hours, Gladwell says, is the figure that comes up time and again as the number of hours it seems to take the brain "to assimilate all that it needs to know to achieve true mastery."[32] This is true in music, professional sports, or any other especially accomplished area in life. It's what separates professionals from the rest.

In any profession, it's important to practice, to keep practicing, and to get the opportunity to practice. Gladwell points out that "even Mozart—the greatest musical prodigy of all time—couldn't hit his stride until he had his ten thousand hours in."[33] Recall the work of Chris Day and his team that highlighted the career stage when teachers were, on average, really striding high? It was the stage that began about 8 or 10 years into the job. And how many hours do you think teachers have been teaching by this point? The exact answer varies a bit depending on the system you are in, but in the main, it's about 10,000! Of course, this doesn't mean that every teacher who has clocked up these hours is necessarily a maestro by this point. It depends on what the hours are like. And it doesn't rule out the prior learning or previous hours that incoming teachers might already have accumulated in sports coaching, youth work, or leadership of young people in general, which might shorten the hours needed to become truly expert when they start teaching for real. But, on average, with these hours behind them, the evidence is clear that teachers have attained higher proficiency than their colleagues who have put in less time.

So it's practice and a great deal of it that develops your *decisional capital,* that makes you a skilled professional and not just a keen amateur. Leave teaching before you've put in your 8 years and you will never develop decisional capital and therefore professional capital to a high level. If recruitment and reward systems in teaching are based on acceptance and even advancement of the idea that many teachers will or should move on after 3–5 years, before their wages rise or their resistance kicks in, then the development of professional capital in individual teachers is prevented, and professional capital is depleted from the system—all for a quick gain under a business capital model that sees public education as a cost instead of an investment.

Decisional capital is also sharpened when it is mediated through inter-action with colleagues (social capital). The decisions get better and better. High-yield strategies become more precise and more embedded when they are developed and deployed in teams that are constantly refining and inter-preting them. At the same time, poor judgments and ineffective practices get discarded along the way. And when clear evidence is lacking or conflict-ing, accumulated collective experience carries much more weight than idio-syncratic experience or little experience at all.

REFLECTIVE PRACTICE

Practice makes perfect, then—but not by itself. You have to have the means of learning from practice and making judgments with new cases as they come. If you are Canadian and over 30, you likely know the name of Lucien Bouchard. Bouchard became premier of Quebec in 1995 just after the people in the province narrowly decided not to separate from the rest of Canada. Bouchard is also one of the most famous casualties of necrotizing fasciitis, or flesh-eating disease, which led, in 1994, to the amputation of his leg. With-out accurate diagnosis and treatment, this disease, in which bacteria eat away a person's flesh at frightening speed, has a high probability of being fatal.

One of us has a daughter who, as a teenager, returned from a camping trip with intense redness on her torso. Within hours, most of her torso had turned violet. She was rushed to the hospital Emergency Room, where flesh-eating disease was one of the suspected diagnoses. In the end, the doc-tors judged it was probably another infection that would respond to strong steroids. They were right—it did. Had their judgment been wrong, however, she would likely be dead by now. So nobody knows more than us that good medical judgment really matters.

Necrotizing fasciitis is not an easy condition to diagnose, as signs on the surface of the skin can be a poor indicator of what is going on beneath. Bos-ton hospital physician and journalist Atul Gawande discussed an interesting case of flesh-eating disease in his first book, *Complications*.[34] The case says a lot about medical judgment. Gawande describes what he and his colleagues did when a 23-year-old woman came to the Emergency Room with a swol-len foot. In many areas of medicine, Gawande points out, the data don't speak for themselves, and medicine often isn't the clinically precise science we imagine it to be. "The gray zones are considerable," he says. Flesh-eating disease is one of these vast gray zones.

Gawande and his colleagues performed lots of tests, all of which pointed to a superficial infection. But something intuitive, deep inside Gawande's gut and contrary to all the objective evidence available, told him it could still be the more serious condition. So, prompted by the patient's parent, the doctors gladly sought another opinion and took a couple of biopsies, which revealed, deep down beneath the skin, traveling up the bone, the signs of this fast-moving, killer disease.

The resulting operation almost certainly saved the young woman's life. But it was an operation brought on not by objective tests alone, or by the certainties of scientific evidence, but by a hunch, a bit of intuition, alongside and in some ways in defiance of that evidence—a hunch that was not shouldered alone but discussed and shared with committed and concerned colleagues.

Medicine, Gawande tells us, is an "imperfect science" that operates in an environment where there is "a great deal of uncertainty about what to do for people."[35] X-rays, scans, tests, and biopsies tell you some things but not everything—they still have to be interpreted, and then there are other signs and symptoms to take into account alongside them. This is where intuition comes in—something seemingly mystical and magical which is actually a perception or a judgment that may be hard to articulate but that is based on years of knowledge and experience.

Intuition isn't always reliable though. Gawande shows that doctors can make spectacularly inaccurate judgments—sometimes with complete confidence. This is when practice matters. If you can, try to avoid having an accident on a Sunday, because that's when the hospital is staffed by junior doctors, and juniors make more errors than experienced colleagues because they have just had less practice. A second opinion also matters—the opportunity to reflect on intuition and to compare it with the experiences and perceptions of colleagues. In other words, it's more likely that practice will make perfect when it is shared and also when it is thoughtful and reflective.

In the 1980s, Boston-born philosopher and erstwhile jazz pianist Donald Schön, who helped found the study of organizational learning, wrote a remarkable series of books about reflective practice and reflective practitioners.[36] Schön was critical of what he called *technical rationality*—the belief that science and objective evidence would provide all the answers in professional practice. He wouldn't be impressed with data warehouses or with the way some administrators worship evidence-based practices today. Instead, the defining core of what it meant to be professional for Schön was to be able to engage in what he called "reflective practice."

Reflective practice, he said, has two aspects—reflecting in action and reflecting on action. *Reflecting in action* is the capacity to walk around a problem while you are right in the middle of it, to think about what you are doing even as you are improvising it. When you have considered whether to speed up or slow down a presentation, to stop and ask a question or tell a joke, to move to the back of the classroom or stay at the front, or to explain an idea another way with another example, you are reflecting in action. *Reflection on action* is reflection after the fact, once the practice has finished. I wonder why the boys don't like writing as much as the girls? Am I drawing answers to questions only from the front three rows and not from the back? Why are some of the children never choosing art as an activity? These are the kinds of questions you pose when you are reflecting on what you have done.

Both of these kinds of reflection are central to professional practice, and both of them benefit from practice. But, in the main, they benefit from having a mentor or coach who can pull you back, slow you down, give you feedback, and cause you to reflect on what you have been doing, why you have done it that way, and how you might do it differently. Get the reflection *on* action right and it enables you to start reflecting *in* action more effectively too. So it's not so much practice that makes perfect then, as practice that is reflective.

Liz MacDonald and Dennis Shirley draw attention to this in their study of mindfulness with a group of urban Boston public school teachers.[37] One of the seven principles of mindful teaching these teachers developed was simply "stopping"—"reflecting on the rush of events and attending to forms of learning . . . that find scant realization" in a test-driven curriculum. What prevents mindfulness and reflection, MacDonald and Shirley say, is not lack of willingness by teachers, but a school environment that is overloaded with tests and targets, awash with data and spreadsheets, and overcome by a frenetic rush of endless interventions.

Of course, people can be just as mindless in low-pressure situations as in high-pressure ones. And a certain amount of pressure can sometimes focus the mind. Our point is that mindfulness must be cultivated and that the norms and conditions of work must deliberately foster it. So it's important that teachers and leaders also engage in a third kind of reflection, which we discussed in a previous book—*reflection about action*—reflection about the things in their environment that distract them from what's important, that get them so immersed in busy activity there is no time left to think, and that are an endless set of responses and reactions to other people's agendas instead of actions driven by purposes that are teachers' own.[38] *Reflection about action* drives you to change the context and conditions of what you practice, so that your practice can improve a lot more.

Reflective practice isn't just an act of will or the result of encouragement. You have to build it into people's practice, make it part of their day. When reflection becomes more structured and systematic, it turns into what German émigré and psychological warfare expert Kurt Lewin first termed *action research* in 1946. Action research, said Lewin, was research designed to solve social problems. It was "comparative research on the conditions and effects of various forms of social action, and research leading to social action." "Research that produces nothing but books," he continued, "will not suffice."[39]

Today, this work in education is known more as *inquiry* or *teacher inquiry*, and it encourages teachers inquiring into their own practice to follow similar processes. Here is an example from the work of Ontario's Literacy Numeracy Secretariat:[40]

A teacher in Ontario engaged in an early primary collaborative inquiry project. This program involves teams of kindergarten, grade 1 and 2 teachers working together to use current research, as well as professional learning and resources, with the intention to increase the thinking, literacy and numeracy skills of their young students.

When the kindergarten and grade one collaborative inquiry began in the fall of 2009 it stirred up a lot of emotions. At the end of the first day of a two-day session, early primary educators across the province expressed trepidation about this new kind of professional learning. Teachers made comments such as "How can we develop an inquiry question that is focused, manageable and applicable to all and is not adding more to our regular practice?" There was a buzz about how to best document student learning to ensure teachers could describe the learning journey of primary students in a meaningful way. The second day, teams were led through a process to begin their inquiry that would be relevant to their classroom. The inquiry initiated profound changes in practice among many educators.

At the end of a two-day session one educator said, "I will carry the 'Inquiry Mindset' into all areas of my teaching—beyond the project we will be engaged in. I have never felt so empowered as a teacher as in the past two days." She continued on with a team of educators from her school in the second year of the project. Her class was engaged as "researchers" who had the opportunity to construct their learning environment and class inquiries with skilful facilitation. The class wanted to learn about making soap, why dinosaurs were not at their local museum, why food packages had numbers on them [bar codes], how computer hard drives work—just to name a few areas they explored within the full day kindergarten program expectations for the year. Their inquiries led this group of young researchers to invite a local soap maker to their classroom to plan, make and market the soap. They also grilled staff at the Royal Ontario Museum via videoconference about their role as museum curators and why dinosaurs weren't found at all museums.

At the spring learning fair the same teacher reflected on her professional journey over the past 2 years and the impact it has made on her students: "This inquiry has become a part of the fabric of our program—it is our program. The inquiry has had a tremendous impact on our practice. We see a new group of learners emerging: confident, capable, and strong. Participation in this inquiry set me on a course— I don't know where it will lead but I love every step. It has empowered me more than words can say. Coming to an understanding of myself as a researcher has assisted me in uncovering skills in my students— curiosity, collaboration, creativity, sustained shared thinking."

This kind of inquiry does not result in being driven by data or becoming a slave to external evidence. Teachers as action researchers or inquirers use external and internally collected evidence to inquire into their practices, assess their effectiveness, identify the reasons for difficulties and also successes, and plan how to improve and make interventions as a result. Action research and inquiry are not activities undertaken in teacher preparation programs that are never used again in "real" teaching; nor are they isolated projects or procedures that educators use when developing an improvement plan for the district, for example. Instead, action research and inquiry are part of the job, integral to teaching, a stance that teachers take, a key part of what it means to be professional and to improve practice on a continuing basis.[41]

In most schools and school systems, this ethic of inquiry as something that is integral to teaching is a distant dream—an unrealistic ideal in a world where teachers are always in their classrooms and never able to stand aside and inquire into what they are doing together. But teacher inquiry *is* a priority in Ontario, not least in work supported by the province's teacher federations, and also in high-performing Alberta, for example, where over 90% of the province's schools are continuously engaged in school-designed innovations that involve inquiry as part of their development and evaluation. In Finland, too, teachers are able to engage in inquiry because, as we have seen, they spend less of their school day in classroom teaching than teachers in most other nations, in contrast to the United States, which has one of the highest figures of all for how much in-class time its teachers spend. If you spend all of your day teaching, you are not going to have much opportunity to inquire into, reflect on, and adjust your practice over time. If you are a hostage to test results, you won't think enough outside the box in ways that would paradoxically help you to get better at those very tests—let alone go beyond them in developing the whole child.

Practice, especially collective reflective practice, then, is integral to decisional capital and, by that token, to professional capital as a whole. In sum, when we add reflective capacity and action research to stocks of human and social capital, we hone our decisional capacity to take informed decisions. Like medicine, teaching is an imperfect science, and we need thinking professionals working together to maximize its effectiveness.

CONCLUSION

Children start school with different amounts of their own human and social capital. In Ontario, for example, more than one in four children arrive in kindergarten with cognitive and emotional difficulties (and they come from all levels of socioeconomic status).[42] In some urban and poor rural areas in the United States, the percentage is dramatically higher: more than one in two are disadvantaged from the beginning. It is obvious that these students, and all students for that matter, will need highly educated teachers who are able to master all the professional capital they can muster to deal with the range of differences they will face.

Teachers won't need much *professional capital* if they will just be drilling whole classes in the basics. But if they are going to develop high-level capabilities in their students, they will need to have learned and acquired a lot of capital themselves. It's not enough for teachers of the disadvantaged and the poor to have a heart of gold. They need to have a treasure chest of knowledge and expertise too. They need to know how to make brilliant connections between the capital children need to get upward access and the existing cultures of these children's families and their communities. To do this well, teachers need considerable human and social capital of their own.

In sum, professional capital is a cornerstone concept that brings together and defines the critical elements of what it takes to create high quality and high performance in all professional practice—including teaching. It is about what you know and can do individually, with whom you know it and do it collectively, and how long you have known it and done it and deliberately gotten better at doing it over time. Professional capital is vital for the future of the teaching profession and of society. The full product of all the elements of professional capital in action is essential (see Figure 5.1, page 88).

If any one of the elements on the right-hand side of the equation is missing, then professional capital will be depleted and the standard of teaching will fall short. Teachers will be short on professional capital if they are underqualified, if they come from the lower end of the graduation range, and if they have not been screened for their emotional capability and for their previous experiences of working with young people. Teachers will be short on professional capital if they spend most of their professional time alone, if they do not get feedback and support from colleagues, and if they are not connected to teachers in other schools. And teachers will be short on professional capital if they do not put in the years required to perfect their practice, and if they are not provided with the coaching, mentoring, and time that helps them reflect on that practice.

In all of this, you learn more and improve more if you are able to work, plan, and make decisions with other teachers rather than having to make everything up or bear every burden by yourself. This is where professional capital and especially social capital meet professional culture or community—and it is the focus of our next chapter. We will examine what professional capital means for the professional culture of a school and for the professional cultures or networks that also connect schools—moving the development of professional capital beyond the transformation of a few teachers to a revolution across whole systems, involving every school.

◆ CHAPTER SIX ◆

Professional Culture
and Communities

CULTURE IS the difference between having bacon and fruit on the same plate in America and regarding this as almost unthinkable in Britain. Culture is about what goes together and what should be kept apart. And often, like bacon and fruit, these distinctions are traditional, unquestioned, and arbitrary.

The arbitrariness of culture is a curse and a blessing. As soon as you grasp that, you realize that it's just when things seem completely fixed that they are actually most open to change. What is the key to transforming any culture? The answer lies in bringing into the open the connection between what people believe and who believes it, and thereby making it necessary for people to examine their own culture and its impact—in this case on the development of professional capital and the learning of adults and children. Being exposed to other people and cultures that are different from and sometimes more effective than one's own is an essential part of this development. Culture, in other words, is affected by the conditions and contexts in which it operates.

If you spend all your time with people who remind you of yourself—people from a similar race, the same profession, or the same high school subject department or elementary grade level—it's likely that over time, you will all come to think the same way and believe the same things, and that these beliefs will become stable and even stale. But if you mix things up a little—if you find friends from different cultural backgrounds, socialize with people from other walks of life, or communicate with colleagues across departments, grade levels, or different schools—then your eyes will be opened and your beliefs will be more open to change as well.

What you believe (the *substance* of a culture) is, in other words, profoundly affected by your relationships with who does or doesn't believe it (the *form* of a culture). Change the form of a culture (the relationships among people) and you have a good chance of changing its content too. Take this case of special education:[1]

Barry Finlay was a quarterback in his university and went on to play five years in the Canadian Football League (CFL). A quarterback must see the relationships among all the players on the field. He's the systems thinker of football. Toward the end of his athletic career, Barry started getting involved in working with young men whom others had found challenging in terms of their discipline or behavior. He enjoyed working with them, empathized with them, and felt he made a difference to these youngsters who hadn't really fit in anywhere else. Barry was now a systems thinker with a moral purpose and a mission.

Barry's teaching experience led him into special education—with kids on the margins who needed some learning support and guidance in their life. Moving on to take his Master's degree in Educational Administration, he focused on organizational learning and on how everything was connected to everything else in the big picture of change. As a principal of a new and innovative high school, Barry then became a systems thinker in action. He organized teaching in Grades 9 and 10 so that students were shared mainly among four teachers who taught as teams, knew what each other was doing, and grasped where all the program was. When substitute teachers came in, for example, they weren't just babysitters, they were slotted right into the whole team. They were now big-picture thinkers too. They all understood how the school worked and what their own contribution was.

Eventually, Barry became Director of Special Education for the whole of his province. Here was his chance to apply his systems thinking to his passion for special education and for supporting all learners. One of his first moves, against some opposition, was to move his office from a separate building, marginalized from the Ministry offices, into the main building itself. If he was outside the mainstream, he reasoned, how could he persuade districts and schools to make special education part of the mainstream themselves? He realized that if he wanted to change people's beliefs about special education, he had to change the relationships and interactions between special education and other personnel—and he realized this had to start right at the top, with himself.

Barry knew how children with special educational needs had often been separated out from other children—"withdrawn" from classes, taught in separate units or distant portable classrooms far away from the rest of the school. Barry presided over a new provincial philosophy that believed that what was essential for some children was good for all of them—that if you wanted to help children with special educational needs, you had to transform the whole school. This provincial philosophy, titled Learning for All K–12, describes an integrating process of assessment and instruction that can be implemented at the district, school, and classroom levels to improve student learning to benefit all students, from high achievers to those who need additional support.[2] Special education teachers worked in teams and in classrooms with regular classroom teachers. They developed senses of shared responsibility for the same children and their progress. Special education teachers started to help all children who found parts of their learning difficult, not just the ones who had been formally identified as having special educational needs. And in school district offices, special education and curriculum departments began to work more closely together—sometimes becoming almost indistinguishable from each other. All of this helped promote the philosophy and practices across the system, where whole-school changes such as providing differentiated instruction or offering assistive or enhancing technologies for all students particularly benefited those with identified disabilities.

Barry Finlay grasped that if you want to change people's practices and beliefs, you have to alter patterns of communication and build new kinds of relationships among them. This may involve changing people's roles or changing the structures of an organization—but the goal is to *reculture* schools, districts, and whole systems so they serve all of their children better.

This chapter is about *reculturing*—a word we invented two decades ago. Moreover, it is about *how* to reculture the professional relationships of a school or a district in order to improve what educators do there.[3] Although we talk here mostly about schools, wider cultures at the district, state, and even national levels also shape school cultures for better or for worse. This is why we furnish action guidelines in Chapter 7 for districts, states, and nations so that they can help transform schools. For now, though, let's stick with school cultures.

We identify six kinds of professional culture in schools and examine their implications for professionalism and student learning. In general, what we will see is that it is better to be collaborative than individualistic as a teacher—but that we need to think harder and deeper about better and worse ways to work collaboratively with one's peers. We present the two main categories of professional culture—individualistic and collaborative—and follow these with a further four subsets of collaborative cultures

- ✦ Individualism
- ✦ Collaborative cultures
  - ✦ Balkanization
  - ✦ Contrived collegiality
  - ✦ Professional learning communities
  - ✦ Clusters, networks, and federations

The best kinds of collaborative cultures build the value and compound the interest on professional capital. Individualistic cultures, or superficial and wrong-headed forms of collaboration, undercut the possibilities of developing and circulating professional capital.

INDIVIDUALISM

Teaching is not the oldest profession. But it has certainly been one of the loneliest. Jean Rudduck once wrote, "education is among the last vocations where it is still legitimate to work by yourself in a space that is secure against invaders."[4] The most common state in teaching used to be one of professional isolation: of working alone, aside from one's colleagues. This state of isolation still exists in more than a few schools today, where teaching is not the "Show Me" state, but the "Only Me" state. Isolation protects teachers to exercise their discretionary judgment in their classrooms, but it also cuts teachers off from the valuable feedback that would help those judgments be wise and effective.

Isolated teachers do get a kind of feedback through periodic formal evaluations, but these are usually sporadic and perfunctory. Performance evaluations coupled to pay and punishment are less valuable still. Teachers won't admit difficulties or seek help if they might be punished in their pay packet for doing so.

Earlier, we said that, like medicine or any advanced profession, teaching isn't an exact science. Uncertainty is in its nature. This uncertainty calls for wise, well-founded judgment. Uncertainty is the parent of professionalism and the enemy of standardization. It is what makes teaching interesting, variable, and challenging—a job that's different every day. But uncertainty encountered alone, in enforced isolation, is uncertainty magnified to unhealthy proportions, because teachers must figure out how to deal with all the uncertainty on their own, with no feedback, advice, or support. If you are alone and uncertain, you get anxious. And if you're always anxious, like a deer in the headlights, you're likely to become rooted to the spot or "stuck."

Susan Rosenholtz undertook a classic study of 78 elementary schools in Tennessee in the 1980s.[5] Based on her findings, she divided the schools into two types: "stuck" and "moving." Stuck schools scored high on measures of uncertainty, were also high on teacher isolation, and did not support improvement. These factors had a negative correlation with student learning gains in literacy and mathematics over a 2-year period. One of the main causes of uncertainty, Rosenholtz found, was the absence of positive feedback:

> Most teachers and principals become so professionally estranged in their workplace isolation that they neglect each other. They do not often compliment, support, and acknowledge each other's positive efforts. Indeed, strong norms of self-reliance even invoke adverse reaction to a teacher's successful performance.[6]

Rosenholtz explained that isolation and uncertainty are associated with what she called "learning impoverished" settings, where teachers learned little from their colleagues and "held little awareness that their standardized instructional practice was in large part the reason they performed none too well."[7]

Uncertainty, isolation, and individualism are a toxic cocktail. Dan Lortie's field-defining book *Schoolteacher* showed that they were closely associated with classroom conservatism, because teachers had no access to new ideas.[8] When teachers are afraid to share their ideas and successes for fear of being perceived as blowing their own horns, when they are reluctant to tell others about a new idea on the grounds that others might steal it or take credit for it, when they are afraid to ask for help because they might be viewed as incompetent, and when they use the same approach year after year even though it is not working—all of these tendencies shore up the walls of individualism and isolation. They institutionalize conservatism.

Isolation and individualism are often attributed to teachers' individual personalities. They are seen as personal flaws or weaknesses. Administrators blame such teachers for being "lone rangers" or "independent contractors." Sometimes this is justified, but more often it's a case of not really understanding why teachers retreat to their own classrooms, or of not being able to tolerate teachers' criticisms of new directions or programs. But if it's not a question of personality, what factors *are* responsible for teacher individualism, then?

- *Architecture.* The architecture of individual buildings, separate egg-crate classrooms, and isolated portables makes it physically hard for teachers to work together. But barriers are easily re-erected in open classrooms, and doors are easily closed after they have been opened. Isolation and individualism are more than a question of bricks and mortar. They are deeply ingrained within the habits and cultures of teaching.
- *Evaluation and self-preservation.* Teachers often associate help with evaluation, and collaboration with supervision and control. The higher the stakes of evaluation in terms of pay and punishment, the less likely it is that teachers will share the strategies that give them comparative advantage or protection, or that they will seek the help that might expose them as weak or as failures. Isolation and individualism are their armor here—their protection against scrutiny and intrusion.

  Dan Lortie said that teacher individualism is "not cocky and assured: it is hesitant and uneasy."[9] In teaching, insecurity comes from the fear of infrequent and unfavorable judgment when there is no other feedback or reality check against one's performance. Insecurity is one of the causes of self-preservation among teachers. Less commonly but more spectacularly, self-interest is another. Here, individualism represents a more willful defense against and defiance of scrutiny that is justified and that would find some teachers badly wanting in effort or effectiveness.

Help can be separated from evaluation, though, by designing and developing more growth-oriented programs of evaluation that focus on improvement rather than on rewards and rankings, leaving high-stakes evaluation for the very worst cases of self-preservation that would then be more open to inspection. Supervisors and senior leaders can also model asking for help themselves as a way to show that everyone needs assistance because the work is inherently difficult. In this way, individualism can be eroded that little bit more.

♦ *Guilt and perfectionism.* Individualism can be a perverse product of teachers setting impossibly high expectations for themselves in a job with poorly defined limits. Teachers have been faced with mounting pressures, ever-rising expectations, and a widening array of responsibilities. Integrating special education students, working with ethnically and linguistically diverse populations, coping with growing amounts of "social work" and emotional problems as support for families outside the school dwindles, and dealing with all the paperwork that results from testing, accountability, data-driven improvement, and bureaucratic regulations—these are just some of the additions to the teacher's role over the years.

Remember the teachers in Chapter 3 who were proud of how much they had raised student achievement by relentless attention to every child, yet who were also utterly exhausted by the effort? These teachers don't need direction from above to motivate them. They drive themselves quite hard enough.

In teaching, patients are never stitched up, bodies are never buried, and cases are never closed. There's always more to be done. Working in the service of others and being surrounded by diffuse expectations, guilt and frustration become part of the work. Here is how one elementary teacher saw it:

> Teaching is a profession that when you go home, you always have stuff that you think about. You think, "I should be doing this". I feel guilty sitting down half the time.[10]

If few teachers are immune from the limitless work that causes guilt and also results from it, isolated teachers can easily get locked into spirals of overwork and guilt until burnout finally defeats them. This affects things as simple as whether teachers come into school or stay away when they are ill.

Many teachers who are ill come into school because they do not want their colleagues to think badly of them, or to seem less committed than other teachers who once came to school when they were even sicker. More than this, substitute teachers can often ignore or wreck the planned lessons that sick teachers have left, meaning there will be extra work when they return. At one highly collaborative high school that one of us studied, though, teachers and colleagues actively cared for each other and each other's families. One teacher described how she and a teaching partner had split the class of a sick colleague between them, taught the students, and marked their work. "I think we are all very supportive of each other's lives in that way, and so is our administration," she said. "It's always been family first."[11] Instead of stoicism and self-sacrifice among isolated and competitive teachers, this school's community balanced work and life by providing mutual emotional support as well as shared curriculum and teaching responsibility so that absences were covered more easily. Guilt is less pernicious when it is dealt with together. We will return to this theme in our discussion of collaboration.

◆ *Pressure and time.* Imposed repetitive change can also exacerbate individualism in teaching because teachers have no time to collaborate anymore.[12] Innumerable standards, test preparation demands, hurried curriculum implementation, and a deluge of data make teachers retreat to the classroom and close the door to meet their obligations—even during break time, when they rush to complete their own work rather than plan with colleagues. Needing more time is not just a cliché. But providing more time will not automatically relieve the sense of pressure that drives teachers back behind their own doors.

So individualism is, on balance, a bad thing. As we said earlier, individual teacher autonomy "behind the classroom door" is a license to be brilliant, but also to be abominable or just plain bland. And from Rosenholtz onward, the evidence is clear: in individualistic cultures, most teachers do not become more brilliantly distinctive from each other. They become increasingly the same, and at the cost of their effectiveness—afraid to take risks or to annoy their colleagues by having their classroom noise levels rise should they try something new.

Individualism is not just an atti-
tude or an affectation, still less a psychological affliction of teachers. It is
rooted in the very conditions and contexts of teachers' work—time, buildings, feedback systems, and so on.

> ◈▷ Eliminating individualism
> should not be about making
> everyone the same and plunging
> them into groupthink.

However, these conditions and traditions have undergone significant change
in the opening years of the 21st century. Peer coaching, mentoring, professional learning communities, and data teams have started to bring teachers
together more and open up new possibilities for teachers, teaching, and
teacher professionalism. When teachers work together, the chances for
increasing *professional capital* are therefore increased significantly. But they
are by no means guaranteed, as we shall see.

One last caveat before we move on—as we seek to eliminate *individualism* (habitual or enforced patterns of working alone), we should not eradi-
cate *individuality* (voicing of disagreement, opportunity for solitude, and
outright quirkiness) along with it. Eliminating individualism should not be
about making everyone the same and plunging them into groupthink. As
well as being worthwhile in its own right, individuality generates creative
disagreement and risk, which are sources of dynamic group learning and
improvement. In the best professional learning communities, we will see,
strong collaboration and distinctive individuality go together in vibrant
communities of innovation and growth.

COLLABORATIVE CULTURES

Susan Rosenholtz, as we noted earlier, drew attention to two distinctive
kinds of school cultures in her sample: stuck and moving. Stuck schools
had lower levels of achievement. Teachers thought teaching was technically
easy, they usually worked alone, and they rarely asked for help. In moving
schools, teachers believed that teaching was difficult, they always sought
help, and they never stopped learning to teach. Support from and communication with colleagues led teachers to have greater confidence and certainty about what they were trying to achieve and the best ways to achieve
it. Certainty wasn't provided by scripts or statistics but by shared support and agreement among teachers themselves. Certainty was situational,

not statistical—arising out of trust, advice, and shared expertise. In moving schools

> it is assumed that improvement in teaching is a collective rather than individual enterprise and that analysis, evaluation and experimentation in concert with colleagues are conditions under which teachers improve.[13]

Rosenholtz's pioneering research has been supported by study after study.[14] Collaborative schools do better than individualistic ones. Within high schools, too, collaborative departments with strong professional communities perform more effectively than weaker ones. Although what counts as collaboration might vary, the overall evidence is consistent—teachers who work in professional cultures of collaboration tend to perform better than teachers who work alone.

Not all kinds of collaboration are equally effective, though. Judith Warren Little has set out a continuum of collaboration from weaker to stronger forms.[15] These comprise:

+ *Scanning and storytelling*—exchanging ideas, anecdotes, and gossip
+ *Help and assistance*—usually when asked
+ *Sharing*—of materials and teaching strategies
+ *Joint work*—where teachers teach, plan, or inquire into teaching together

If collaboration is limited to anecdotes, giving help only when asked, or pooling existing ideas without examining or extending them, she says, collaboration will reproduce the status quo instead of challenging it. It is ultimately joint work that leads to improvement through exploring challenging questions about practice together—although the other kinds of collaboration may be prerequisites for it.

So, if informal collaboration or what is widely referred to as "sharing practice" is left to itself, it can become loose, unfocused, and inward-looking. Equally, as we shall see later, if there is no attention to the informal underpinnings of a collaborative school culture, collaboration can become awkward, artificial, and even oppressive. The trick is how to synchronize and sequence the informal and formal aspects in a positive combination.

Although informal aspects of collaboration have their risks, Jennifer Nias was one of the first to point out, in 1989, that they are absolutely integral to building a sustained collaborative culture in a school.[16] Collaborative cultures are to be found everywhere in the life of the schools that have them—in the gestures, jokes, and glances that signal empathy and understanding; in hard work and personal interest shown outside classroom doors and in school corridors; in recognition of birthdays and other little ceremonies; in accepting the connection between personal lives and professional ones; in overt praise, recognition, and gratitude; and in sharing and discussion of ideas and resources.

In collaborative cultures, failure and uncertainty are not protected and defended, but instead are shared and discussed with a view to gaining help and support. Collaborative cultures require broad agreement on values, but they also tolerate and to some extent actively encourage disagreement within these limits. Schools characterized by collaborative cultures are also places of hard work and dedication, collective responsibility, and pride in the school.

Collaborative cultures don't railroad other people's agendas and purposes through teachers. They acknowledge that teachers have purposes and commitments of their own. Ironically, disagreement is more frequent in schools with collaborative cultures because purposes, values, and their relationship to practice are always up for discussion. But this disagreement is made possible by the bedrock of fundamental security on which staff relationships rest—in the knowledge that open discussions and temporary disagreements will not threaten continuing relationships.

So there's no use hurling teachers into meetings to compare their students' work or discuss disturbing data together unless a basic platform of secure relationships has been established that will open these teachers up rather than shut them down. It's pointless and expensive putting everyone in a district through a packaged workshop on how to become professional learning communities if some of the principals have not been able or willing to build trust and respect with and among their teachers. Walkthroughs and instructional rounds are other quick-fix technologies that will again produce pitifully low returns unless there has been prior investment in knowing one's staff and colleagues and building relationships with them. And without underlying trust, respect, or sheer time to build relationships, leaders who instigate what are now called challenging or courageous conversations with their teachers about expectations, strategies, or results will learn all too quickly that what is challenging to them can come across as just downright offensive to their teachers.

So, usually, trust and relationships come first. But they don't happen aside from actual behavior. Getting behaviors going that demonstrate trust, and building new norms founded on trust, are perhaps the best ways to increase trust—provided that better trust is truly one of the intentions. We will return to these issues in our later discussions of contrived collegiality and professional learning communities.

Finding the time to develop collaboration, trust, and respect doesn't just happen accidentally or completely spontaneously—though it is possible to create platforms where spontaneous collaboration will occur. Meetings between special education and regular classroom teachers, a systemwide initiative supporting school-designed innovation in the province of Alberta, or local curriculum development processes in Finland that lead to a shared ethic of responsibility are just some of the examples of how systems can support deep collaboration grounded in trust and respect.

Collaborative cultures not only *can* be informal but they also *must always* be informal because without investment in underlying relationships, collaboration will be stilted, forced, and even damaging. These underlying relationships include caring for staff as individuals and making allowances for personal circumstances such as bereavements, other family crises, or just bad days. Collaborative cultures are not pressure cookers of guilt and perfectionism, but slow-boiling pots that allow vulnerabilities to be voiced and doubts to be articulated.

To sum up, collaborative cultures build social capital and therefore also *professional capital* in a school's community. They accumulate and circulate knowledge and ideas, as well as assistance and support, that help teachers become more effective, increase their confidence, and encourage them to be more open to and actively engaged in improvement and change. Collaborative cultures value individuals and individuality because they value people in their own right and for how they contribute to the group. As we will see, collaborative cultures do require attention to the structures and formal organization of school life, but their underlying sources of strength are informal in relationships, conversation, expressions of interest, provisions of support, and ultimately the mobilization of collective expertise and commitment to improve the lives and life chances of students. Talk together, plan together, work together—that's the simple key. The bigger challenge is how to get everyone doing that.

Whatever the particulars of one kind of collaboration or another, on average, collaborative cultures are still more effective than noncollaborative ones. But not all forms of collaboration are valuable. Some kinds of collaboration are best avoided. Others are wastes of time and limited in their impact. Still others are really way stations to be surpassed in the pursuit of more ambitious forms. We examine four different forms of collaboration next, along with their respective strengths and limitations—balkanization, contrived collegiality, professional learning communities, and clusters/networks/federations.

Balkanization

In some schools, while teachers associate more closely with some of their colleagues than they do in a culture of individualism, they do so in particular groups more than in the school as a whole. These schools have what we call *balkanized* teacher cultures—cultures made up of separate and sometimes competing groups, jockeying for position and supremacy like loosely connected Balkan states.[17]

Teachers in balkanized cultures attach their loyalties and identities to particular groups of their colleagues with whom they work most closely, share most time, and socialize most often in the staffroom or department workroom. The existence of tightly insulated subgroups in a school often reflects and reinforces very different outlooks on learning, teaching strategies, discipline, and curriculum. In balkanized cultures, teachers may not be *isolated,* but they are quite *insulated.*

Balkanized cultures are not confined to traditional teachers. Innovative teachers who see themselves as being ahead of or above their colleagues can also segment themselves in ways that hinder whole-school development. Indeed, this is one of the classic reasons for the fading and failure of innovative schools and programs over time—a sheer inability to manage envy![18]

Balkanization leads to poor communication, indifference, or subgroups going their separate ways. This, in turn, produces poor continuity in tracking and reviewing students' progress and inconsistent expectations for their performance and behavior. Balkanization can generate squabbles over space (room allocations, storage space, online access), time (priority in scheduling), and resources (budgets, student numbers, and so on). The urgency and necessity of defending territory and status against claims from other groups explains the great seriousness teachers attach to apparently "petty" disputes over things like cupboard space in a school corridor.

Balkanized cultures are a familiar feature of high school life, mainly because of the strong subject department structures on which high schools are based. This is one of the reasons that high schools are so notoriously hard to change. These cultures are not confined to high schools, though. In elementary schools, teachers are often separated into different grades and divisions—primary, junior, and intermediate—making cooperation across grades difficult and rare, and continuity in curriculum over a child's life disconcertingly weak. Continuity has been dealt with in written standards and programs rather than through the interactions and relationships among teachers who have taught the children and know them best.

The search for collective responsibility for student learning across grades is one way to circumvent these dangers of balkanization. So too is flexibility in moving teachers between different grades over the years, to widen their networks and extend their empathy for how other kinds of teachers teach. Collective responsibility is partly a matter of moral purpose and will, but there are also strategic actions that can bring it about:

- Discussing examples of student work, or reviewing ongoing data on individual student performance, in ways that provide a forum for cross-grade conversations
- Releasing teachers from the same or different grades to plan and meet together at the same time
- Asking teachers to cover for colleagues in different grades so that, for example, intermediate teachers can learn and appreciate how challenging it is to teach very young children
- Organizing shared projects across grades for half a day each week so that children from different grades and their teachers engage in joint work together
- Initiating interdisciplinary innovations in high schools that can bring together teachers from different subject departments around work that inspires and excites them
- Having senior curriculum and special education staff in the district work together on districtwide initiatives to set an example for similar joint work between special education and classroom teachers at the school level concerning students and curriculum they have in common

Arrangements such as these reaffirm two central principles that under-pin collaborative staff relationships. First, routine experiences of joint work with others are a better route toward understanding and cooperation than either rational persuasion to consider other teachers' viewpoints, or relying on formal procedures alone to secure continuity and alignment. Second, in places such as Finland, Alberta, and Ontario, educators understand that teacher development is inseparable from curriculum development. It's not the job of bureaucrats or a few elite teacher representatives to develop cur-riculum while classroom teachers deliver it. Instead, within clear common guidelines, teachers and schools create, think about, and inquire into cur-riculum and pedagogy together. Otherwise, how can we expect children to develop 21st-century skills of innovation and creativity if their teachers don't enjoy the same opportunity?

Contrived Collegiality

Some years ago, one of us was invited to dinner with a group of principals in Australia. Midway through the main course, one of the principals said, "Do you mind if I ask some advice?" He described problems he was having with a teacher who refused to collaborate, even though, paradoxically, the disserta-tion the teacher had recently completed for his graduate degree was on pro-fessional collaboration. When asked to give some examples, the principal said:

> "Well, at the start of staff meetings, we usually begin with an ice-breaking activity, and he refuses to do it."
>
> Back came the probing questions: "How long have you been at your school? What are the relationships among the other teachers like?"
>
> "Actually, they're very good. I've been there a few years and we have worked a lot together. The trust levels are really high."
>
> "So perhaps there's no ice to break, then!" came the reply.
>
> "That's funny," the principal said. "You may be right. He keeps accusing me of this thing . . . What does he call it? Contrived colle-giality!"
>
> "I have bad news for you," was the response. "I invented the term!"

Because collaborative cultures don't evolve quickly, they can be unat-tractive for administrators seeking swift solutions. Collaborative cultures are difficult to pin down in time and space, living as they do in the informal interstices of school life. They are also unpredictable in their consequences. The curriculum that will be developed, the learning that will be fostered, and the innovations that will be created cannot be planned or predicted exactly in advance.

For some administrators, this unpredictability can be disconcerting. What is developed by these collaborative cultures may not always correspond to administrators' own preferences or current school district priorities. Just as votes in an election can go against you, so can collaborative cultures. Therefore, administrators often prefer forms of collegiality they feel they can control—meetings with an agenda, working groups you can list on paper, or data teams that produce specific results. These more regulated kinds of collaboration are what we have meant and still mean by *contrived collegiality*.[19]

Contrived collegiality is characterized by formal, specific bureaucratic procedures to increase the attention being given to joint teacher planning and other forms of working together. It can be seen in initiatives like peer coaching, mentoring schemes, and data-driven team meetings. These administrative contrivances can get collegiality going in schools where little or none existed before. They are meant to encourage greater association among teachers and to foster more sharing, learning, and improvement of skills and expertise. Contrived collegiality is also meant to help deliver new approaches and techniques from the outside into a more responsive environment.

Contrived collegiality is double-edged, though. It has positive and negative possibilities depending on how it is used. At its best, it is a useful way to kick-start collaborative relationships between teachers where few had existed before. It is a way of putting teachers in touch. Principals can then build on those elements of recognition, trust, and support to focus conversations and activity more tightly around teaching and learning. To avoid confusion here, we prefer to call this *arranged collegiality*—a stepping stone to deeper forms of working together.[20]

Collaborative cultures don't happen by themselves. Some deliberate or even required arrangement is usually necessary in establishing them. Shrewd scheduling releases the right people to have an opportunity to plan together. Principals can use their own time to cover classes and facilitate this planning. Arrangements and expectations can be established for special education teachers to meet with regular classroom teachers. Protocols can be written to have teachers examine students' work in their respective classes. These kinds of arrangements make it more likely (though not certain) that high-trust collaborative cultures will develop.

Arranged collegiality can also disturb collective complacency and extend what teachers collaborate about. By looking at achievement data, examining achievement profiles of particular students, or comparing how different teachers might assess examples of students' assignments, arranged collegiality can sharpen the focus of joint work. At its worst, though, when arranged collegiality turns into contrived collegiality, it can become a slick administrative surrogate for collaborative teacher cultures.

Collaborative cultures take much more time, care, and sensitivity than speedily implemented changes or hurriedly assembled teams allow. As we shall see shortly, professional learning communities can be stilted caricatures of the vibrant cultures of deliberation and dialogue that they could really be. Building collaborative cultures is a patient developmental journey. There are no easy shortcuts.

Of course, as we have argued, collaborative cultures do require some guidance and intervention. But this supports, facilitates, and creates opportunities for teachers to work together. Collaborative cultures don't mandate collegial support and partnership through fear mongering and force. On the other hand, the pursuit of collaborative cultures is not a soft endeavor. As we will see in the guidelines for action in Chapter 7, teachers must push as well as pull each other toward stronger professional cultures.

Let's dig a little deeper. In some of the most questionable kinds of what we more precisely term contrived collegiality, colleagueship and partnership are administratively imposed, creating a degree of inflexibility that violates the discretionary judgment that is central to teacher professionalism and professional capital, and thus are ultimately superficial and short-lived. There are many examples of imposed collegiality that sail under the convenient flag of collaboration. Here are three of them:

1. *Coaching.* Peer coaching relationships can take many different forms, some more empowering than others. Some of these don't just encourage teachers to work together on improvements they identify, but also mandate that they work together to deliver prescribed literacy programs with *fidelity*. Here is a U.S. coach and some teachers discussing their struggles in using mandated common planning time so that they could respond to short vignettes about their work with a prescribed vocabulary curriculum, Word

Generation. The coach's job is to steer an agenda related to the district's goals within a mandated common planning period, but where there is shortage of time more generally. The case comes from work one of us did with writing partner Jane Skelton.[21]

> *Coach:* I struggle with having to get the conversation going. Sometimes I feel like I say a lot. I do a lot of "okay." Time is always the constraint. It's always the big factor. I've always struggled with what are the questions you have to bring forth in the moment to get things going. You don't want to say too much. You don't want to say too little. Getting other folks to talk—that's my struggle. I feel pressures to have other folks speak. So I feel like I say too much up front (Almost all of the teachers nodded in agreement.)

Time is not the only problem here. Teachers have to deal with many other initiatives and everyday demands such as "kids coming down the hallway" or parents waiting for attention, as well as the literacy requirements, and because of budget cuts, they are not even sure they will be keeping their jobs or where they will be working the following year.

> *Teacher 7:* When we come in here, we have to switch off from that other stuff. We know it's Word Generation, and [we have to] focus on what we're doing.

> *Teacher 1:* We have so many team meetings. We're at the service of the parents and if the parents come, it's just a matter of us being in two places at once.

> *Teacher 4:* You have common planning time, you have cluster time, and there's no real sacredness to it. So everything comes before it, and you're flying by the seat of your pants. And, you sit down for a couple of minutes and you want to participate and you find yourself, like everybody else, waiting for the kids to be coming back from gym. So you can never really be relaxed.

> *Teacher 3:* And then with this year and everyone trying to figure out their job, our minds are in different places.

> *Teacher 4:* Finding work.

Teacher 2: The [writing prompts] still have to be corrected.

Coach: About coming from one place to the next—[the common planning time] tends to be very coach-driven. I think that there are places where I try to invite, but I think that folks feel overloaded with what they are trying to do outside of these meetings. I know that we had talked about questions [related to the vocabulary issues] and a couple of folks had brought them back. You get caught up in things. And so when you think about doing that collaborative piece. . . . I mean, they had a parent show up this morning. They had an [individual education plan] meeting this morning. And I feel lots of times, it's like, "Can you handle this so we can deal with the parent and go to the [individual education plan] meeting? And kind of bring it back together for us week by week so that we can remain focused." (The teachers were silent.)

Coaching in the context of mandated reform can often fall short of its ideals, therefore, leading to hurried, anxious, and one-sided interactions, in required time periods that draw teachers away from compelling classroom concerns in a system where even basic job security can no longer be counted on. Passive resistance results in the form of withholding full attention or not responding to the coach's requests to complete a survey on what students were learning. It is easy to argue that teachers are just dragging their feet in acquiring new and much-needed technical *skills*. But in this case, they are actually digging in their heels to assert a contrary *will* that opposes the enforced transportation of unwanted programs and practices into their classrooms, especially at a time when their very jobs are up in the air.

2. *Peer pressure.* Peer pressure of certain kinds can be a highly valuable ingredient of positive professional collaboration—when peers who are knowledgeable about your practice and share your instructional goals help you and even push you to be the best you can be. The processes of what are called *cognitive coaching* and *challenge coaching* can provide feedback that will deepen reflection, provoke inquiry, and question existing assumptions. But sometimes, peer coaching can be just another technical way to implement an external mandate—with peer coaches or system literacy coaches now acting as messengers of compliance with enforced external reforms. An interesting example of this kind of peer-mediated accountability comes from a place where both of us have done extensive current and long-standing work—Ontario—but the source derives from other commentators at McKinsey & Company.[22] We quote directly:

> This is the story of a teacher who joined a primary school that had established the routines of collaborative practice as part of its literacy and numeracy strategy—these were professional learning communities through which teachers jointly reviewed student work and developed teaching methods. In that teacher's first week in the new school two of his colleagues visited him and suggested that he should use word walls because they had both found them to be effective. When, two weeks later, he had not yet put up the word walls, his colleagues visited him again, this time urging him more strongly to put up the word walls, sitting him down to share why this was the practice in their school and the difference it had made for students. A few weeks later, by then well into the school term, he had still not put up the word walls. His colleagues stopped by again after school, this time simply saying, "We are here to put up your word walls and we can help you to plan how to use them." As professionals in that school, they had developed a model of instruction that they found effective . . . so they expected others to use it too. Their commitment was to all students and to their professional norms—not just to their own students in their own classrooms—and they were willing to hold each other accountable for practices that they found effective.

What are we to make of this? Is it a case of opening the door to a new world of instructional effectiveness for the teacher in question, or is it too pushy, contrived collegiality? There isn't really enough information to go on in McKinsey & Company's description, but in a way, that's exactly the point. We hear the triumphant account from the peers who pushed their incoming colleague, but there are no words as to how this process was experienced by the colleague himself, or whether he became a better teacher as a result. It's a somewhat self-congratulatory account by the pushers, not the pushed.

We don't know how well these peers know, understand, and have come to grips with the details of their colleague's practice, but we do hear about infrequent visits and contacts—"two weeks later" and "a few weeks later"—suggesting that these may have had some of the features of the drive-by observations that are all too common in many coaching, supervision, and evaluation situations. Then there is the question of whether these educators see themselves truly as professional peers at all if they can take it upon themselves to be "sitting him down." This is very different from the behavior of Finnish teachers, who work together as peers in a "society of experts." And we don't hear about what approaches to literacy this teacher already uses, whether they are effective or not, and how rich or not they might be. All we know is whether or not the teacher has a word wall—an easily observable item, torn out of context, that can be quickly ticked off a checklist by transient and micromanaging peers who may quite possibly be acting like the clipboard kings and queens we described earlier.

Of course, it's perfectly possible that these peers did have deep understandings of and engagements with their colleague's practice and that the use of a word wall was just one well-articulated part of all of this. But we hear none of this. In this case, as in too many cases, it simply seems to come down to whether or not the teacher has a word wall: an example of contrived collegiality at its pushiest, most superficial, and groupthink-like extreme. And in the way the example is presented by McKinsey & Company, it uses the admirable principle of positive pressure to issue a license for pressure that the pushers decide on.

3. *Planning time.* Some years ago, one of us had an intriguing opportunity to study the impact of a policy to increase teachers' planning time in elementary schools. Would teachers use it to plan collaboratively, as one district intended, or to keep on planning alone? What would happen if the traditional contextual barrier of time for collaboration was taken down? Would more time allotment away from face-to-face interaction with students put an end to teacher individualism?[23]

One dedicated elementary school principal gave up his own time to cover for his third-grade teachers so they could plan together, by taking the whole grade himself, for half a morning, every week. One day, he walked down the hallway to see how they were getting on with the planning. The principal was shocked to discover that his teachers weren't planning together at all but working, planning, and grading students' work alone.

When they were challenged, the teachers asked him to trust them. They had been planning together, they said, but just then, at that moment, it was more important for them to work alone. Their principal was neither persuaded nor appeased. Having invested so much of his own time to allow them to plan together, he felt his trust had been abused when they did not and so he decided he would now regulate and monitor the planning time instead.

Was this a fair decision? In reality, planning time like any other scheduled time has complicated relationships to teachers' work and lives that principals cannot always see. In the wider study that was undertaken, many teachers did not see planning time as the best time to plan at all. Planning periods were usually fairly short—40 minutes or less. Many minutes were often lost looking after classes until the covering teacher arrived, taking children to the gym and supervising them while they changed, walking across to the staffroom if the teacher's own classroom was in use, and so on. This time was often regarded as too short for sustained planning, either with colleagues or alone. So these teachers preferred to plan at other times, such as lunch period or after school. Official planning time was used more to clear the decks of the innumerable small tasks such as photocopying or contacting parents that could be dispatched less efficiently at other times, especially when many teachers were clamoring for the same resources. If teachers cleared the decks during official planning time, they felt able to do more sustained planning at other points in the day.

But even this situation of finding planning time at lunch or after school didn't suit everyone. Planning time during the school day was ideal for other teachers. Teachers who coached sports teams, for example, had little opportunity to meet with colleagues at any other time. Pressing family responsibilities made it difficult for a number of female teachers to stay long after school to plan with colleagues at that time (even though many went to great inconvenience to do so). Official planning time therefore worked better for them.

Clearly, there is no magic administrative formula for perfect planning time. No set of bureaucratic rules or union contracts can meaningfully stipulate it. The important principle, rather, is to set expectations for *collegial tasks* (through discussion and development with teachers) rather than overmanaging the specifics of *collegial time.* It's about setting common expectations for goals, directions, and a collegial culture, and also about creating additional time that will make it possible to address and meet these expectations—without preempting teachers' discretionary professional judgment about how to deploy that time most effectively in the circumstances they know best. In the final analysis, our point is that collective deliberation must become *job embedded* into the profession of teaching. It must become just as regular a practice as classroom teaching—as is true in all the top-performing countries.

SOME CRITICS of the concept of contrived collegiality (which they often misread and misrepresent as contrived *congeniality*) wrongly claim that it is being used as a verbal weapon to defend teachers' right to teach any way they like (to shore up their individual classroom autonomy, that is).[24] As the arguments we have presented make very clear, nothing could be further from the truth. But the principle that collegiality usually has to be organized, expected, and arranged—often (but not always) by administrators—should not be used to justify and to fail to challenge the excesses and abuses of contrivance. Authentic professional collaboration is doubtful when it is based on external agendas that administrators decide, at times of their choosing, and in relation to purposes in which teachers have no control, such as test score thresholds.

To contrive something is to do more than merely organize and arrange it. Deliberate change requires deliberate measures. But to make things contrived is to push them quite a bit further. It is to make them unnatural, false, artificial, even forced. Contrived collegiality is collaboration on steroids. In the end, the drawbacks and benefits of arranged collegiality (at its best) and contrived collegiality (at its worst) are not to be found in whether or not particular structures or practices are suddenly introduced—such as planning times, protocols, or procedures for analyzing data. The differences between merely arranged and artificially contrived or forced collegiality are to be found in whether there is already enough trust, respect, and understanding in a culture for any new structures or arrangements to have the capacity to move that culture ahead.

This is not a question of whether administrators or teachers should be the driving force behind professional collaboration. There are risks (as well as benefits) on both sides. When administrators lead the charge, as we have seen, the interactions can become forced and backfire. When collaboration is left strictly to teachers, it can lack bite. In the end, somebody has to lead collaboration, and neither group should ignore or override the other.

The issue then is that if there is any pressure, whether it is exerted by principals or by peers, what distinguishes good pressure from bad pressure (as by the literacy coach in the example)? Pressure from peers is inherently no better than pressure from principals or other administrative leaders if the pressure is of the wrong kind, exerted in the wrong way. The same goes for the positive pressure of arrangement rather than enforced contrivance—what it is, is more important than who initiates it.

These seemingly abstract issues have been addressed by Amanda Datnow in a study of the dynamics of data-driven teams in two school districts.[25] Using the concepts of collaborative cultures and contrived collegiality as a touchstone for her team's analysis, she found that while the collaboration promoted by both districts was administratively regulated and designed to meet the districts' purposes through such devices as mandated meeting times and prescribed questions within meeting protocols, many of the negative effects normally associated with contrived collegiality did not take hold. Rather, "what began as contrived meetings to discuss data evolved into spaces for more genuine collaborative activity wherein teachers challenged each other, raised questions, and shared ideas for teaching."[26]

The explanation for this finding is interesting. There was already quality, integrity, and long-term stability in the leadership of these districts, even before the introduction of data-driven improvement. The districts had pursued continuous improvement for some time and been able to "develop trust among teachers, assuage their concerns about how the data reflected upon them as individual teachers, and promote a positive orientation towards data use."[27] Strong collaborative cultures were the foundation underpinning the immediate efforts at data-driven contrived collegiality.

We do not yet know how best to develop and sustain these collaborative cultures over long periods of time. Because of this difficulty, contrived or at least arranged collegiality (often without the necessary foundation of trusting and respectful relationships) is likely to characterize many early attempts for many years to come. When it is used in a facilitative, not controlling, way, contrived (or arranged) collegiality can provide a starting point and a necessary first step toward building collaborative cultures with focus and depth. One of the most significant, sustained, and systemically broad efforts to do that has taken the form of *professional learning communities*, places where the pushes and pulls of different kinds of collegiality come through with real intensity.

Professional Learning Communities

What have we learned so far about collaborative cultures and social capital? Two basic lessons stand out. First, a lot of the work of building collaborative cultures is informal. It's about developing trust and relationships, and it takes time. But if all this is left entirely to spontaneity and chance, a lot of collaborative effort will dissipate and provide no benefit to anyone. Second, the strong collaboration of joint work can benefit from deliberate arrangements of meetings, teams, structures, and protocols, but if these are hurried, imposed, or forced, or if they are used in the absence of commitments to building better relationships, then they too will be ineffective.

Strong and positive collaboration is not about whether everyone has a word wall, or a set of posted standards, or not. It's about whether teachers are committed to, inquisitive about, and increasingly knowledgeable and well informed about becoming better practitioners together, using and deeply understanding all the technologies and strategies that can help them with this. Collaboration can be too warm and too cold. We need to find the sweet spot that's "just right" in between. The place where all these scenarios play out these days is in professional learning communities.

Since the origins of the terms *professional community, learning community,* and *professional learning community* in the 1990s, professional learning communities have spread like wildfire. Sometimes they have been a means to develop teachers' overall capacity for inquiry, improvement, and change. Sometimes they have been used as a strategy to implement external reforms—especially in tested literacy and mathematics. Sometimes they have just been a flourish of new vocabulary. Indeed, we have worked in districts that have been called such-and-such a school district one year and such-and-such a learning community the next—but only the name has changed!

Originally, the inventor of the term *professional learning community,* Shirley Hord, simply meant that a PLC, as it later came to be called, would be a place where teachers inquired together into how to improve their practice in areas of importance to them, and then implemented what they learned to make it happen.[28] In the spirit of this simple starting point, we see PLCs as comprising three elements. They are:

1. *Communities.* Where educators work in continuing groups and relationships (not merely transient teams), where they are committed

to and have collective responsibility for a common educational purpose, where they are committed to improving their practice in relation to that purpose, and where they are committed to respecting
and caring for each others' lives and dignity as professionals and as
people.

2. *Learning* communities. Where improvement is driven by the commitment to improving students' learning, well-being, and achievement; where the process of improvement is heavily informed by
professional learning and inquiry into students' learning and into
effective principles of teaching and learning in general; and where
any problems are addressed through organizational learning in
which everyone in the organization learns their way out of problems instead of jumping for off-the-shelf, quick-fix solutions.

3. *Professional* learning communities. Where collaborative improvements and decisions are informed by but not dependent on scientific and statistical evidence, where they are guided by experienced
collective judgment, and where they are pushed forward by grown-
up, challenging conversations about effective and ineffective
practice.

Professional capital is and should be about all three of the listed elements. Since the intellectual origins of PLCs, their strategic development
and dissemination have owed a lot to the energetic efforts of PLC champions and consultants Rick and Becky Dufour and Bob Eaker. They have
worked with district after district in the United States and elsewhere to set
clear goals, get teachers working together as teams, gather data, discern
where the problems are, and design interventions. The Dufour team has also
published several well-documented examples of school and district success
driven by PLC concepts, strategies, and practices.[29]

Sadly, however, their strategies have often been imposed simplistically
and heavy-handedly by overzealous administrations. Too often, they have
become yet one more "program to be implemented" rather than a process to
be developed. Sociologist Robert Merton called this *goal displacement—*
when the original purpose is displaced and the innovation or means to that
end becomes the new end in itself.[30]

One clear example comes out of Alberta. In a research team that one of
us led to review the province's groundbreaking school improvement initiative, Dennis Sumara and Brent Davis undertook an in-depth study of three

contrasting school districts and how they each approached school-based innovation within the province's wider initiative.[31] One of them, which they called Arrowhead, decided what their schools' innovations would be—professional learning communities—and imposed them on everyone. Leadership money was spent on moving one or two teachers from the schools to be coordinators in the district office (in another district, by contrast, the money was spent on providing bits of time for lots of teachers to interact and inquire into their practice together within and across their schools) and on bringing in well-known external trainers to do multi-day workshops with school teams. The aim was to achieve alignment in the district. But, in practice, the only time the schools met each other was during the workshops, and because leadership was concentrated in the district office and imposed from the top, none of the schools knew what the others were doing. Ironically, the district ended up getting very little alignment at all because the PLCs were laid on, there was not enough leadership to spread around, and the only learning that was going on was from the external consultants. These PLCs were superficial. They neither built on nor developed any kind of deep change in the cultures of their schools or their district.

Diane Woods's research pinpoints how PLCs, like many reforms, are often viewed more favorably by people at the top relative to those on the ground.[32] Charles Naylor, a professional development leader for the British Columbia Teachers' Federation, has seen how the importation and implementation of professional learning communities has fared in high-capacity, high-performing Canada, and he is not impressed with the results.[33] The worst proponents of PLCs, he says, avoid connecting them to innovative and ambitious learning goals but stick to the technicalities of specifying narrow performance goals, defining a focus, examining data, and establishing teams.

We recognize a dilemma here. This is tough terrain. If someone doesn't push PLCs, there is a worry that individually autonomous teachers may not get around to purposeful interaction. This push might come from administrators if capacity in a school or a group of schools has been weak and teachers have little prior experience with professional collaboration. It might equally be teacher leaders who may have to push their administrators to give them time to collaborate on learning agendas about which they are more knowledgeable than their principals. We have seen this in the case of the California Teachers Association, whose responsibility to turn around the lowest performing schools in their state has sometimes required teachers to spearhead collaborative improvement despite the resistance or indifference of school administrators who are uncomfortable with ceding professional control to their more instructionally knowledgeable teachers.[34]

Still, whether it's administrators or peers, do we really want improvement to happen as a result of a bunch of change pushers? Why does change always have to be driven or pushed from somewhere else or by someone else? In the Beyond Expectations study, which one of us conducted with Alma Harris, one of the organizations is an extraordinary and highly successful craft brewery featured on the Discovery Channel—the makers of Dogfish Head beer. Our research team members who conducted this case are Corrie Johnson and Alex Gurn.[35]

> At Dogfish Head Craft Brewery, the Dogfish way of creating "off-centered ales for off-centered people" is all about living life counter-intuitively, against the grain. Dogfish Head's employment of 'opposite-approach strategies' works to turn conventional industry practice on its head and circumvent the big three US beer companies' attempts at structured market domination. For instance, instead of adopting conventional *push* strategies of marketing, which advertise the product far and wide, Dogfish Head uses *pull*-marketing at craft . . . beer events and the like that devote time face to face with people and develop a cult following. "From the outset, it's still this fun, funky thing that people just gravitate to."

It sounds like tough talk to be saying we need to be *pushing* things all the time, either from above or from one's peers. But professional learning communities, collaboration, and change in general are as much about *pulling* people toward interesting change by the excitement of the process, the inspirational feeling of the engagement, the connection to people's passions and purposes, the provision of time that is not consumed by classroom responsibilities or mandated change agendas, and the creation of not just a spreadsheet of higher test scores but also a culture of engaged and successful learners, like the wizard learners at Limeside Primary School in England that we discussed in Chapter 3.[36] Create positive energy and excitement in relation to a commonly valued goal and you will always *pull* lots of people toward you.

In educational change, it is sometimes said that human beings, like physical objects, usually prefer to be at rest, to remain just where they are. In line with the laws of physics, some kind of force will therefore be required to move them. What kind of force should it be, and who should exert it? Should teachers be pushed, pulled, dragged, drawn, or lifted? Is a great shove needed to move them forward and keep doing so, or will just a well placed nudge be enough to get them moving by their own momentum?

If pushing or pressure is excessive and amounts to shoving people, it can border on bullying and abuse—like the example earlier of "sitting" someone down until he agreed to have a word wall. In their widely used book *Nudge: Improving Decisions About Health, Wealth and Happiness,* Richard Taylor and Cass Sunstein argue against two flawed theories of change that under-pin many administrative and policy efforts to alter behavior.[37] Except where it is absolutely necessary and the protection of public safety is at risk, they argue, attempts to alter behavior by the first strategy of compulsion or force usually backfire by generating resistance to and avoidance of change. We have seen this, for example, in models of policy delivery where standardized tests or other key performance indicators are linked to high-stakes system targets for improvement, with punitive consequences for those who fall short. Force as a strong shove drives people to game the system and produce the appearance of compliance, even and including when force is applied to requirements for professional collaboration.

The opposite of overwhelming force is unlimited choice. This, too, say the authors of *Nudge,* is a detrimental option. In *The Paradox of Choice,* Barry Schwartz argues and shows that too much choice can be bad for us.[38] It makes us confused, frustrated, and unhappy, because out of all the options available, we can never be truly sure we have made the right or completely the best choice—be it shoes for our feet or schools for our children. More than this, say Taylor and Sunstein, when consumers are overwhelmed, they will often make choices, or fail to make choices, in ways that turn out to be bad for them—especially when the results of those choices are long term and can easily be overshadowed by other choices that yield short-term rewards. This, they say, is why people often choose to purchase and con-sume foods that are bad for their health, or why they fail to review their pension fund investments to safeguard their long-term retirement.

What the authors of *Nudge* argue for instead of inescapable force and unlimited choice is ways to "nudge" or prod people's choices in one direc-tion rather than another, reducing the range of choice and increasing the probability that people will themselves then choose the behaviors that are in the best interests of themselves or those they serve. Some of these nudges are normative: they are in the language we use and the expectations we set.

Others are structural: they are arrangements of the organizational or physical environment to make some choices more likely than others. Placing fruit rather than candy bars next to the supermarket checkout shifts the likelihood of what people will buy, on impulse, as they line up to pay. Making the best rather than the worst pension option the default option for those who don't actively choose, again instigates a structure that channels people's own choices into more beneficial areas rather than harmful ones. Nudging, say Taylor and Sunstein, isn't meant to be a way to deceive consumers or hoodwink people into harming themselves. It is a way to deliberately organize and arrange the structures and norms of organizations to increase personal benefit and public good. Nudging is arranged collegiality; shoving is contrived collegiality.

In general, we need to move the debate away from pushing PLCs per se and into the arena of developing professional capital, which, in its more advanced forms, means that teachers will challenge each other as well as challenge their leaders as part and parcel of the give and take of continuous improvement. Again, there needn't be an ideological battle between tender words and tough talk, between pushing and shoving and pulling or also nudging change forward. Usually, what will be involved from different quarters is a bit of push, a bit of pull, and a bit of push back. And when all the forces come together, the results can be dynamic. All of this is evident in an Ontario school district that has been studied as part of an investigation with Henry Braun of special education reform strategies in 10 (of the 72) districts in the province. Case writer Matt Welch captures the nuances when one man's push and pull becomes a push too far for his colleagues:[39]

Dave Perkins (a pseudonym and composite of two district administrators) is Director (superintendent) of a Northern Canadian school district that has 24 elementary and secondary schools with a 40% population of First Nations (aboriginal) students in a far-flung territory the size of France. He's the kind of guy who looks more at home in a snowmobile than sitting down with a spreadsheet, but he cares passionately about students and social justice.

We investigated how Dave's district used project funding for whole-school approaches to special education reform. Every district took a different approach. Dave's district initially used its resources for supply (or substitute) teacher coverage to allow both general and special education teachers to attend PLC meetings together and for "capacity building" more generally. The reflective aspects of PLCs in this district allowed teachers to increase their awareness that the significant language challenges of their aboriginal students were less a matter of inherent and insurmountable cognitive impairment, but rather a developmental and experiential issue that could be addressed collaboratively as well as pedagogically.

Dave and his colleagues *pulled* teachers in by having flexible formats and focal points in different schools and by funding ample release time to break down the separation between special education and curriculum staff: "sharing strategies, supporting each other, talking about at-risk kids, talking about special needs." They also *pushed* frank discussion about teaching strategies and about expectations for aboriginal students' learning.

> There was a lot more self-direction in the PLCs coming from teachers. It was more "Let's make sure we're focused and make sure we're doing something and our school energies are all being harnessed and directed in unison rather than us all paddling our own little canoes in different directions."

As teachers reflected on their students' performance data, collaborated, and discussed students' needs, the task of improving students' writing no longer mainly meant reviewing student performance on practice prompts or drills related to the high-stakes standardized tests. Rather, as the PLC process "unfolded, we began to see more and more connection between early language development as oral language development [and] reading development, writing development, and overall literacy development." Staff became increasingly aware that many aboriginal students of low socioeconomic status were entering school with very little existing language capacity whatsoever. During walkthroughs, staff presented early childhood classrooms where groups of students were using a variety of tools to build literacy skills (e.g., computers, board games, and manipulatives). Younger students now had their needs brought to the fore, and teachers began to see the connection to measured literacy performance in later grades.

PLCs could sometimes become quite confrontational, but mainly in a productive way. The district's data administrator described how it was:

Very confrontational for one teacher—not in a negative way, but they definitely felt that they needed to be able to defend the way that they wanted to mark and grade student work. And she walked away from the table understanding that she wasn't using a criterion-based assessment even though she had developed a rubric but [the grade was] based on the effort that they were working on. That was her peers at the table. She didn't go away upset. She went away saying, "I need to rethink this."

Facilitating the challenging work that enabled teachers to have productive and frank conversations took time. In the words of one teacher:

Pushing people outside of their comfort zone, as difficult as it is, truly is successful because in time we were able to see changes in the content of discussion and the quality of the discussions that were happening around the table, but it took a lot of time.

Teachers said they were more frequently "listening to colleagues and watching what they're doing," and described how they were "more willing" to try colleagues' ideas since they had built "relation-ships." One said, "if we're going to be an effective school we need those relationships."

You would think that all this would make the superintendent and his staff self-congratulatory about their success. Yet the pressures in bringing about changes through "frank" conversations were by no means always seen as positive and productive. The special education coordinator for the district talked about this tension:

Teachers definitely are feeling that they're under more scrutiny, more pressure from senior administration. Principals regularly are in classrooms. They're doing walkthroughs. They're look-ing for specific things. They want to see evidence that guided reading is happening. They want to see evidence of all of the initiatives that the board is working on. There is a lot of pres-sure on teachers to make changes and they certainly are feel-ing that pressure.

When this superintendent met with the research team and all his fellow district superintendents from elsewhere, he spoke movingly about how valuable the case study reports had been to him and his district. "I thought I was having challenging conversations with my staff," he said, to open up practice and raise expectations. "But since I read this report," he continued, "I realize that what I intended to be challenging conversations have sometimes been experienced as oppressive conversations." "That is just the perception of some of my staff," he went on, "but perception is reality and I have to learn from this and take it very seriously."

Courageous leaders of PLCs are not bullying and self-congratulatory. They are humble and self-reflective. When push comes to shove, they know and are alert to when they have overstepped the mark and gone too far; they know when they need to remain committed but not push too heavily and too hard. As a wise principal we know once said to her principal colleagues, "don't use your power just because you can!"

There are some powerful concluding lessons from this example about PLCs, their nature, and their momentum. They have that back-and-forth feel that permeates much of our analysis of professional collaboration and community—between the relative contribution of pressure and support, push and pull, focus and flexibility, relationships and results. This culminating example shows how unproductive it is to take ideological sides on these issues—to talk tough because it appeals to policymakers and administrators, or to use kinder words that appeal more to the profession, to pitch change ideas to teachers on the one hand or to administrators on the other. In the district we have described,

- Teachers are *pulled* into something they find energizing, that they are given time for, and that respects their collective (not individual) professional autonomy and discretion; yet they are also *pushed* to review or revise what has been more or less effective for them, and to acquire practices from other colleagues who may be doing some things better.
- PLCs have a clear *focus,* but this is collectively and *flexibly* determined by the community—not administratively imposed on everyone, in a standardized way, from outside.
- There is a sense of *urgency* about challenging teachers' practice, yet also a *patient* realization that the essential trust and relationships that underpin PLCs can only develop over time.

◆ The superintendent is *firm and persistent* enough to challenge his teachers and leaders with frankness, yet *humble and open* enough to know when he has to pull back because he has gone too far and shoved too hard.

We have found these elements of the yin and yang of change leadership in our other studies of especially effective leadership. In dynamic times, change leaders are confident *and* humble, resolute *and* empathetic, collaborative *and* competitive. Such professional capital is sophisticated yet accessible to those who practice it. All in all, the current PLC movement should be reconsidered and reconfigured in terms of how well it can become grounded not in implementing outsiders' agendas but in promoting professional capital and all of its three components—decisional, human, and social.

Clusters, Networks, and Federations

It's not a good thing when teachers work alone. Nor is it good when schools operate in isolation either, no matter how collaborative they are internally. Teachers improve when they collaborate with and learn from other teachers. Schools also improve when they collaborate with and learn from other schools—but not always. Just as collaboration between teachers can be weak, unfocused, or excessively contrived, the same is true for collaboration among schools.

In the past, in the United States especially, school-to-school networks have often been professionally energizing for their participants, but they have been less convincing in terms of their impact on student achievement—so system administrators are understandably neither enthusiastic nor generous when someone comes along proposing a new idea for school networks.[40] At the same time, whenever a new reform is introduced, part of the design often includes ways to share practice across schools—so districts and state departments are inclined to believe they have already invested in school-to-school interaction, failing to appreciate that merely sharing practice carries little guarantee of impact or success. Despite a few exceptions, school networks have a poor track record, then, and it is not easy to get policy makers today to reinvest in them.

However, just like professional collaboration within schools, collaboration across schools can be highly effective, but only if you go about it in the right way. It's another way to circulate professional capital. Fortunately, across the world, we now have some very positive examples of school-to-school collaborations that have had a profound impact on improving and spreading *best* practice, and also on developing and disseminating innovative *next* practice. Some of the best have been developed in England. England got tired of trying to raise achievement and turn around underperforming schools through top-down strategies of intervention. When the national trajectory of achievement results hit a plateau, the Labour government was eager to explore alternative approaches that could raise achievement by schools helping schools through lateral, peer-driven assistance and interaction. The most successful of a number of early efforts on this score was a project called Raising Achievement/Transforming Learning (RATL), which was led by an inspirational and highly successful former headteacher (principal), David Crossley.

In 2005, with Dennis Shirley, one of us was asked to undertake an evaluation of this groundbreaking project. Crossley's network, we found, was not just a loose assemblage of schools that were encouraged to share practice. It had a clear change architecture. Specifically, RATL

- *Invited* (but did not enforce) participation by 300 underachieving secondary schools that were identified by indicators of performance dips
- *Networked* schools together through conferences and programs of inter-visitation, so that schools in the same boat could support each other
- *Made available* (but didn't assign) *mentor schools* and leaders to provide coaching assistance and offer practical solutions
- *Provided* visionary *inspiration* and motivation at network conferences as well as *technical* systems and *assistance* for analyzing student achievement and other school-level data
- *Injected* a range of experience-driven and *practically proven strategies* for raising achievement and transforming learning
- *Incentivized* participation through modest funding for both the helped and the helping schools, to be spent at the principal's professional discretion, provided it was on improvement

Crossley and his RATL leaders designed a unique model that yielded early and measurable benefits in student achievement in two-thirds of project schools, which improved in terms of student achievement at double the rate of the national average within 2 years. And even the schools that didn't improve reinforced the basic design thrust—they were geographically isolated or didn't know how to network. RATL had a *push–pull* architecture. Schools were *pulled* into it by the discretionary funding, voluntary participation, common bonding, professional inspiration, peer assistance, practical strategies, and technical support. They were also *pushed* forward by transparent processes of participation and collective visibility of measured results. Crossley has now taken versions of this architecture to the United States, beginning with 33 low-performing schools in the Metro Nashville Public Schools district.

In England, the RATL initiative was quickly followed by an impressive National Leaders of Education (NLE) Program, introduced by the National College for School Leadership, under its head, Steve Munby.[41] Here, 600 outstanding headteachers (principals) who had been successful in assisting other schools worked closely with struggling partners to improve learning and results—not through sending in hit-and-run teams with checklists and quick-fixes but by working alongside the existing administration day by day over sustained periods to make practice better. Some of these NLEs even took over the schools they supported. The many schools that participated experienced significant achievement gains as a result. England's current coalition government likes the strategy so much that is has asked the National College to establish a more systematic version that goes under the name of National Teaching Schools, which have *alliances* of schools, teaching schools *networks,* and *job-share* partnerships.[42] These are all shared investments in common success.

With our colleague Alan Boyle, we recently filmed a cluster (what the British system calls a federation) of primary schools in the London borough of Hackney. St. John/St. James school had significantly improved under successful school leadership.[43] It went from being in the worst category of "Special Measures" (England's nomenclature for failing schools) to having the top rating of "outstanding." When the local authority (or school district) contemplated what to do with a second school that was in Special Measures, they decided that St. John/St. James should partner with that school— with the St. John/St. James school head becoming "executive head" of both schools. The turnaround was so successful that a third and then a fourth school was added to the federation. There is one executive head, with each of the other three schools having principals who report to her. Teachers are routinely involved in helping each other across the schools, and the whole group of schools has become a breeding ground for the development of future school leaders (heads).

England's innovative energy in developing robust architectures of improvement—where schools work with schools, professionals work with professionals, and the strong help the weak—has been admirable in terms of the number of schools showing improved learning and achievement. But the danger of spreading out any strategy that shows great promise and a high success rate is then to mandate, legislate, or universalize it, or to hook it up to purposes other than those for which it was originally designed. Of course, this inclination is an understandable but nonetheless flawed response to the equally great danger that new networks involve only small numbers of enthusiasts and that they never become more than small pockets of success (or failure) that affect only parts of the overall system. But the overreaction of mandating networks or clusters takes away the collective professional responsibility and autonomy—the dynamic force of professional capital—that made the original networks and federations successful, and replaces them with old systems of bureaucratic compliance that have almost never worked in the past.

So, for example, the coalition government in England is attempting to turn all schools into "Academies" with the expectation that they will form clusters with one or more other schools. Many Academies are being arranged in chains of similarly branded schools under the influence of corporate or other part-funders, who often install their own leadership to replace the leadership of the school that each Academy replaced. In these instances, it has been pointed out, schools may be more inclined to assist and have loyalty to distant partners in the chain, rather than to schools outside the chain but within the same community.[44] These chains represent an elaborate version of the *business capital* approach where pockets of competitors try to outdo each other.

The displacement of the original purposes and successes of British school networks and federations by markets and mandates means that the results of this initiative are now a very mixed bag! Indeed Chris Chapman's research on the effectiveness of different types of school federations shows that only those that have designs and principles close to the original architecture evident in RATL actually yield positive results.[45]

Outside England, other countries and jurisdictions have also employed the same principle of schools learning from each other in systemic designs that promote win–win relationships, focused inquiry, and widespread development. Two examples documented by OECD and McKinsey & Company come from Asia:[46]

> Shanghai—a city of over 20 million—literally came from nowhere in the period 2006 to 2009 to become the world's highest performing system in the PISA/OECD assessment of 15-year-olds in literacy. One of the ways they did this was to pair high-capacity schools with lower capacity schools and enable them to work together in a non-judgmental relationship.

> In Singapore, every one of its more than 400 schools is in a formal network of 12–14 schools with a full-time coordinator to run the cluster. Here, talented people work purposefully to leverage each other's knowledge while focusing on personalized learning for all students. Effective collaboration requires teachers with strong capabilities. In McKinsey & Company's description of this case, one Singaporean educator made clear that "we could not have implemented professional learning communities as effectively in the 1980s. We did not have the skill levels in schools for it, and it may have backfired. However our teachers and leaders are highly skilled now, and therefore we have shifted to peer collaboration and it works."

These Asian examples seem as inspiring as the English ones. We need to be careful, of course, about how we transplant principles of success from Southeast and East Asia to non-Asian contexts—as we should be cautious about transplanting any reforms internationally. Many Asian cultures, for example, have a traditional and historical respect for teachers, a traditional family focus on learning and achievement, and an established deference to hierarchical authority. So educational mandates work out differently here than they do in many other cultures—even when the mandate is to collaborate. Even so, it is encouraging that federations, networks, and clusters can be as widespread and effective in cultures as different as Anglo-Saxon and Asian ones.

There are yet more examples of successful peer-to-peer improvement in places such as Finland, where there is a national network of innovation; Alberta, where the province's schools, now in their fourth 3-year cycle of school-designed innovation, are concentrating on networking innovative practices within and across school districts; and York Region School District, just north of Toronto, which has all of its almost 200 schools in clusters of 6–8 schools. So the reach of these ways of circulating and sharing professional capital across cultures is considerable. Where it is difficult to establish cross-school networks or indeed any kind of professionally collaborative behavior is in countries that have been, within the memory of one or two generations, former despotisms or dictatorships, where fear and corruption were (or still are) widespread and habits of suspicion and compliance are deeply ingrained; or in places where there is a deep-seated political culture of top-down control or competitive individualism.

In the United States, there are a few small pockets of school clusters within districts, but they are not nearly as formally structured as in the previous examples, and they are still very much the exception. Sanger Unified School District near Fresno, California, a district that one of us has filmed, has every one of its 15 schools in small clusters of 3 or 4 schools that meet regularly and learn from each other.[47] The student achievement results are consistently impressive.

All these examples are *systemic*—the whole system of schools sets about improving on a comprehensive and mutually supportive basis. Some systems mandate federations or clusters, but mandating professional changes like these is likely to be counterproductive in cultures that do not defer to hierarchical authority as a habit of mind. In the main, then, in our view, complete participation or almost complete participation in networked professional capital should be an energetic aspiration and normative expectation within a system's professional culture, rather than a bureaucratically enforced mandate. These forms of learning together can be powerful system builders leading to the mutual development of new capabilities and commitments, or they can become the system-level equivalent of comfortable collaboration (shared practice) or excessively contrived collegiality, which all too often characterizes collaborative efforts within schools. When you circulate professional capital freely, energetically, and inclusively, you get wholesale professional improvement at its best.

This can be true even in very large-scale systems that appear to be and often are, in some respects, competitive. This competitiveness, we believe, is not just an obstacle that can be overcome, but a force, when it is not of a win–lose nature, that can actually be capitalized upon. This occurs when two powerful forces come together: collective responsibility and collaborative competition—or what the business literature calls *co-opetition*.[48]

Collective responsibility con-sists of the enlargement and deep-ening of identity beyond oneself. When individual teachers within a school start identifying with all students in the school, not just those in their own classroom, that is collective responsibility. When

> ◆▷ . . . collective responsibility is not just a commitment; it is the exercise of capabilities on a deep and wide scale. It encompasses positive competition: challenging the limits of what is humanly and professionally possible.

individual school principals become almost as concerned about the success of other schools in their cluster as they are about their own school, we see enlarged commitment again. When districts see themselves as part of a state's or country's quest for success for all their students and as part of the nation's or state's development of its common identity, we see the force of collective responsibility once more. Moreover, as countries around the world attempt to learn from each other, and openly share what they know, we see the makings of a global identity that will contribute powerfully to the future of humankind.

But collective responsibility is not just a commitment; it is the exercise of capabilities on a deep and wide scale. It encompasses positive competi-tion: challenging the limits of what is humanly and professionally possible. In every healthy cluster or network that we have studied or been part of, there has also been a powerful tendency to try to compete, but in a spirit of how we can outdo ourselves as well as each other, for the good of the whole, or even the good of the game, to use a sports analogy. We call this "collab-orative competition," co-opetition, or friendly rivalry, because concepts both of collaboration and competition come together to form an unbeatable combination.

We certainly have seen many bad forms of win–lose competition that in-clude self-centeredness, widespread cheating, divisive effects of performance-based pay, envy and jealousy, unwillingness to offer assistance to struggling neighbors, and, like a spoiled child, finding yourself all alone with no one to share all your expensive toys (books, interactive whiteboards, sporting facilities, or highly skilled teachers) when you keep all your goodies for yourself. But when you get collective responsibility on the rise, and em-brace strong developmental strategies in pursuit of a noble cause, you also get a kind of "Moral Olympics" where there is almost no ceiling to what can be accomplished.

This is the kind of professional capital worth fighting for—collective responsibility and capability, as well as collaborative competition or friendly rivalry for the good of everyone in the system.

CONCLUSION

So what have we learned about the role of professional culture and community in developing and circulating the professional capital that raises achievement, improves learning, and propagates innovation? A professional culture, we have seen, connects the way people perform their work to the people they are, the purposes they pursue, the colleagues they have, and how they do or do not improve.

In the old days, and still too much today, the professional culture of teaching was one of individual classroom autonomy, unquestioned experience, and unassailable knowledge and expertise. Nowadays, professional cultures are more and more collaborative. Teachers may still actually teach alone for much of the time, but the power of the group—and all of the group's insight, knowledge, experience, and support—is always with them. The best groups are diverse, full of unique individuals bringing their different insights, capabilities, and classroom teaching strategies together around a common purpose. They are places where teachers share collective responsibility for all their students—with teachers in other subjects and grades, and with teaching assistants as well. They are places where teachers constantly inquire into learning and problems together, drawing on their different experiences of particular children or strategies, and on what the evidence they can collect is telling them—about the best way to approach a child, a difficult curriculum concept, an unfamiliar innovation, or a group of learners who are falling behind. And they are places where teachers don't just endure but actively enjoy challenging and being challenged by their colleagues and their administrators when results are disappointing, levels of commitment and standards of professionalism start to wane, old habits are not supported by the evidence of what's effective, change efforts seem headed in the wrong direction, behavior is personally inconsiderate, or there are just better ideas around that need to be embraced in order to push things ahead.

Professional learning communities need an architecture or design if they are going to be productive. They have to be organized and arranged. As in

Finland, time allocations in the school day must honor teachers' need to have time outside of the classroom together to inquire into their practice and how to improve it. Team meetings need a commonly agreed purpose and agenda. Staff meetings need to look more like high-quality professional learning experiences than places to deliver announcements. Teachers have to be drawn or pulled into these communities and nudged along by them, as well as driven or pushed by them. In the very best cases, teaching itself is often collaborative. It's the joint work that Judith Warren Little recommended—with integrated projects moving across grade levels, middle school teachers working in teams who share and often teach large groups of students together, and special educational resource teachers working alongside grade-level teachers in the regular classroom setting, for example. In all these, professional collaboration is structured, expected—simply the way of working that teaching now must be.

The days when individual teachers could just do anything they liked, good or bad, right or wrong, are numbered, and in many places are now gone altogether. Teaching is a profession with shared purposes, collective responsibility, and mutual learning. Teaching is no longer a job where you can hog the children all to yourself. If that's what you still believe, then it's time to leave for another profession, because unless you share the responsibility and emotional rewards with your colleagues, you're no longer really a professional at all.

But the new expectation that professional cultures have to be ones of *collective* autonomy, transparency, and responsibility, that have to be deliberately arranged and structured around these principles, should not be a license for administrative bullying and abuse, or enforced contrivance either. Professional learning communities are not professional data communities or professional test score communities. They are not places for administrators to impose questionable district agendas that gather teachers together after busy days in class to pore over spreadsheets simply so they can come up with quick interventions that will raise test scores in a few weeks or less. They are not places where overloaded literacy coaches convene hurried meetings with harried teachers who scarcely have time to refocus from the preceding class before they have to rush off to the next one. Nor are they places where principals and superintendents convert challenging conversations into hectoring harangues, and where all the challenges come from above, with no comebacks or reciprocal challenges allowed from teachers themselves.

This discussion also brings the current emphasis on the "principal as instructional leader" into sharp relief. Policies are being passed left, right, and center that school leaders must spend stipulated percentages of their time in classrooms, use checklists in observing teaching, engage in walk-throughs, participate in instructional rounds, and the like. We have disturbing news for advocates of these policies: while these practices can increase individual leaders' knowledge and capability in some areas, their impact on schoolwide student achievement is at best questionable!

Consider the practicalities. In a school of any size, how can principals get around to observe all teachers? How can they have the expertise to be influential across different subjects? And if they do get very good, what is their legacy when they eventually depart?

Consider the evidence. Recall Leana's study of the impact of social capital in New York City schools. She found that principals who spent their instructional time monitoring and mentoring individual teachers had no impact on schoolwide student achievement. The more effective principals were those who defined their roles as facilitators of teacher success in terms of accessing resources, focusing on teachers' teamwork, and building relationships with parents and the community. They knew their people and how to galvanize them together, but they didn't need to know all the ins and outs of their people's practice. In brief, the effective principals were successful because they went about systematically developing *internal and external social capital*.[49]

Other research evidence supports Leana's conclusions. Two of the world's most prominent researchers on school leadership, Vivianne Robinson and Ken Leithwood, have spent four decades coming to the unequivocal conclusion that the most successful principals affect student achievement indirectly through teachers. In her massive meta-analyses of the impact of principals on student achievement, Robinson found that one factor was twice as powerful as any other—namely, the degree to which principals "promoted and participated in teacher learning and development."[50] Similarly, in his study of the characteristics of high-performing school districts, Leithwood found that high performers incorporated three core processes into their work: widely shared system directions (vision goals), building curricula and instruction in relation to the shared goals, and ensuring systematic use of evidence to inform decisions and solve problems.[51]

Principals don't need frontal lobotomies or any other strategy that might convert them into instructional leaders. They need to know how to identify, develop, select, and connect their people—a leadership challenge that is more powerful yet also more doable. The role of the principal, in other words, is indirect but nonetheless explicit: to build the professional capital of the school's teachers and its community.

Thus, the core principles that draw on and build professional capital in schools are the same as those that cultivate and circulate professional capital throughout an entire system—be it a district, a province, a state, or a nation. They are about developing your commitments and capabilities, pushing and pulling your peers, exercising collective responsibility together, and collaborating with your competitors across the whole system for the greater good that transcends us all. In our large-scale research and development work on high-performing educational systems and other organizations, we have been encouraged about the possibilities for transforming the cultures of schools and school systems, and thereby transforming the culture of the teaching profession as a whole. We are talking about a system change of deep cultural proportions.

What we have found in the best of the large-scale examples is educators, students, and communities working and fighting together to achieve outstanding results and high performance. There are many forces and barriers that stand in the way and we have seen more than a few of them: underinvestment in personal and collective capability, divisive self-interest and self-protection, toxic cultures of individualism and isolation, power plays of contrived collegiality and divide-and-rule reward systems, political short-termism, and sheer inertia.

Chapters 4, 5, and 6 have been a deep and probing journey into the lives of teachers—their careers, the nature of their work, and the place of the profession in society. Insight can stir action, but we need a more overt plan too. There have been many glimpses of what to do and what not to do throughout our text—how to push and also pull people forward, how to invest in developing teachers beyond a few short years so all the investment will pay off in handsome returns for students' learning, how to focus on developing professional quality collectively rather than rewarding a few outstanding teachers individually, how to avoid the extremes of comfortable collaboration and contrived collegiality, how to build networks of teachers and their schools that are robust and outcomes-oriented rather than frivolous or unnecessarily forced, and how to combine collaboration with competition instead of seeing them as opposites. We have also provided many examples from around the world of these positive and practical strategies at work in instances of high professional performance and professional capital.

Our analysis has pointed out right and wrong actions, and shown how easy it is to mistake one for the other, or to slip onto the wrong side of moral purpose. But knowing and recognizing right from wrong, good from bad is not the same as working out a coherent plan of action to get things right and do things right. Ideals and analyses matter massively, but without strategy they are just pontifications. Many so-called system strategies turn out not to be strategies at all. Aside from often being based on the wrong diagnosis or analysis and even the wrong purpose, these plans do not incorporate concrete actions. We have shown how easy it is to slide into contrived collegiality, and we have demonstrated that even seemingly good intentions such as developing principals as instructional leaders can easily go awry.

We promised earlier that we would try to supply both a new and inspiring vision of the future of the profession, and a road map to enact and sustain such a vision. It's time now to bring vision and action together. There is something for everyone, but it must be coordinated in the same direction. We believe that it is both timely and essential to move into the future with frankness and full force. We are at the crossroads to the future. We know what road to follow and which directions we must avoid. It is time to stop gazing at the signposts and stride into action.

CHAPTER SEVEN

Enacting Change

IT'S TIME to invest and reinvest in your own and your colleagues' professional capital—for the good of yourself and your whole profession! And it's time to persuade, push, pull, and nudge the public and policy makers to invest in teachers' professional capital as well. Children need it, teachers will thrive on it, and achieving a productive economy and cohesive society demands it. In this action chapter, we briefly review the new agenda. Then, we consider how change occurs in practice. Finally, we offer three sets of action guidelines for teachers and teacher leaders; for school and district administrators; and for government, state, and union or federation leaders. In short, we set out a vision and define multiple pathways of action to bring it into being.

THE PROFESSIONAL CAPITAL AGENDA

Every so often a new idea comes along that changes the existing terrain. We believe that professional capital is such an idea. We have presented two visions of teaching. One is based on what we call *business capital*, and, we argue, this model provides short-term payoff at best. It is an asset that depletes quickly and requires constant replenishment. The other vision is based on what we call *professional capital*—capital that is regenerative.

In 1792, a young man from a farming family in Massachusetts headed out West to spread apple seeds and then religious teachings along the frontier. He became known as Johnny Appleseed, and his name was eponymously attached to practices of propagating new seeds of thought in unfamiliar territory.[1] With this book we issue the Johnny Appleseed challenge for professional capital. What we have attempted to do is seize the issue,

confront the problem, present a clear alternative, describe successful examples, and draw in the reader's attention—all to help the idea spread.

We hope we have shown that we are not one-dimensional about the
problem or its solution. There is no one party to blame for the present situation. There is no simple right answer. We have shown what the job and the
career of teaching are alike. On the one hand, we have said that it is essential
to empathize with, embolden, and empower the teaching profession. We
have also said that it is necessary to push, prod, and pull the professional
capital agenda forward.

Teachers are at the heart of the quality agenda, but we have demonstrated that this matter is being horribly stereotyped as policy makers in
more and more countries opt for individualistic, competitive, and coercive
solutions through a combination of sticks and carrots. We have offered
much more powerful concepts that include developing individual *human*
capital but argue this can only be achieved on any scale by unleashing the
force of *social* capital that will develop professional capabilities among the
many, as well as *decisional* capital that will cultivate it and perfect it over
prolonged periods. If you want to get big things done, get the group to do it,
we said. And invest in the process, because to be done well, as in medicine
or engineering, it will take time.

We stressed the necessity of focusing on the whole career. People must
be prepared properly and rigorously at the beginning. They have to be
pulled into and kept in the critical mid-career phase when investment in
their years of practice brings them to peak performance. And the later
stages of teachers' careers have to be rethought so that there are opportunities for renewal, alternative ways of continuing to be engaged with education, and availability of gracious retreats from classroom life when teachers
have a secure enough platform to take on another productive career ahead.
We made it clear that the focus must be on the *entire profession*. Initial
teacher education and working conditions throughout the lives of teachers
must together build the profession as a whole.

We have directly challenged mainstream models in the United States
and elsewhere. We have confronted the business capital short-termism that
underpins them and that is spilling over into other countries that are bur-
dened with debt and looking for easy savings in the public sector.

Although we honor the profession as a profession, we also say that it
is not nearly good enough for the job it needs to do today. Professional
autonomy can no longer be individual autonomy. Specialized knowledge

and language can no longer be used self-servingly to mystify parents and mesmerize the public, who will simply resort to test scores when they feel there is no other kind of transparency. Working by the rulebook doesn't only protect teachers from unproductive after-school meetings that are mandated to implement wave after wave of different external agendas. It also prevents positive professional development that is professionally collaborative and effective and that benefits the most disadvantaged students. The profession that defined the Baby Boomers' past must step aside for a modern profession that best serves our children's and our nations' future. We have therefore raised the bar for what teachers should expect of themselves. We have neutralized the negative arguments and stereotypes that undermine the complexity and the dignity of teaching, and built a counter case that has all the ingredients to bring together professionals, administrators, and government leaders who have too often stood apart from or against each other.

The evidence—our own and other people's—is strong, affirming, challenging, and inspiring. But this is not enough to get action on the scale that will be needed. How does transformational change occur of the kind we are talking about? Something can't just be said to be a game changer; it has to actually change the game!

HOW CHANGE OCCURS

We don't want to write a whole new book on how change occurs. We have done that before. What we are talking about here is a specific kind of change that is more akin to a "movement." Successful movements occur when dissatisfactions with and tensions of the current system reach a breaking point. As the strain of the system grows worse, rebellious acts crop up, but we are also detecting the beginnings of pockets of positive alternatives, often on the periphery.

At some point, and we believe that point is now, there is enough dissatisfaction, and enough of an image of the alternative, that more and more people are willing to try it. Breakthroughs are generated by both bottom-up and top-down forces, albeit both in the minority at the start. In other words, at the beginning, it will be a broken front with a few brave souls from different quarters operating in semi-independent packs, widening and growing the appetite for the new order, and eventually coalescing in a majority force that carries the day. It is what a principal in Singapore described to one of us as "structured insurgency." This is Social Movement Theory 101. It has a long history and we have written about it before, but let's take a closer look.

In Chapter 1 we referred to Rosenberg's book *Join the Club: How Peer Pressure Can Change the World*. Rosenberg dismisses what she calls the typical approach to solving a social ill, which focuses on giving people more information and attempting to motivate them through fear. Essentially, Rosenberg's alternative, fundamentally compatible with ours, is that if you want to change human behavior you need to "help . . . people obtain what they most care about: the respect of their peers."[2] Thus, professional capital, once you get it started, acts as a bootstrap that pulls up greater change. It has its own generative power because peers are positively influencing peers through transparent, purposeful, and energizing interaction.

In the early stages, this process will not be smooth, which is all the more reason for the combination of pressure and support that Rosenberg so insightfully captures. She observes that successful social movements persuade people to act in support of a shared common cause in the future, even though the immediate steps are psychologically difficult or dangerous in the beginning. The basis of any successful large-scale reform, then, is going to be built on shared experiences, trusting relationships, and personal and social responsibility, as well as transparency. What pulls people in, teachers all the more so, is doing important work with committed and excited colleagues and leaders engaged in activities that require creativity to solve complex problems and that make a real difference. Obstacles are expected, but they inspire determination rather than inflicting defeat.

The change we are talking about will necessitate that early instigators are prepared to overcome stereotypes as well as the fatalism and fear of others. The goal is to change the thinking of others in a way that generates more positive peer power and leads to partnership with former adversaries. The ring of power expands as people experience success on a scale never before obtained. As Rosenberg states, identification motivates people much more than information or abstract visions.

Enough seeds of professional capital are already in place and are beginning to germinate. What we have done here is to supply the concept that grounds this work. It's time now to talk about how to turn the ideas into action.

ACTION GUIDELINES

In the pages that follow, we offer three sets of compatible action guidelines—for teachers; for school and district administrators; and for state, government, and union/federation leaders. You can't take effective action by simply jumping into a set of action guidelines. One of us wrote a book on the critical importance of starting with your own practice—practice drives practice, good practice drives even better practice.[3] You have to start, then, by revisiting and reflecting on your own practice and soaking in the key concepts we have been discussing in previous chapters. Do you have any of the bad habits we identified? Do you have elements of professional capital that you could build on? What are the strengths and weaknesses of your own setting in terms of the issues we have been surfacing?

The best place to begin is always with yourself. Your own experiences, frustrations, ideals, and sense of self are the crucial starting points. This is what Mary Parker Follett was getting at in 1927 in an exasperating exchange with some graduate students when she was teaching a seminar at Harvard.[4] In her books, she had identified three action principles:

- Seek power with, and possible integration with, both sides of a polarity
- Instead of marshalling outside experts, use information to advance transparency of operations in your own situation
- Use effective leadership so it is not about commanding obedience but rather about "giving expression to external realities and the interior aspirations of others"

So far, so good, but the graduate students wanted to go straight into action by applying the principles. Parker Follett, however, challenged the students to learn by watching and interpreting their own experience. "Experiment, record, pool" was her motto. The students would have none of it. They saw little value in sorting through their own experiences when they already had the valuable framework of principles from Parker Follett to guide their thinking. Finally, Parker Follett had had enough:

I have not sat and read books on philosophy and decided that the deepest fundamental principles were three. I have simply for about

25 years been watching boards and groups and have decided. I am giving my experience. I am not giving philosophy out of a book.[5]

In that spirit, we ask that you examine and learn from your individual and shared experience as you contemplate the concepts and action guidelines we are about to offer. A book can introduce you to a new domain, but it is only by opening up your own experiences and those of others that new possibilities can be embraced and enacted.

The next insight from Follett is to acknowledge polarities, confront them, embrace them, and finally transcend them. It is mistreatment or perceived mistreatment that results in polarization over time, when it eventually takes on a life of its own. The battle for the future of the teaching profession in the United States is defined by just such a polarization at the present time. At the crossroads of the top of the world, where the future of entire generations is at stake, political and professional adversaries are locked in wars of uncompromising words and reciprocal resistance. But we believe there are cracks in these walls that are a result of the growing realization on all sides that the present situation is intolerable. Hundreds of years of war in Northern Ireland finally came to an end when ordinary people who became leaders on both sides realized that the pain had become unbearable and no more blood should be shed. After years of external pressure and internal conflict, the citizens and government of South Africa eventually also came up with a solution to apartheid that did not end in one side being vanquished by the other.

The conflicts surrounding the future of the teaching profession—where defenders of a high-status, autonomous, and secure profession are facing off against government proponents and corporate lobbyists advancing cheaper, younger, and less secure alternatives—may be less bloody, but they are just as significant, for they are a battle for the future soul of the world.

As people try to understand their opponents' standpoints, the old stereotypes will still flare up from time to time: Why do we all have to pay for the incompetent teachers you protect? When will you ever support a change that's not just about more jobs, more money, or easier work? How can you moan about the job being so hard when you get weeks and weeks of vacation each summer? Or on the other side: The job's so much harder and all-consuming than what you remember from way back when. The private sector screwed up our economy—why should public servants pay the price? If it wasn't for all the spreadsheets and paperwork you throw in front of us, we'd be able to get our work with children done to the standard that everyone wants.

> ◆❯ The fundamental goal is to do things that bridge the chasm, reach for partnership, and replace polarization with integration—in ways that make every effort to respect each other's positions without capitulating to them.

We can and we will get beyond these two positions. The fundamental goal is to do things that bridge the chasm, reach for partnership, and replace polarization with integration—in ways that make every effort to respect each other's positions without capitulating to them. To make headway at the beginning, both sides will need to give each other "more respect than they have earned," so to speak, if new breakthroughs are to occur. Indeed, it is not when resources are abundant that breakthroughs are most likely, but when money is genuinely scarce. Perhaps the pushing and pushing back has gone far enough, and now it's time to pull together, to work on building your professional capital—human, social, and decisional—as an asset that will keep on yielding returns, with interest.

Guidelines for Teachers

The professional capital revolution has to be bottom-up as much as top-down. In *What's Worth Fighting For in Your School,* we had a dozen guidelines for action for teachers, and most of them still apply. But the agenda now is sharper and more pronounced. In the spirit of "simplexity"—a small number of key ideas that gel together—we offer 10 core guidelines for action here:[6]

1. Become a true pro.
2. Start with yourself: examine your own experience.
3. Be a mindful teacher.
4. Build your human capital through social capital.
5. Push and pull your peers.
6. Invest in and accumulate your decisional capital.
7. Manage up: help your leaders be the best they can be.
8. Take the first step.
9. Surprise yourself.
10. Connect everything back to your students.

1. *Become a true pro.* Good teachers are dedicated. They care about their subjects and their students. They put in endless extra hours. It is a lot. But it is not enough. Not if you want to teach like a pro. Teaching like a pro means preparing yourself properly: putting in years of study and practice until you reach your 10,000 hours of highly accomplished performance, and then honing your skills even more as you help develop the next generation of teachers. Teaching like a pro is not a temporary engagement, an afterthought leading to a few quick weeks of training, or something to do first or along the way until a better option comes along. Teaching like a pro means connecting with the latest research evidence, inquiring into your own practice—with other colleagues and other schools, down the street and across the world—to find new ideas, get advice, and sift what works from what doesn't. Teaching like a pro is not just about how many hours you put in, but more about what you do with those hours. It's an investment of attention to study, practice, and learning from colleagues. It's an investment in yourself and in the students you serve. It's a capital investment. The system isn't out there. The system is you!

2. *Start with yourself: examine your own experience.* Many years ago, our former colleague David Hunt wrote a deeply insightful book called *Beginning with Ourselves.*[7] His argument was simple. In the passion we often feel to change things or to change other people, the best and most important place to begin is with changing ourselves. Mahatma Gandhi put this profoundly: "Be the change you want to see in the world." You must start with yourself. And the place to begin that process is by examining your own experience:

- Are you truly teaching like a pro?
- What steps can you take to deepen both your commitment and your expertise? Given a choice between reading or hearing about the latest advances in differentiated instruction on the one hand, or producing a more perfect display of children's work on the other, which would you choose?
- When did you last undertake further certification in your own time?
- Is what you are doing working? How do you know?
- How do you share what you have been recently learning outside your school with your colleagues?

Name three concrete actions you might take to become more effective—
at least one that you can do on your own and one that involves one or more
colleagues.

3. *Be a mindful teacher.* We live in a culture of presentism.[8] There's no
time to plan for the future or reflect on the past. We want it all and we want
it now. In the rush of everyday events—deadlines, email, instant results, and
Twitter—we can easily become alienated from our deepest needs and feelings. Teaching is no exception, and in many ways it is worse. Philip Jackson
once said that teaching has always been characterized by "immediacy."[9]
There are always things to be done, decisions to be made, children's needs to
be met—not just every day, but every minute and every second too. This is
the stuff of teaching. Mounting paperwork, endless reports, escalating targets, and accelerated demands for turnaround in low-performing schools
exacerbate these problems even further. There is no let-up. The energy,
activity, and judgment this all calls for can be invigorating sometimes, but
the constant pressure can also drain us dry. It can rob us of the time to take
stock, to be mindful of what we are really doing and why. And if we don't
have the time to be mindful, we are not able to be mindful of how to create
the time for mindfulness either. It's a vicious cycle.

Often, when we say we don't have time for something, it's an evasion.
What we mean is, we have more convenient or immediately rewarding
things to do with that time. As authors and teachers, we are not immune.
We get quicker returns for giving a speech, writing a short op-ed piece for
the newspaper, providing consultancy advice, updating our websites, writing blogs, or just answering our email. Instant applause, an article in the
paper next day, or an empty inbox—all these things give us the appearance
of professional completion and satisfaction. Writing a book like this is much
more challenging. Days are spent facing what William Faulkner called the
tyranny of the blank page,[10] hours are consumed by ditching more sen-
tences than you have created, ideas become ones that you can't at first agree
on, there are weeks of sweating and crafting, and months before you get a
final response from your readers. But without these longer-term engagements, there would be no ideas or good ideas to talk about, no visitors to
our websites, less email to respond to, no impact, not even any applause.

Can you enact some of the core principles of Mindful Teaching developed by Liz MacDonald and Dennis Shirley with a group of Boston Public
School teachers?[11] That is,

- Do you check that what you do in your classroom is *authentically aligned* with your beliefs and your values, more than just technically aligned with the district's plans and requirements?
- Do you practice *stopping* by meditating, listening to music, or just taking long walks to regain a sense of perspective?
- Are you *open-minded* so you don't stereotype and stigmatize your superiors or opponents who sometimes seem responsible for your frustrations, and do you try to see things from their point of view as well?
- Do you invest in developing your own *professional expertise* within and beyond the school day?
- And do you take time to sit down with colleagues so you can take *collective responsibility* for all the students you have in common together?

Be mindful. Begin with yourself.

4. *Build your human capital through social capital.* Start by taking an inventory of your own strengths and weaknesses as a pro. New standards for teachers, and the best teacher appraisal schemes that are focused more around promoting professional growth than assigning competitive rewards, can be useful tools for this purpose. You may want to conduct such an inventory with one or more of your peers. In this way, individual human capital turns into collective social capital—building the capabilities of yourself and your peers together.

Commit to working with your colleagues in multiple and overlapping ways:

- Plan a unit with a grade partner.
- Engage in peer observation and inquiry.
- Start an innovative unit of work with three or four colleagues.
- Go as a team on an external professional development opportunity and, still as a team, try to apply some of what you learned there when you return.
- Discuss examples of students' work and compare how you would assess them.
- With the special education resource teacher, develop a closer in-class relationship around the children you have in common.

- At staff social events, sit beside and talk to a colleague who may be older or younger than you are or who may have a different approach to his or her teaching than you do.
- Become involved as a mentor or a peer coach for other teachers.
- Join a school improvement team.
- Connect online and share lesson plans with teachers in your own school or with a school elsewhere.

All of these things build the relationships, networks, ideas, and understanding that comprise social capital and that make teachers collectively more effective over time. Social capital produces more and more human capital as well as creating a powerhouse of collective efficacy.

5. *Push and pull your peers.* Creating a revolution in professional capital is going to take some pushing and pulling. You don't have to push specific practices, but you may have to push for new norms and ways of interacting. Don't be shy about initiating a conversation about teaching like a pro. What could it mean in your situation? What two or three specific things could be done to further it? Remember that peer respect is the biggest lever for changing behavior. What you want to do, then, is create opportunities to increase purposeful peer interaction, help establish and consolidate new norms of teachers working together, and build respect for each other. You want to pull or draw people in with the energy and excitement of your own committed practice and also push and nudge them forward with your relentless commitment to being better and doing better for all your students. But don't let push turn to shove so that you become a bullying and abusive colleague rather than an appropriately challenging one. And let your patience wear thin over time with teachers who persist in old habits, refuse to consider alternatives, won't work with colleagues, and have no interest in learning to teach like a pro.

In pushing and pulling peers you have to grapple with the paradox of trust. We have seen from Bryk and Schneider's research that high-trust school systems perform far better than low-trust systems.[12] Teams typically don't perform well in environments of low trust. Trust takes a lot of time to build, but if you wait all this time, many children might suffer in the meantime and, indeed, many of the people in whom the time has been invested to build trust may move on and leave. It takes trust to build trust. So if we don't already have it, are we condemned to remain stuck or to have to wait an eternity for change?

The answer can be found in learning to *trust processes as well as people.* In traditional societies, families, and communities, trust develops slowly over time—like living in a village. You learn who the people are you can rely on, the ones who will never let you down. Building trust in this way with colleagues is also important as a foundation for teamwork and change—meeting socially as well as professionally, getting to know your peers as people with lives and not just as performers of tasks, and so on. But in large schools, with virtual networks and highly mobile systems, it is much more difficult to know all of the adults well and build trust in this way. Leaders get promoted, key people move on, and if all the trust in a culture is invested in particular individuals, massive instability will result when they leave. More-over, if you only work with people you already trust, they are likely to be very similar to you and you will learn less from them than you would from peers who are a bit different.

So you have to trust processes of peer interaction as well as trusting particular people. These processes are ones that maximize the organization's collective capabilities and improve its problem-solving capacities. They include improved communication, shared responsibility for particular students' progress, moderating one another's assessments, peer observations, networking with outside environments, shared innovation projects, and so on. Trust in people remains important, but trust in the process supersedes it. Trust the process, and most of the time you will end up trusting the people too. That's how you embrace the paradox of trust and learn to push and pull your peers, by pushing and pulling yourself.

6. Invest in and accumulate your decisional capital. What decisions do you currently control? The list may be longer than you think—not just within your own classroom, but in your school and broader professional life too. Now, extend your sphere of influence. Small steps will do. Maybe the extension will concern the use of data in improving instruction, or the choice of certain teaching methods. Some of this extension should include peers. Decisional capital concerns the judgments that are most central to teaching and learning.

Developing decisional capital—being able to make very good judgments about teaching, learning, and children—is partly a matter of time. As one of us knows from experience, it's relatively easy, with a bit of practice, to pick up a few guitar chords over a few weeks and strum out a passable tune. But becoming a master guitar player requires widening the range and learning the much harder bar chords, as well as how to pick and not just strum. It got too hard when this stage was reached, and because the goal was not to be Eric Clapton and have a professional music career, the guitar playing didn't need to advance beyond three-chord riffs. This is what it's like to be an amateur, not a pro.

Many teachers—up to half in urban school districts—throw themselves into the job enthusiastically, often with little preparation, and find at first that they are having an impact, in a way. But after 2–3 years, there is a lot more to the job than they thought, and they start to realize and begin to worry about just how much they don't know. The work, they find, involves much more than the instructional equivalent of a few basic riffs and so, sadly, they leave. If you're a young teacher who has reached this point, please don't leave. It's by the fourth or fifth year that all the practice you have been doing starts to pay off and gives you a platform for acquiring new strategies and skills that will help you reach more of your students better.

And if you find some of your peers or your leaders unhelpful or frustrating, this point is also typically the time when teachers begin to see beyond their own classrooms and start to be able to influence the things in the school that influence them—policies, scheduling, collegial respect, and parental support to mention just a few. If you leave teaching after 3 years or less, you're not teaching like a pro. Stick it out if you possibly can—in another school, perhaps—but stick it out all the same, not for the sake of sheer endurance but because this is how you and the profession that has called you will establish and advance your expertise.

The other part of decisional capital, remember, is about getting feedback on your practice—and reflecting on it with peers. The most powerful way to build your decisional capital is to do it with others—with principals, coaches, and peers within and outside your school. So join or initiate anything you can to receive the feedback that will enable you to improve as you practice over time. Perhaps this will be a grade partner, or a university teacher education partner, or a professional development organization—but quality feedback from trusted peers will magnify your decisional capital over time, and if you reciprocate with your colleagues, it will develop their decisional capital too. In short, seek opportunities to give and receive feedback as much as you can.

7. Manage up: help your leaders be the best they can be. One of the hardest parts of any professional work is "managing up"—dealing with the people above you. Some people see this as a matter of damage containment. But others see it as an opportunity to acquire support for the causes they are passionate about. Remember the principal in Chapter 2 who was passionate about supporting her students with special educational needs and got her teachers to take collective responsibility for all their students' achievement? When she was called to the school district office, she saw it as an opportunity to press them for the assistive technologies that would help her special education students succeed. And in other schools who had started committing to innovations that benefited special education students in Ontario, when new principals were transferred into several of the schools that were studied, it was often high-performing teaching teams who kept the initiatives alive—educating the incoming principals about their benefits, instead of waiting to see what these new principals would do next.

We have talked throughout about the need for strategies to reduce polarization and achieve greater partnership. This means teachers reaching out to school and district administrators to support collaborative learning wherever they can. It means fighting and resisting corrupt or controlling administrations when their policies are unworkable or indefensible. But even and especially when there is resistance, it is vital not simply to oppose an issue, or to insist that everything should remain just as it is, but to come up with clear and compelling alternatives, such as teacher-union-run pilot schools, or assessment of performance by fairer means than student test scores, or better data rather than no data at all. Teaching like a pro is about taking charge, in relation to colleagues and even superiors, just as much as with children.

8. Take the first step. One definition of leadership is doing something first, before anyone else is willing or able to. When British explorer Ernest Shackleton brought all his men back safely from their aborted expedition to the South Pole, after their ship had been trapped and then sunk in the Antarctic ice, he persuaded his men to leave behind their weighty possessions as they dragged a small cutter over hundreds of miles of ice flows to seek possible safety.[13] But the only way he could persuade his men to give up the personal possessions that they truly valued and that comforted them, was by first burying his own most treasured possessions in the snow in front of them. Shackleton was prepared to go first.

If something for your school is worth starting, then take the lead and start it, in any way you can. Ask for help from someone before offering assistance to them (this then models that it's OK for anyone to ask for help). If you are one of the most expert and experienced teachers in the school, take on one of the most difficult classes that had previously been handed to newcomers, instead of keeping the easiest classes for yourself. This will raise the status of the class, drawing other experienced teachers to teach it—and it will produce better results with that class. When the storm is closing in, it may feel safer inside the tent than outside, but once supplies are dwindling, someone will have to take the first step. At Grange Secondary School in Oldham, as described in Chapter 3, teachers believed nothing could be done about the low attendance rate, until Graeme Hollinshead and his leadership partner got in their cars and rounded up the missing students themselves. They took the first step. Many great teachers and leaders do. Can you?

9. Surprise yourself. Teaching is a profession brimming with positive emotions such as satisfaction, joy, and pride. The most underestimated of these emotions, perhaps, is surprise. This is the emotion we often feel when something pleasant happens that we truly didn't expect. In life, we experience surprise at moments like proposals of marriage, or when we win a contest, or when our sports team unexpectedly triumphs over far superior opposition. Kindnesses and compliments from strangers can be cause for surprise too. In teaching, we are surprised when a child says something especially eloquent or unusual, when he reveals something about his family or his life that we were not aware of, or when she displays a talent we never knew she had. It is not the incremental gain in our students' achievement that surprises and delights us, but the leaps in their imagination or understanding.

If you just deliver a narrow and prescribed curriculum that concentrates excessively on driving through the basics and teaching to the test, you will rarely be surprised. So teach something else as well, even for just 30 minutes a week, even if it's officially frowned upon. If you keep teaching the same way, by yourself each year, you will be less and less surprised, so find some teaching partners, plan lessons with them, and swap or combine classes when you can. If you always hang around with the same group, within school and also socially, even if they are fellow innovators, you will seal yourself off from other colleagues and sources of influence and fail to be surprised. So start an innovation with a different colleague, or team-teach a class with someone who shares your goals but has a different style. Learn from your differences. Seek out variety. Avoid groupthink. And do this across schools too. Don't turn your school into a little island that has no contact with any others. And don't wait for your principal to make connections outside the school for you either. Join networks of teachers across schools and learn how practice is different there. Take a day or two of your vacation to visit and learn from a school in another country with a different teaching season (and claim it as a legitimate taxable expense when you get back!). Get permission and support from your principal and your district if you can, but don't let that stop you if you can't.

10. *Connect everything back to your students.* The purpose of teaching like a pro is to improve what you can do for your students. This needs to be kept front and center all the time. When you teach like a pro, international school visitations are not just enjoyable junkets but must be judged on their benefits for students. What did you learn from your visit, how will you share it with your colleagues, and what are your plans for following through? When you teach like a pro, further study or higher degrees are not about accumulating more qualifications, bolstering your CV, or increasing your pay and status, but about developing your own capability, enlarging your professional community, and increasing your capacity to benefit the learners you will touch in the future. Likewise, professional learning communities should be neither inconsequential talking shops nor a statistical world of scores and spreadsheets that take on a life of their own, far removed from real students. PLCs should be places where focused conversations and inquiries, supported by data and experience, lead to improvements and interventions that benefit real students whom the community shares in common.

Guidelines for School and District Leaders

The guidelines for teachers all apply equally to leaders in districts and in schools—being mindful, reflective, and professional; building social capital by pushing and pulling one's peers; seeking variety; managing up; being prepared to take the first step; and connecting everything back to students. They are about building and circulating professional capital by changing the cultures of whole schools and entire districts. We set out six guidelines here that follow directly from the professional capital agenda.

1. Promote professional capital vigorously and courageously.
2. Know your people: understand their culture.
3. Secure leadership stability and sustainability.

4. Beware of contrived collegiality (and other irritating associates).
5. Reach out beyond your borders.
6. Be evidence-informed, not data-driven.

1. Promote professional capital vigorously and courageously. Professional capital involves a change of culture in your school and in your district:

- Do you want to keep turning over young teachers every 2 or 3 years because it will save on salaries and keep the culture young and compliant? Or are you committed to developing the quality, qualifications, and capabilities of your teachers until they soar to even greater heights, whether they stay with you or move on to another position?
- Is your professional learning community just a device for responding to the district's pressure for higher and higher test scores, or is your first priority creating engaging and successful learning for all your students?
- Do your teachers see that you are always learning, always collaborating, by being engaged in and not just observing their professional development, and by working with your peers in other districts and schools, or are you communicating to them that collaboration is something they should do but that you don't practice yourself?
- Do you initiate conversations with other schools and districts about achievement data, new research, and leading edge innovation, or do you wait for them to contact you first?
- Are you a hungry learner or just a harried manager?
- Do you just react to or resist your senior managers, or do you manage upward to promote their own professional capital?

As a school or district leader, if you grow professional capital, your job can actually become both easier and more powerful. Build capital though others and you *all* get more done and derive more satisfaction in doing it. Professional capital becomes your legacy.

2. Know your people: understand their culture. With our colleague Alan Boyle, one of us has studied the dramatic performance turnaround of the London Borough of Tower Hamlets, which went from being the 149th-ranked district out of 149 in 1996, to being positioned at or above the national average on all key indicators 10 years later and still to this day.[14]

Among the many reasons for this remarkable turnaround is the relationship between the schools and the district's administration. Knowledge of and presence in the schools by district staff provide support, build trust, and ground intervention in consistent and direct personal knowledge and communication more than in the numerical data that eventually appear on spreadsheets. Time and again, school leaders say they trust and are trusted by the district, and district leaders say the same. One of Tower Hamlet's district leaders sums it up well. It's "not just about the data. It's actually knowing the school, knowing the community, knowing about history, knowing about the staff—all of that." Think of all the crises that can be averted and emails that can be saved because of the face-to-face conversations that occur around teaching and learning every day, in real schools.

In the same study of performance beyond expectations, corporate leaders have said that you cannot make demands of people you do not know. Think about that. How far do you imagine you would get as a teacher if you set high expectations of a class of 14-year-olds you had no relationship with and did not know? Beyond an initial period of shock and awe, perhaps, how long do you think a principal could sustain his or her teachers' commitment to profound improvement if the principal did not know or show an interest in the teachers as people, was never in their classes just to learn what they were doing rather than to judge their performance, only ever came by on a walkthrough or an instructional round, never participated as a learner with teachers in professional development, and only communicated with teachers when something was problematic rather than responding routinely to the practice that the principal saw?

Then ratchet that thinking up to the district's relationship with the schools! Instead of sitting down with spreadsheets, firing off emails, and staggering from meeting to meeting, shouldn't district administrators be spending more time in schools? Administrators keep on saying that principals should be instructional leaders—shouldn't they be instructional leaders too? Impossible, you say? Too much paperwork? Too much administration? Too many initiatives to respond to? There are many ways to deal with all of this—giving up just one morning a week for school visits might be a start. But let's take just one example—from a network of schools that tackled the problem head on in something called the SAM Schools Project.[15]

Based in Jefferson County Public Schools in Kentucky, but spread out all over the United States, more than 300 SAM schools (SAM stands for School Administration Manager) have sought to raise student achievement by increasing the proportion of time principals spend directly on teaching and learning. In the United States, on average, school principals devote less than a quarter of their time to teaching and learning issues. They work inside their offices or out-side their schools on management and paperwork issues instead. SAM schools do three simple things. They hand off many of these administrative duties to trained existing staff members to free up the principal for learning-related work; they use tracking systems so principals can have a dashboard that helps them and their colleagues learn and review together how they are actually allocating their time; and they have reflective coaches—sometimes a retired principal, sometimes a rotating student responsibility—who will get principals to focus on their time priorities and if necessary cajole them into leaving meetings and handing things off to their administrative sup-port team, to allow them to get to their next class.

In the first 2 years, admittedly with the benefit of foundation funding, principals moved to spending an average of 70% of their time on instructionally related activities, and rates of student achieve-ment doubled. Although the project is now self-funded, gains in both areas are still statistically significant.

Recall the findings we reported earlier on leadership effects—leaders who are closely connected to student learning and their teachers' learning have the greatest positive effects on student achievement. They know their teach-ers and help them build and circulate their professional capital. The point about the SAM project is not one of old-fashioned instructional leadership—about leaders knowing and being able to personally monitor the details of good practice when they see it. The point is about leaders taking time to know their people and what their people do, and to know how to bring out the best from those people collectively.

But getting to know people takes time. SAM tackles the principal's time trap in a simple and strategic way. In England, changes in school leadership structures have also taken a lot of the finance, politics, physical plant respon-sibilities, and routine paperwork out of the principal's (headteacher's) hands so these individuals can be more effective leaders of learning. Unless princi-pals and headteachers remain connected to teachers' and students' learning, their own professional capital will atrophy over time. You can only develop other people's professional capital if you continue to invest in your own. Stay invested, keep it circulating—that's the way you get the stock to rise.

3. *Secure leadership stability and sustainability.* Leadership in U.S. urban schools and school districts turns over at a frightening rate. Elsewhere, as one of us has found, regularized rotation of principals by their districts every 3–5 years has more of a negative than positive effect on improvement efforts. The same is true of political leadership. As McKinsey & Company found out in their report on *How the World's Most Improved Educational Systems Keep Getting Better,* school systems that show a strong record of improvement benefit from the injection of new political or strategic leadership that then stays around.[16]

> Once installed, they have staying power: the median tenure of the new strategic leaders is six years and that of the new political leaders is seven years, thereby enabling continuity in the reform process and development of the system pedagogy. This is in stark contrast to the norm. For example, the average tenure for superintendents of urban school districts in the US is nearly three years.

In the Beyond Expectations study (which also included a review of the research on schools that didn't perform so well), most of the organizations benefited from leaders who had strong knowledge of and attachment to what the organizations did—either by having worked there a long time, or by having returned to the organization after having worked there earlier. What was clear in business, education, and sports was that desperately replacing the leader again and again did not yield any benefits. Indeed, belief in the silver bullet of leadership replacement is one of the six fallacies of organizational change we described in Chapter 3.

Stable and sustainable (not stagnant and stale) leadership does not drag a school or a system from one initiative to another, condemning its educators to manic depressive mood swings rather then consistency of orientation and focus. It goes beyond politics and short-termism to build long-term professional capital across whole cohorts of teachers, develop social capital among them as communities, establish trust with the teachers and schools they know well, and guide teachers and leaders through their careers as professionals and as people. Stable and sustainable leadership prospers when there are incentives of recognition, support, and reward in the most troubled communities, encouraging principals and system leaders to *stay rather than move* up and move on. Stable and sustainable leadership also prospers when, as in England, we break down the outdated assumption of one principal–one school, and allow the leader of a highly successful school (with the right resourcing and significant additional reward, of course) to take on a second struggling school and a third without leaving the first school entirely behind. This, of course, means completely overhauling the outdated line-management structures of U.S. schools that have administration overly concentrated in the state, then the district, then passed down once more for implementation purposes to isolated and scattered principals in disconnected schools.

4. Beware of contrived collegiality (and other irritating associates). Professional capital is not an end in itself. It is a *means* of developing the profession as it effectively increases learning and the life chances of all children. Beware of any district leader or leadership team who comes back from a conference and says, "Let's all do PLCs!" A much more basic conversation must take place with respect to aspirations for the teaching force in this district, and how they integrate with improving teachers' practice and raising achievement for all children.

It's the same with a school vision. Sometimes, when principals say the school has a shared vision, they mean "I have a vision. You share it." Now, of course, if the school has had no vision, if people have felt lost, they are sometimes all too ready for an incoming leader to set out a vision, to take them somewhere, almost anywhere, in fact. One of the defining characteristics of effective leadership is being able to provide some direction, and setting out a vision is part of that.

However, "my vision," "my teachers," and "my school" are proprietary claims that suggest the principal actually owns the school rather than it being everyone's collective responsibility. With visions as singular as this, teachers can quickly learn to suppress their voice. Management becomes manipulation. Collaboration turns into contrived collegiality. Worst of all, when teachers conform to the principal's vision, this takes away the opportunity for the principal's own learning—for the development of his or her own professional capital. This learning might include the possible realization that parts of the vision may be flawed and that some teachers' visions may be as valid or more valid. It's a courageous act of leadership when, as we have occasionally seen, an incoming principal acknowledges that some of the teachers may be light years ahead in their knowledge of teaching and learning, and in their existing habits of collaboration, compared to him or her.

But the opposite can be just as true. Teachers may have spent years in classroom isolation or being segregated into small cliques. In cases like this, school and district leaders sometimes see themselves as (and they sometimes are) the rightful instigators of collaborative learning cultures. As teacher capacity grows stronger, though, individually and collectively, as a formal leader, you can make yourself less indispensable as the direct cause of good things. Put positively, the time comes to take the risk of trusting the process of teachers innovating together, and of standing back to let this happen. Collective empowerment and responsibility combined with non-judgmental transparency is one of the fairest and most authentic forms of accountability we know. The greater the capacity of teachers, the more *peers* become the source of innovation. Administrators work toward that goal and then do everything possible to sustain and deepen this capability in their teachers.

In the end, effective school and district leadership locates and procures professional capital wherever it exists. This capital does not all have to be the leader's own. The leader's job is to locate it, circulate it so it becomes common property of the group, and see its yield increase in the quality of teaching and learning that is evident throughout the school or the system. Ultimately, developing professional capital is about helping people to help themselves and help their students more effectively; it is not about manipulating them into complying with externally imposed requirements or delivering someone else's vision.

5. *Reach out beyond your borders.* The dream dilemma of many school leaders is this: What do I do when my school is performing well? Where do we go next when we have raised student achievement, created and sustained a range of successful curriculum innovations, developed teacher and student leadership, and all the staff seem fulfilled and happy? The answer, says David Carter, Executive Principal of the Cabot Learning Federation of five secondary schools in the Bristol area of England, is "You help another school."[17]

Helping another school nearby or on the other side of the world contributes to social justice and keeps everyone moving forward, learning, and improving. Cabot was originally just one Academy. Now, sponsored by a university and the luxury brand of Rolls Royce, it's a federation of five schools. This isn't imperialism or colonialism—a kind of capital we do not support. It's a way to help others and help yourself at the same time, constantly building capacity as those who were once helped become the helpers themselves.

U.S. districts and state departments still have difficulty coming to grips with this. They still want to concentrate resources in the central office more than in the schools. They want command and control to go down from the bureaucracy into sets of separate schools. They are working with an increasingly digital and networked profession, but they are trying to cling to power in an analog bureaucratic system.

Ideally, districts should create learning clusters of schools. Even in the poorest parts of the world, where teachers have immense class sizes and almost no resources, gathering them occasionally in clusters (when the other job demands of these underpaid teachers permit it) is one way to share and learn from each other's practice, and to develop at least a little professional capital. But if district leaders do not foster school networks at the beginning, you may have to be the one who connects informally with other principals and schools. Principals as a group can be enormously influential within and across their districts, independently of district leadership if necessary.

Singapore sends out its leaders across the world to study, learn from thoughtful leaders, and visit leading edge systems and schools. It's a nation of global capitalists and global professional capitalists. Learning globally from each other is becoming a new habit. Alberta and Finland—two of the highest educational performers in the world—have created a formal, signed partnership, not to smugly celebrate their joint success but to keep learning from each other and pushing one another further forward. Year after year, in our own systems and institutions, we are both delighted to host visiting leaders on study scholarships from their governments in Australia, New Zealand, Singapore, the Netherlands, Scandinavia, and the United Kingdom—leaders who connect with the best ideas and practices from overseas and consider adapting and recombining them in their own countries. All of these educators are moving beyond their borders, learning from other countries, to stay at the cutting edge. In the United States, most school and district leaders can scarcely get out of their district or their state, never mind their country, if they want to pick up outstanding ideas from elsewhere. If the United States doesn't want its educational performance to sink still further, this professional isolationism and protectionism must change. Otherwise, without a free trade of professional ideas, the nation's overprotected professional capital will simply deplete.

Continuous progress is always a balance between taking advantage of the close commitment of peers you are working with on the one hand, without getting insular or unimaginative on the other. You have to have both: disciplined group focus, and exploration of new ideas in a more loosely structured manner. In his grand sweep of *Where Ideas Come From,* Steve Johnson traces the origin of innovations in the period from 1400 to the year 2000.[18] He found that increasingly, over time, new ideas come from loosely connected networks that enable people to learn from "the adjacent possible." What this means for professional capital is that we need to do two things: (1) focus specifically and relentlessly on the implementation of practices that we have selected, and (2) at the same time, sponsor loosely connected exploration of possible new ideas for the future through action research and through global connections to educators and other learners in other countries.

So, if in doubt, join a cluster or start a cluster. If you feel like you're reaching the peak of your success, help another school beside you or far away. Even if you're struggling, seek out fellow strugglers too, so you can find assistance together, knowing there are many others like you. Give up some vacation time for an educational visit overseas. Learn about and from another culture. Host a visit or exchange from an international partner. Develop a unit of work with a school across the ocean or even just across the nation. What's worth fighting for is usually what's already out there somewhere. You just have to reach out for it, and get ready to learn something new.

6. Be evidence-informed, not data-driven. In North America, in district after district, data warehouses are being created—places that store vast quantities of data, especially about student achievement. More and more principals have a dashboard on their laptop or tablet computer where they can examine performance and progress data in real time. Elementary schools are being asked and often required to erect data walls where student performance is transparent and can be tracked from red through amber to green in terms of how satisfactory each student's progress is. Armed with all these data, principals, learning teams, and inspectors go through their schools with checklists, on instructional rounds and walkthroughs, looking for visible evidence in classroom artifacts of what the data have been suggesting to them. Professional learning communities examine spreadsheets of achievement and attendance data together, looking for gaps and shortfalls—places where they can quickly intervene.

It's good to have data to help you make better, more-informed decisions and to allow you to intervene before it's too late. It's good to be able to learn more, in real time, about how your students are doing. It's time to look at the data seriously and not just rely on your intuition. But just remember four things as you do so:

- First, as a district or a school, don't overload yourself with data so that you have no room, as a community, to think about or discuss anything else. You can't know everything about everybody face to face; and you can't know everything about everybody with statistical data either. Decide what data you need, use the information prudently and judiciously, and you will make better judgments as a result.

- Second, remember that the point of data is to help you know your students. Again, we have to avoid goal displacement, where data analysis becomes an end in itself. Finland doesn't need this profusion of data so teachers can know their students well—it just has smaller class sizes, collective responsibility, and a lack of external administration and initiatives that would distract teachers from the task at hand (though when Finland's classrooms get more diverse, its teachers may find that data become useful after all). We are not advising that we should follow Finland's lead and dump all our data—we just need to remember that there are children behind the numbers and if the data aren't helping us know our children better, or if we are so busy analyzing data that we have less time to be with the children, then we are getting sidetracked down the wrong path.

- Third, there is a tendency for data walls and teachers' analysis of them to draw people's attention only to shortfalls, problems, and deficits. That, after all, is where these systems began, in industrial manufacturing, to pay relentless attention to identifying and eliminating defects. The best use of evidence, including data walls, doesn't ignore those who are falling behind. But it does direct more discussions about evidence toward improving learning for everyone: not just those who are falling behind, but those in the middle and those who are surging ahead as well. When data are used to promote progress for all and not only to track those who might be falling behind, this benefits learning and achievement for all students and strengthens feelings of professional success (thereby building yet more professional capital and confidence as well).

◆ Last, performance data and professional learning communities can narrow your focus excessively to what the data are about—usually tested literacy, mathematics, and science. The data on these basics and the discussions in PLCs that arise from them therefore need to be supplemented by other kinds of data, on other aspects of learning, and by knowledge of children and learning that is also based on shrewd experience and not easily quantifiable at all. In the end, it's important to be informed by the evidence, not numbed by the numbers. "Put the faces on data," we say, and do it for each and every student.[19] Make evidence human and inclusive, and it becomes a powerful strategy for building professional knowledge of one's students and professional motivation to serve them better.

The advice of the former chief of all of England's school inspectors, Christine Gilbert, in a country that has been progressively eliminating its standardized tests before age 15, perhaps says it best of all:

data are only numbers on a page, or a spreadsheet on a screen. They only measure what has been tested. And people often only test what they feel they can measure. The challenge for schools, and for inspectors, is to understand the data available and get behind the figures to explore the strengths and weaknesses they indicate.[20]

Guidelines for State, National, and International Organizations

Finally, we move to the grand designs of national and even international strategy. In *What's Worth Fighting For in Your School*, we didn't address these, as most educational change then took place at the school level. The game has now changed. Global competition and knowledge of what successful countries are doing to get quality results have caused all countries to examine their policies and strategies for improving their school systems. For a decade and more, the focus on large-scale reform has gained in prominence. Because some governments have clearly shown the way, and because the stakes are increasingly high with transparent results exposing those who are lagging behind, governments at all levels have a clear moral responsibility to get it right.

The guidelines we offer here are based on our own experience of being engaged directly in system reform with many countries, states, and provinces.

The agenda is becoming clearer to both of us, and we offer eight guidelines from this work:

1. Know where you're going.
2. Break your own mold.
3. Obey the law of subsidiarity: push and partner, stimulate and steer.
4. Redesign the professional career.
5. Bring teachers back in.
6. Be the change.
7. Pay people properly where they serve the greatest need.
8. Get out and about more.

1. *Know where you're going.* If you don't know where you're going as a state or a country, how do you expect your teachers and schools to know where *they* are going? It's not enough and not even right to be driven by what is the least costly, by how high you can be ranked on PISA—top five, Number One, or just better than the country next door—or by what will get you through the next election. So the very first thing, as a system, and as a state or a country, is to know who you are, where you are going, and why, and to understand and articulate with relentless inspiration that a high-quality educational system and high-quality teachers are an inalienable part of this. In places like Singapore, Finland, South Korea, and to some extent Canada, this sense of national direction and nation-building places teachers front and center in their societies; it gives them status in the eyes of the public; it draws the very best and most capable people to the work. It is a magnet for human capital. So stop trashing and attacking teachers. Start saying why your nation needs them. Tell people over and over that teaching is a complex and difficult job, but one of the best jobs there is—in its daily rewards and in how it serves the nation. Remember the teachers who inspired you and helped make you what you are today as a national or state leader, and remind the public of their influence. Public statements of where you are going have to include building the teaching profession and its professional capital. Teachers, all 100% of them, are your nation builders.

2. *Break your own mold.* We have made it clear that politically popular stances based on being tough on teachers, establishing no-nonsense accountability, and hammering the system with testing simply do not work. No successful country ever leads with these ideas. Therefore, we call on a few brave politicians to publicly acknowledge that the emperor has no clothes. If practically every state has a waiver from your national policy, it's like giving every high school student a hall pass. You can say goodbye to having any credibility at all. These politicians—governors, chief state superintendents, federation and union leaders, and others—need, on the one hand, to denounce excessive testing and punitive accountability, as they now do in England and Alberta, after these had been among the most tested systems in the world—and, on the other hand, to promulgate capacity building, collective development of the teaching profession, and high expectations. These politicians need to make professional capital their new political platform.

Professional capital resolves the age-old top-down–bottom-up dilemma. By developing professional capital, you create a system of *collective autonomy* wherein the group at the local level acts with discretion and internal accountability while defining itself as part and parcel of the larger system. In this way, the distinction between the top and the bottom begins to disappear.

A big difference between successful systems and unsuccessful ones is that the former have a clear sense of direction and a high degree of coherence, and an interconnected set of policies and strategies as well as an embedded culture of improvement that provides that direction and coherence. They have what we called the right drivers for change. The wrong drivers change the surface, whereas the right drivers change the culture, as we explained in our example of inserting individualistic teacher appraisal schemes into negative school or system cultures. Teacher appraisal may have an important part to play, but only if working hand in hand with developing the professional culture and professional capital of the schools.

In sum, the opposite of wrong drivers is professional capital on the rise. So the task is to review and modify policies and related strategies so that they are built around the development, accumulation, and circulation of professional capital. Let's start a bit of structured insurgency with a few brave and bold politicians, then connect them together as kindred spirits at all levels of the system to become a movement of gargantuan proportions.

3. Obey the law of subsidiarity: push and partner, stimulate and steer.

In political science, the principle of subsidiarity is one in which issues should be addressed and resolved by the least centralized competent authority among people who are closest to that issue. Anglo-Saxon jurisdictions (though not all of them) have been inclined in recent years to drive and deliver policies designed in great detail centrally from the top, with a plethora of targets and interventions in every sector of public life. Interestingly, jurisdictions that have adopted this approach, or more old-fashioned forms of top-down bureaucracy before them, are among the least effective in terms of educational performance. Practicing subsidiarity, by contrast, means not just training people so they can implement everything the center has decided, but enabling them and supporting them wherever possible to make effective decisions themselves, then connecting them together to create coherence as they do so. A good example is Finland and its more than 300 Local Education Authorities that extend from small municipalities to entire cities. In our OECD review of Finland, one of us observed:

> Municipal leadership takes on extraordinary importance, in the words of the [Central] Department staff, as it "tries to support every school to be successful." Social and health authorities have to work together within municipalities and so do schools. Schools are obliged to present how they cooperate with other schools. In the city of Javenpää, for example, all comprehensive schools follow the municipal level common curriculum which has been created in a city-wide effort with the participation of several hundreds of teachers, led by the municipal department of education.
>
> Some of the municipal leaders have explicit and pronounced concepts about how school leadership should be organised and improved and they take effective steps to achieve these ideas. We saw, for instance, a very strong commitment by the head of the education department of a municipality in favor of school-level collective leadership. She demands that all schools establish and operate executive teams. When meeting the leaders of the schools in order to discuss questions related with their work, she prefers to meet the whole team instead of only with the principal. In this municipality, professional development is provided and purchased not only for the principal but also for all members of the executive teams. Leadership at municipal level is shared, among others, between professional administrators and elected politicians. Through this linkage, education is connected to broader community affairs. This connection is reinforced by the integration of educational administration into overall local administration including urban planning, local economic development, health and social care, housing or culture.

In the municipalities we visited, systemic leadership rests on principles of *subsidiarity*: within a broad vision, legislative arrangements and funding structures, decision-making is moved to the level of those most able to secure implementation of them in practice.[21]

This isn't just a Finnish fantasy. It's about developing, gathering, and drawing on collective professional capital to administer and improve a system by increasingly highly capable people who understand it the best. It's about securing joined-up thinking and action between health and other public and community services, as well as local economic strategy. It's not about elevated central experts driving through disconnected initiatives with dreamed-up targets from an Olympian height far removed from the front line. The center steers, provides clear and firm direction, establishes and supports frameworks and expectations for peer-to-peer interaction, and then leaves the locals to get on with it as far as they can and as much as they should.

In situations that are stagnant or divisive, starting with decentralization may not always or even usually be the right answer—except where excessive centralization has already been a cause of the stagnation, perhaps. At the beginning, if central leaders do have a good grasp of the right drivers, the first phase may need to involve "pushing and partnering." This is how Ontario launched its system reform in 2003. On the heels of a divisive battle between government and teachers, and following on from flat-lined performance, the new government embarked on an assertive reform agenda, but it also recognized that respecting teachers and building partnerships with the education sector was the key to success. In other words, they pushed and partnered in combination.[22]

As capacity increases, and professional capital accumulates, the strategy can then shift to obey the law of the subsidiarity, remembering that the center is still highly involved—now with the task to "stimulate and steer" in order to engage the power of lateral interaction at the local level and gain corresponding participation in wider networks, including two-way partnerships between local and central levels. At that point, a point that many high-performing countries have already reached or approached, there is a truly transformative change: systems thinking in action, among almost everyone. It is then that teachers act with pervasive professional capital, and central leaders oversee and steer the system to the greater good of all.

4. Redesign the professional career. U.S. policy makers and advisors want to adopt the *business capital* approach to redesigning the teaching profession, concentrating on the front end. This puts more emphasis on teaching as a short, flexible, temporary, and inexpensive career that won't incur taxpayer liability in expensive pensions for teachers when they get older. Teacher unions and organizations, with their Baby Boomer leaders, want to define teaching as a lifelong career (at least in terms of working life), where long and dedicated service is rewarded with financial security at the end, and they rightly defend their public pensions when debt-burdened governments try to attack them. There is no clearer example than this of the polarization we described earlier. Irresistible force meets immovable object. Stalemate.

But if we follow the evidence presented in this book and think a bit more laterally, there is a third solution hiding in the middle. When are teachers at their peak? When are they most likely to have perfected their decisional capital? The answer, we found, was between 8 and 20 or so years in the profession. So perhaps this is where we need to concentrate some of our strategic efforts—not just at the beginning and end of the career, but in the high-performing middle. Assuming a system has, in line with strategies we set out earlier, been able to draw in high-quality entrants to the teaching profession, we need to ask how it can then keep them beyond the vulnerable fall-out point at about 3 years, so they will stay long enough for their capital to really start accumulating. Here are a few proposals:

+ Provide coaching, mentoring, and networking support for early career teachers in years 3 and 4, not just in the first two years.
+ Create early opportunities for aspiring and emerging leaders' programs, not just to fast-track people into principalships through what are conceptualized as leadership "pipelines" (a nonprofessional capital term if we ever heard one) but to empower and energize them with leadership capabilities now—as leadership organizations in the United Kingdom and Australia, for example, are already doing, along with teacher union and federation pioneers in Canada and the United States.
+ Intensify and accelerate professional learning through grants for further study, internships, and exchanges with other schools and systems, as well as small bursaries to attend conferences and visit other outstanding schools overseas.

- Insert a significant accelerator into the pay trajectory, between about years 4 and 6, that, conditional on satisfactory peer review, rewards teachers who are eager to stay.

Having said all this, we cannot ignore the clear indicators of tail-off in commitment and efficacy that seem to kick in after about 20 years in the job. Again, stereotypes and polarization can easily characterize proposed solutions for this phase, with people arguing these older teachers have been worn down by years of insensitive reforms on the one hand, or that they have sat on the laurels of their anticipated pensions on the other. It's important to remember, with Michael Huberman, that this is not a homogeneous group, and that multiple strategies are likely to be helpful in addressing it. For example:

- *Construct multiple (though flexible) career tracks* for teachers that offer leadership and development opportunities in different spheres such as curriculum leadership, new teacher mentoring, master teaching, and so on, over time, and that enable the long-term teachers to find the right niche or a different niche for themselves as they age and mature.
- *Provide employee assistance and counseling support services,* as many Canadian systems already do, to support teachers with the many personal problems such as health issues, aging parents, or demanding adolescents, that can distract them professionally at this stage of life and that can otherwise strike them out.
- *Offer sabbatical and other tax-supported leave incentives* so that teachers, after an agreed amount of service, can (as some Canadian teachers have done) have periodic renewal through travel or further study, by enabling them to receive 4 years of their salary over 5 years, with the next year away being funded by the savings of the preceding ones (Australia compels *all* public sector workers to take a funded leave every 10 years!).
- Follow the lead of the armed services and *offer an attractive mid-term retirement plan,* for those who wish to leave the profession after 20–25 years, that may be insufficient to support complete retirement, but that will provide a strong financial platform for teachers to apply their skills to the challenge of another career in business, publishing, universities, counseling, or the nonprofit sector, perhaps.

5. Bring teachers back in. In March 2011, a promising summit was held in New York City sponsored by the U.S. federal government and OECD. Government officials, union and federation leaders, and academics from over a dozen countries participated in addressing the question of *Building a High-Quality Teaching Profession: Lessons from Around the World.*[23] The first three sections of the ensuing report addressed the usual matters of attracting and retaining talent. A not-so-innocent fourth section was entitled "teacher engagement in education reform." This section essentially said that all of the successful countries involve teachers and their unions or associations in setting and supporting the reform agenda. The same is true in the United States, as a number of reports recognize—the highest performing state is actually the most unionized, and many lower performing states are not unionized at all. Of course, it is not unions per se, or any other kind of professional association, that make the difference, but rather the quality and strength of the relationship between local and national governments on the one hand and the teaching profession as a whole. And strong unions or federations that are well led and that focus on developing professional capital for the good of all students are more likely to help bring about the transformation we are advocating. Unionization is not a determinant variable; it all depends on how union membership interacts with other professional capital factors we have been discussing.

Government and union leaders from the United States who participated in the international panels noted in awe, or shock, that almost none of the big things that successful countries were doing were evident on any scale in the United States. Almost 2 years later, nothing has been done to rectify the situation. Professional capital builds teacher skill, ownership, and responsibility. The opposite seems to be happening—silver bullets as capital punishment—as the wrong drivers and fatal fallacies decimate the profession. It is time to bite the bullet, not shoot it. Building collective professional capital is the only force equal to the task of whole-system reform that benefits all children.

In effect, you cannot get anywhere without widespread teacher ownership. The pursuit of professional capital furnishes a golden opportunity to rally everyone around a common agenda. This will be tough politics at the outset because of the current polarization. Involvement is not so much about the old cliché of "ownership," although it is also certainly that. The more fundamental gain is that the very expertise that is required can only come through the *subsidiarity* of involved participation and development. How on earth can you change teaching and teachers, who are on the front lines of their profession every day, unless you involve, engage, and empower teachers and their unions or associations themselves?

The problem is not insoluble. Effective educational reform can be accomplished by robust partnerships between management and labor. A case in point is Illinois Senate Bill 7, signed into force in June 2011, and involving unions, administrators, and school boards working together to produce legislation that overhauls many aspects of teacher hiring and teachers' work. In *Reforming Public School Systems Through Sustained Union–Management Collaboration*, the Center for American Progress shows how such labor–management partnerships can improve public education systems.[24] The varied school districts studied by the authors had long-term collaborative partnerships between administration and local teacher unions, centered on school improvement, student achievement, and teacher quality. Recommendations and lessons from the study were:

- ◆ Shared decision-making in school improvement should take place both at the district level as well in the schools themselves.
- ◆ Successful union–management collaboration in public school reform must focus on substantive areas affecting the quality of teaching or student achievement.
- ◆ The development of peer-to-peer networks of teachers will improve the quality of instruction.
- ◆ Formal structures at the district and school levels must coexist with strong cultures of collaboration, with school boards and the community, to inform approaches to planning and decision making, as well as hiring decisions.
- ◆ It is important to employ a strong, honest broker in the process who is respected by both (or all) sides and has strong substantive knowledge.

Some of the most "evolved" teacher evaluation systems have actually developed through local collective bargaining, and they show positive impacts in improved instructional performance of teachers needing improvement and self-selection out of those who don't improve sufficiently after agreed-upon supports have been provided.[25] Of course, these are still only exceptions. Not enough has happened yet on the ground or on a scale that can make an impressive difference.

Both the American Federation of Teachers (AFT) and the National Education Association (NEA) are showing more than vital signs of engaging with the political capital agenda. For example, NEA's *Transforming Teaching: Connecting Professional Responsibility with Student Learning* calls for "collective accountability" and "collaborative autonomy."[26] These are fine words. Now we must turn them into action.

This brings us back to what's worth fighting for. Let's make collective commitment, responsibility, and expertise or capability the key considerations in relation to the moral purpose of educational change—moving beyond polarities and stereotypes without political innocence but with absolute moral commitment to serve all students well. Enable teachers as valued professionals to inspire each other and the people around them through this commonly held, yet locally pursued moral agenda. Bite the silver bullet and spit it out: *collusion trumps collision* when it comes to professional capital.

6. *Be the change.* Schools, districts, governments—each level needs to be capable and credible; to be morally consistent, culturally connected, and strategically aligned. Each needs new capacities for the obvious reason that it will be impossible to have good partnerships without each party being capable, but also because you can't be credible if you can't model what you are requesting of others. Remember former football player Barry Finlay? He knew that he couldn't allow his own office to remain on the margins of the Ministry if he was going to convince district leaders and teachers in schools that special education and regular curriculum staff or classroom teachers had to work together in an integrated way. Now consider the opposite:

- If government parties cannot reach across the aisles for the sake of education or the country's economy, how can they expect unions or federations and policy makers to work together as well?
- How can state departments credibly promote differentiated instruction when they persist with high-stakes standardized testing?
- What does it say about how teachers should treat their students if districts and state departments keep on ranking, punishing, and shaming struggling schools?

Be the change you want to be, and like Gandhi himself, start at the top.

New capabilities and commitments have been portrayed throughout our book. It is time that they apply at the highest levels of policy as well as inside the smallest schools:

- Building a team focus within your organization as distinct from having separate silos
- Being good at two-way partnership where exchange of information is open and influence is mutual
- Pulling and pushing people forward without under- or overcooking how you do it
- Honing in on the knowledge base of research and experience, and on strategies that promote the spread of excellent practice
- Refining and reviewing your judgments and your capacity to make them over time
- Being transparently and collectively responsible to your students, to each other, and to the public at large

7. Pay people properly where they serve the greatest need. Professional capital is not all about pay. We saw in Chapter 2 from Daniel Pink's work that people get their drive not from more and more pay, but they need to have enough pay so that it is not a disincentive. The point about pay, in developed countries at least, is that as in Finland, it doesn't have to be stellar, but it has to be good enough. In less developed countries, though, pay is absolutely critical.

Report after report from international, economically driven organizations makes recommendation after recommendation for improving education in countries that have pitifully low levels of educational investment. Their strategies include decentralization, a strong and strict framework of curriculum standards, data to guide decision making, standardized testing, a few networks or clusters here, a pilot project or two on teacher inquiry there. None of these cost much money. But in countries with classes of 50 or 100, where many teachers are barely one step ahead of their students, where principals can be corrupt, or where teachers don't even show up at all because they can't get transportation or because they have to work at other jobs, the elephant in the room is teachers' pay.

International organizations and lending banks would rather tinker with standards and data any day of the week than go remotely near this question. In developing countries, teachers are often absent, poorly performing, and unable to find the time to develop their skills, work in teams together, or prepare their lessons properly because they have to make a living somehow by holding down other jobs in addition to their teaching positions because teaching doesn't pay enough for them to survive. If we can end the war in

Northern Ireland, bring down the Iron Curtain, and put a stop to apartheid, surely we can gather the collective will—a massive global social movement of will—to end the calumny and the ignominy of appallingly low teacher pay that denies children and future generations any kind of quality public education throughout the developing countries of the world. We have started to make significant progress in giving all children access to primary education in developing countries; it is now time to concentrate on providing access to *quality* education.

In the very few developing countries and emerging economies where pay scales are reaching acceptable levels, the issue is more about providing incentives for the best teachers and principals to work in the most challenging schools. Professional capital is at its strongest when those who have it consider it a badge of honor to be successful in the most difficult schools. In the long run, when professional capital flourishes, this distinction will be unnecessary because the entire teaching profession will have become collectively committed to whole-system reform.

8. *Get out and about more.* Professional capital is about constantly learning from your own efforts, and from the efforts and achievements of others, wherever they are in the world. It includes periodic stock taking about how the system is doing and what could be done better, and now it also involves countries sharing with and learning from each other, by comparing data and observing examples of and studying reports on each other's practice.

OECD's PISA program has stimulated the appetite of more and more countries to learn from each other, especially about the practices, principles, and strategies that lie behind the numbers of high-performing countries. The United States is finally in the game now, as in the New York City summit it called on the teaching profession, mentioned earlier. And after our own work and the work of one or two others on documenting examples of high performance in Canada, the United Kingdom, Finland, and elsewhere, other scholars, commentators, and consultants based in the United States are now joining the international comparison discussion as well. The revelation is that those countries that are front runners are also among the most aggressive in both sharing what they know and seeking insights from their global partners. They don't sit back and say, "We're great. We already have all the answers. We have nothing to learn from anyone else." Like high-performing schools and teachers, they are always reaching out, even and especially when they are at the top of their game, for new insights, original ideas, ways to become better still. With improved quality data, and greater openness to sharing and exchanging ideas and practice on an international scale, this is a perfect time for professional capital to go global. The larger agenda is, after all, not about improving one's own country but really about building a better, more socially just world for all.

ENACTING THE FUTURE

Our whole book is about enacting a new future for the teaching profession and its role in social justice and global prosperity. To do this, we must develop, accumulate, invest, and circulate professional capital. There is a lot at stake here. Unequal societies are worse off on almost every measure of well-being. In an assessment of the degree of economic inequality in 17 of the most developed countries, using the Gini coefficient, the United States and England were dead last. The Scandinavian countries were at the top. Canada placed 13th, in the middle.[27] The same patterns apply on UNICEF's measures of well-being at age 15. Who are at the top once more? The northern European nations. And which countries are rock bottom? You've got it—the United Kingdom and the United States. Canada once more came out in the middle. It did well on material wealth and tested achievement, but not nearly so well in self-regard, risk taking, or mental health.[28] If we take educational inequality—the size of the discrepancy between high and low achievers within a country—the United States and England are again among the most unequal as reported by OECD/PISA and have, if anything, been getting worse over the years.[29]

We don't think it is any exaggeration to say that if the United States and United Kingdom continue down the path of widening discrepancies between the best and the worst off, we will see more and more riots on the streets of the kind that made London's Burning in August 2011 into a frightening reality, not a children's song. Professional capital is about enacting more equal, higher attaining, more healthy countries in just about every way that counts. This is why successful countries treat their teachers as nation builders, and how they come to yield high returns in prosperity, social cohesion, and social justice. In high-performing, socially just, and cohesive countries, teachers are not merely dedicated, or even champions. Teachers are complete professionals. They are true pros who are well prepared, sufficiently paid, properly supported, continuously learning, collectively responsible, and shrewd in their judgments after years of inquiry and practice.

It's time to articulate a bold and inspiring vision, at the very top, that education is a public good and the collective responsibility of everyone in society. Declare that testing has gone too far and technology is not the easy answer; that a great society is built on truly great teachers who exude professional capital; that stripping off public education assets,

> ◆> We can treat teaching as just a short-term investment of business capital, and finance the present by mortgaging our children's future. Or we can make teaching a sustainable investment for professional capital, and give birth to a world of many happy returns to come.

most of all the assets of our people, to benefit the short-term business capital interests of test-producing companies, technology conglomerates, and charter school or free school start-ups, is not a wise or worthy way for us to go; that if we want to be among the world's best, we must start to behave like the world's best. Say these things loud; say them clear; say them now, from the very top, before it's too late.

In a way, in this book we have traced what's worth fighting for to its very roots. No fight is more fundamental to the future of society than the one we have proposed. The action guidelines we have provided furnish an agenda in which we all, individually and in groups, have a role to play. There is a lot at stake.

Nelson Mandela once tellingly observed, "There can be no keener revelation of a society's soul, than the way in which it treats its children."[30] It is clear and proven that the number one factor that makes the greatest difference to children's lives and children's futures within our schools is the children's teachers. So we should also say:

> There can be no keener revelation of a society's soul than the way in which it treats its children *and their teachers*.

We can treat teaching as just a short-term investment of business capital, and finance the present by mortgaging our children's future. Or we can make teaching a sustainable investment for professional capital, and give birth to a world of many happy returns to come. The choice is ours. The consequences will be profound. The responsibility belongs to all of us. The task appears formidable, but the rewards can be great. Professional capital is an accumulating asset. Let's make it our prime political, professional, and public investment.

Notes

PREFACE

1. Fullan, M., & Hargreaves, A. (1996), *What's worth fighting for in your school* (New York: Teachers College Press).

2. British Cabinet Minister Oliver Letwin, quoted in *The Guardian* (2011, July 30), Public sector workers need 'discipline and fear', says Oliver Letwin, retrieved from http://www.guardian.co.uk/politics/2011/jul/30/public-sector-jobs-oliver-letwin.

3. Tucker, M. S. (2011, May), *Standing on the shoulders of giants: An American agenda for education reform* (Washington, DC: National Center on Education and the Economy), p. 15, retrieved from http://www.ncee.org/wp-content/uploads/2011/05/Standing-on-the-Shoulders-of-Giants-An-American-Agenda-for-Education-Reform.pdf.

In *Aftershock,* former U.S. Secretary of Labor Robert Reich has undertaken an extensive analysis of U.S. responses to the global economic collapse. This response, he argues, protects very high income inequalities and prevents wealth, consumption, and economic growth circulating throughout the society; instead, it reduces any squeeze on existing profits by attacking pensions, social security, and other public sector services. See Reich, R. B. (2010), *Aftershock: The next economy and America's future* (New York: Alfred A. Knopf).

4. There will be a detailed discussion later of the themes in this topic. However, on perverse incentives, see Bird, S. M., Cox, D., Farewell, V. T., Goldstein, H., Holt, T., & Smith, P. C. (2005), Performance indicators: Good, bad, and ugly. *Journal of the Royal Statistical Society: Series A (Statistics in Society), 168*(1), 1–27.

5. Irving Janis coined "groupthink" in 1972 to refer to faculty decisions caused by group pressure. See Janis, I. L. (1972), *Victims of groupthink* (New York: Houghton Mifflin); and Janis, I. L. (1982), *Groupthink: Psychological studies of policy decisions and fiascoes* (2nd ed.) (New York: Houghton Mifflin).

6. Bion, W. R. (1961), *Experiences in groups* (London: Tavistock).

7. Mourshed, M., Chijioke, C., & Barber, M. (2010), *How the world's most improved school systems keep getting better* (London: McKinsey & Company), retrieved from http://mckinseyonsociety.com/downloads/reports/Education/How-the-Worlds-Most-Improved-School-Systems-Keep-Getting-Better_Download-version_Final.pdf.

CHAPTER 1: A CAPITAL IDEA

1. The "$500 billion market" comment was made by News Corporation Chairman and CEO Rupert Murdoch in a press release after his company acquired Wireless Generation, an education technology company, retrieved from http://www.newscorp.com/news/news_464.html.

2. Odden, A. R. (2011), *The strategic management of human capital in education: Improving instructional practice and student learning in schools* (New York: Routledge). See also the recommendations for career development–based pay from Harvard's Next Generation of Teachers Project, such as those in Johnson, S. M., & Papay, J. (2010), Merit pay for a new generation, *Education Leadership, 6*(8), 48–52.

3. Leana, C. R. (2011, Fall), The missing link in school reform, *Stanford Social Innovation Review,* p. 34.

4. Yarrow, A. (2009), State of mind: America's teaching corps, *Education Week, 29*(8), 21–23.

5. The attrition rates of Teach for America (TfA) members have been reported to be 80% or more after their third or fourth year according to Darling-Hammond, L., Holtzman, D. J., Gatlin, S. J., & Heilig, J. V. (2005), Does teacher preparation matter? Evidence about teacher certification, Teach for America, and teacher effectiveness, *Educational Policy Analysis Archives, 13*(42), 1–48, retrieved from http://epaa.asu.edu/ojs/article/view/147/273.

The most recent data for TfA attrition rates are discussed in Chapter 2 and were originally reported in Donaldson, M. L., & Johnson, S. M. (2011), TfA teachers: How long do they teach? Why do they leave? *Phi Delta Kappa International,* web only, retrieved from http://www.edweek.org/ew/articles/2011/10/04/kappan_donaldson.html.

Attrition rates of alternatively certified teachers are also documented in Heilig, J. V., & Jez, S. J. (2010), *Teach for America: A review of the evidence* (East Lansing, MI: Great Lakes Center for Education Research & Practice), retrieved from http://www.greatlakescenter.org/docs/Policy_Briefs/Heilig_TeachForAmerica.pdf. See also Kane, T. J., Rockoff, J. E., & Staiger, D. O. (2008), What does certification tell us about teacher effectiveness? Evidence from New York City, *Economics of Education Review, 27*(6), 615–631.

For McKinsey & Company's international and market research–based perspective on teacher recruitment, compensation, and development of educators, see Auguste, B., Kihn, P., & Miller, M. (2010), *Closing the talent gap: Attracting and retaining top-third graduates to careers in teaching* (London: McKinsey & Company), retrieved from http://mckinseyonsociety.com/downloads/reports/Education/Closing_the_talent_gap.pdf.

6. Critiques of conventional teacher education acknowledge the existence of some very good programs, but they leap a little too quickly to a strategy of replacement by alternate paths rather than reformation or restructuring. For a recent example of this discussion, see Otterman, S. (2011, July 21), Ed schools' pedagogical puzzle,

The New York Times, retrieved from http://www.nytimes.com/2011/07/24/education/edlife/edl-24teacher-t.html?_r=2&adxnnl=1&hpw=&adxnnlx=1318450581-HtTtxD7BMmw5imtTseaGxg.

7. A report on the impact of the California Teachers' Association's strategy is included in Shirley, D., & Hargreaves, A. (in press), *The global fourth way* (Thousand Oaks, CA: Corwin Press).

On Alberta, see the review of the Alberta Initiative for School Improvement in Hargreaves, A., Crocker, R., Davis, B., McEwen, L., Sahlberg, P., Shirley, D., & Sumara, D., with Hughes, M. (2009), *The learning mosaic: A multiple perspectives review of the Alberta Initiative for School Improvement (AISI),* retrieved from http://education.alberta.ca/media/1133263/the%20learning%20mosaic.pdf.

For the role of teacher inquiry among 1,500 teachers in Ontario, see Lieberman, A. (2010, June), Teachers, learners, leaders. *Educational Leadership, 67*(9), retrieved from http://www.ascd.org/publications/educational-leadership/summer10/vol67/num09/Teachers,-Learners,-Leaders.aspx.

On schemes in the United States, see Rubinstein, S., & McCarthy, J. (2011), *Reforming public school systems through sustained union–management collaboration.* Washington, DC: Center for American Progress, retrieved from http://www.americanprogress.org/issues/2011/07/pdf/collaboration.pdf.

8. Fullan, M. (2011), *The moral imperative realized* (Thousand Oaks, CA: Corwin Press).

9. Rosenberg, T. (2011), *Join the club: How peer pressure can transform the world* (New York: W. W. Norton).

10. Rosenberg, *Join the club,* p. xix.

11. Follett, M. P. (1998; first published 1918), *The new state: Group organization, the solution of popular government* (University Park: Pennsylvania State University Press).

12. Blasé, J., & Blasé, J. R. (2002), *Breaking the silence: Overcoming the problem of principal mistreatment of teachers* (Thousand Oaks, CA: Corwin Press).

13. This widely used quotation has an unclear and unidentified single source, but is widely believed to have been made as an aside in an interview and has since been disseminated more widely. Retrieved from www.interculturalstudies.org/Mead.

14. Briskin, A., Erickson, S., Ott, J., & Callanan, T. (2009), *The power of collective wisdom and the trap of collective folly* (San Francisco: Berrett-Koehler).

15. Briskin et al., *The power of collective wisdom,* p. 131.

16. Briskin et al., *The power of collective wisdom,* p. 193.

CHAPTER 2: COMPETING VIEWS OF TEACHING

1. This book will repeatedly return to high-performing systems on well-regarded international assessments of student performance in order to establish comparisons with strategies being pursued in lower performing systems like the

United States and England. One of these systems is Finland—the world's highest performing non-Asian country on the Organization for Economic Cooperation and Development's (OECD) Programme for International Student Assessment (PISA) tests of student achievement at age 15 in different countries. With a population of a little over 5 million—just under the average of a U.S. state, where most educational policy is actually made—Finland was the world's top performer until 2009, when three new Asian jurisdictions were added to the comparisons for the first time, though Finland's position still remains extremely high. One of us undertook the first external review of Finland's system in explaining the reasons for its success in 2007. See Hargreaves, A., Halász, G., & Pont, B. (2008), The Finnish approach to system leadership, *in* B. Pont, D. Nusche, & D. Hopkins (Eds.), *Improving school leadership, Vol. 2: Case studies on system leadership* (pp. 69–109) (Paris: OECD). See also Hargreaves, A., & Shirley, D. (2009), *The fourth way* (Thousand Oaks, CA: Corwin Press).

For other increasingly prominent international assessments of and explanations for Finland's performance and what we can learn from it, see "Finland: Slow and steady reform for consistently high results," chapter 5 *in* OECD (2011), *Strong performers and successful reformers in education*: *Lessons from PISA for the United States* (Paris: OECD), retrieved from http://www.oecd.org/dataoecd/32/50/46623978.pdf.

See also *The Finnish phenomenon: Inside the world's most surprising school system* (http://www.youtube.com/watch?v=bcC2l8zioIw). This is a short film by documentary filmmaker Bob Compton and Dr. Tony Wagner of Harvard University. In the film, Dr. Wagner provides the viewer with an inside perspective on the Finnish education system.

For information on Finland's education system and key analyses by Finnish insider Pasi Sahlberg, see Aho, E., Pitkänen, K., & Sahlberg, P. (2006), *Policy development and reform principles of basic and secondary education in Finland since 1968* (Washington, DC: World Bank); and also Sahlberg, P. (2011), *Finnish lessons: What can the world learn from educational change in Finland?* (New York: Teachers College Press).

For other reports on high-performing education systems, see Mourshed, M., Chijioke, C., & Barber, M. (2010), *How the world's most improved school systems keep getting better* (London: McKinsey & Company), retrieved from http://mckinseyon society.com/downloads/reports/Education/How-the-Worlds-Most-Improved -School-Systems-Keep-Getting-Better_Download-version_Final.pdf; and Barber, M., & Mourshed, M. (2007), *How the world's best-performing school systems come out on top* (London: McKinsey & Company), retrieved from http://mckinseyonsociety.com/ downloads/reports/Education/Worlds_School_Systems_Final.pdf.

See also Tucker, *Standing on the shoulders of giants.*

2. Singapore is one of the top-performing countries on OECD's international PISA assessments of 2009. The two Asian jurisdictions above it—Hong Kong and Shanghai—are part of China. At the time of writing this book, one of us had recently

undertaken a month long review of Singapore's educational system. This will be reported in Shirley & Hargreaves, *The global fourth way.*

3. Some of the international sources listed earlier in relation to Finland, also set out data on and explanations for Singapore's success. See especially OECD, *Strong performers and successful reformers in education*; Barber & Mourshed, *How the world's best-performing school systems come out on top*; and Mourshed et al., *How the world's most improved school systems keep getting better.*

4. An excellent body of work addressing the ethics of collegiality in these terms is that of Elizabeth Campbell at the University of Toronto. See especially Campbell, E. (1996), Ethical issues of collegial loyalty as one view of teacher professionalism, *Teachers and Teaching, 2*(2), 191–208.

5. Sanders, W. L. (1998), Value-added assessment, *The School Administrator, 55*(11), 24–32; and Sanders, W. L., & Rivers, J. C. (1996), *Cumulative and residual effects of teachers on future academic achievement* (Knoxville: University of Tennessee Value-Added Research and Assessment Center).

Classic references in the wider debate on measuring teacher effects include: Hanushek, E. A. (1992), The trade-off between child quantity and quality, *Journal of Political Economy, 100*(1), 84–117; and Hanushek, E. A., Kain, J. F., & Rivkin, S. G. (1998, August), *Teachers, schools, and academic achievement,* Working Paper 6691 (Cambridge, MA: National Bureau of Economic Research), retrieved from http://www.nber.org/papers/w6691.pdf.

More recent work includes: Carey, K. (2004), The real value of teachers: Using new information about teacher effectiveness to close the achievement gap, *Thinking K–16, 8*(1) (Washington, DC: The Education Trust); Braun, H. I. (2005), *Using student progress to evaluate teachers: A primer on value-added models* (Princeton, NJ: Educational Testing Service); Walsh, K. (2007), *If wishes were horses: The reality behind teacher quality findings* (Washington, DC: National Council for Teacher Quality); and Koretz, D. (2008, Fall), A measured approach: Value-added measures are a promising improvement, but no one measure can evaluate teacher performance, *The American Educator,* 18–39. More recently, John Hattie examined more than 800 meta-analyses in this area over a 15-year period. In one of six key points, he notes that "Teachers are among the most powerful influences in learning." See Hattie, J. (2009), *Visible learning: A synthesis of over 800 meta-analyses relating to student achievement* (London: Routledge), p. 238.

6. Felch, J. (2010, August 14), How good is your child's teacher? The *Times* crunches the numbers, *L.A. Times,* retrieved from http://latimesblogs.latimes.com/lanow/2010/08/times-evaluates-teachers.html.

7. On teacher recruitment in high-performing Finland, Singapore, South Korea, and Canada, see Auguste et al., *Closing the talent gap.*

8. Kangasniemi, S. (2008, 27 February), Millä ammatilla pääsee naimisiin? [With which profession to get married?], *Helsingin Sanomat Koulutusliite,* pp. 4–6.

9. Levin, B., & Naylor, N. (2007), Using resources effectively in education, *in* J. Burger, C. F. Webber, & P. Klinck (Eds.), *Intelligent leadership: Constructs for thinking education leaders* (pp. 143–158) (Dordrecht, the Netherlands: Springer).

10. The source for these data is Donaldson & Johnson, TfA teachers: How long do they teach?

For additional references on the attrition rates for TfA teachers, see Darling-Hammond, Does teacher preparation matter? The attrition rates of alternatively certified teachers are also reported in Heilig & Jez, *Teach for America: A review of the evidence*; and Kane et al., What does certification tell us about teacher effectiveness?

11. For literature on merit pay, see Gatz, D. B. (2011, Summer), Performance pay: Path to improvement. *Kappa Delta Pi, 156–161.*

Jesse Rothstein has written about the issues with value-added measures. See Rothstein, J. (2008), *Teacher quality in educational production: Tracking, decay, and student achievement* (Cambridge, MA: Princeton University and NBER), retrieved from http://www.irs.princeton.edu/pubs/pdfs/25ers.pdf. See also Viadero, V. (2009, July), Value-added gauge of teaching probed, *Education Week, 28*(36), 1–13.

Other seminal pieces on merit pay date as far back as the 1980s: for example, Murnane, R. J., & Cohen, D. K. (1986), Merit pay and the evaluation problem: Why most merit pay plans fail and a few survive, *Harvard Educational Review, 56*(1), 1–17.

For background and proposals for teacher compensation, see Johnson, S. M., & Papay, J. P. (2009, October), *Redesigning teacher pay: A system for the next generation of educators* (Washington, DC: Economic Policy Institute); and Johnson, S. M., & Liu, E. (2004), What teaching pays, what teaching costs, *in* S. M. Johnson & The Project on the Next Generation of Teachers, *Finders and keepers: Helping new teachers survive and thrive in our schools* (pp. 49–68) (San Francisco: Jossey-Bass).

12. Pink, D. H. (2009), *Drive: The surprising truth about what motivates us* (New York: Riverhead Books).

13. Severson, K. (2011, July 5), Systematic cheating is found in Atlanta's school system. *New York Times,* retrieved from http://www.nytimes.com/2011/07/06/education/06atlanta.html.

14. Braun, H., Chudowsky, N., & Koenig, J. (Eds.) (2010), *Getting value out of value-added* (Washington, DC: National Academies Press); and McCaffrey, D. F., Sass, T. R., Lockwood, J. R., & Mhaly, K. (2009), *The inter-temporal variability of teacher effect estimates,* Working Paper 2009-03 (Nashville, TN: National Center on Performance Incentives), retrieved from http://www.performanceincentives.org/data/files/news/PapersNews/200903_McCaffrey_etAl_TeacherEffectEstimate1.pdf.

15. Deal, T., & Kennedy, A. A. (1982), *Corporate cultures: The rite and rituals of corporate life* (New York: Basic Books).

16. The Beyond Expectations study is documented in a report for the National College for School Leadership in the United Kingdom (http://www.nationalcollege .org.uk/index/leadershiplibrary/leadingschools/school-improvement/international -perspectives-on-developing-high-quality-leadership/performance-beyond-expecta

tions.htm). The study examines 18 organizations in education, business, and sport that perform better than they did, better than comparable peers, and/or better than might be expected given levels of resources and support. The co-directors of the project were Andy Hargreaves and Alma Harris. The project team and case workers— some of whose case report writing has been excerpted and edited for this book— comprise Alan Boyle, Katherine Ghent, Janet Goodall, Alex Gurn, Corrie Stone-Johnson, Lori McEwen, and Michelle Reich.

On whole-system reform, see Fullan, M. (2010), *All systems go: The change imperative for whole system reform* (Thousand Oaks, CA: Corwin Press).

CHAPTER 3: STEREOTYPES OF TEACHING

1. Lemov, D., & Atkins, N. (2010), *Teach like a champion: 49 techniques that put students on the path to college* (San Francisco: John Wiley & Sons).

2. See Sarason, S. B. (1999), *Teaching as a performing art* (New York: Teachers College Press).

3. In this 1989 film directed by Peter Weir, Robin Williams plays an inspirational English teacher, John Keating, who encourages his students to "seize the day" and change their lives of conformity through his teaching of poetry and literature (http://en.wikipedia.org/wiki/Dead_Poet%27s_Society; http://www.imdb.com/title/tt0097165/).

4. In the BBC Two production of *The Choir,* Gareth Malone is a choir master who persuades a "stolidly unmusical community" to form a choir (http://www.telegraph.co.uk/culture/tvandradio/6207545/BBC-Twos-The-Choir-and-the-man-who-taught-the-world-to-sing.html; http://www.bbc.co.uk/programmes/b008y125).

5. See Waller, W. (1932), *The sociology of teaching* (Hoboken, NJ: Wiley), p. 10.

6. Waller, *The sociology of teaching*, p. 385.

7. Waller, *The sociology of teaching*, p. 391.

8. Waller, *The sociology of teaching*, p. 61.

9. The Happiness Index comes from a relatively new survey conducted annually by City & Guilds in the United Kingdom. In the United Kingdom, over the past 5 years, the vocation with the happiest people has been hairdressers, which has ranked in the top two places every year except one; beauty therapists also have a consistently high ranking (http://www.cityandguilds.com/24635.html?search_term).

10. Waller, *The sociology of teaching*, p. 375.

11. This example is edited and adapted from Hargreaves, A. (2003), *Teaching in the knowledge society: Education in the age of insecurity* (New York: Teachers College Press).

12. This example is taken from a study in Ontario of whole-school educational reforms that also benefit students with special educational needs. The directors of the project are Andy Hargreaves and Henry Braun. In addition to the directors, the

other case writers who have been compiling cases of implementation in 10 Ontario districts—almost a seventh of all the districts on Ontario—include Alex Gurn, Maureen Hughes, Karen Lam, Kathryn Sallis, and Matthew Welch. The work of particular writers is cited wherever it appears in this text. This example was written by Andy Hargreaves, the coauthor of this book.

13. This example is taken from the Beyond Expectations study. The original case material was written by Andy Hargreaves.

14. This material is edited and adapted from Fullan & Hargreaves, *What's worth fighting for in your school.*

15. The argument in this subsection comes from a study one of us conducted of secondary school reform in Ontario and New York State in the late 1990s and early 2000s under regimes of increasing standardization and market competition. See chapters 3 and 4 in Hargreaves, *Teaching in the knowledge society.*

16. Payne, C. M. (2008), *So much reform, so little change: The persistence of failure in urban schools* (Cambridge, MA: Harvard Education Press).

17. Payne's reference to "11 sick days per year, nearly double the national average, with most people being afflicted on either Monday or Friday" was originally taken from Houston, J. (1989, January 12), Teacher absenteeism on rise in city, *The Chicago Tribune,* retrieved from http://articles.chicagotribune.com/1989-01-12/news/ 8902240720_1_chicago-teachers-day-to-day-substitutes-los-angeles-teachers.

18. The last two quotes in this paragraph were reported in *The Chicago Tribune* on June 18, 2004. The remarks were made by then incoming union president Susan Stewart. Retrieved from http://articles.chicagotribune.com/2004-06-18/news/040 6180067_1_labor-union-union-funds-union-dues.

19. Shirley, D. (2009), *Report accompanying public testimony to the Education Committee of the California State Assembly on the Race to the Top* (Chestnut Hill, MA: Author).

20. On the attrition rates of TfA members, see note 7 for Chapter 1. In relation to Teach First in the United Kingdom, Professor Alan Smithers of Buckingham University reports that 86 of the 149 entrants to Teach First in 2005–2006 had left after 3 years. Teach First, he concluded, is "not the solution to the supply and quality of teachers." See BBC News (2011, August 10), Too few trainee teachers end up in schools, says report, retrieved from http://www.bbc.co.uk/news/education-14461935.

21. See Miller, A. (2009), *Principal turnover, student achievement and teacher retention* (Princeton, NJ: Industrial Relations Section, Firestone Library), retrieved from http://irs.princeton.edu/seminars/pdfs/miller.pdf; Weinstein, M., Jacobowitz, R., Ely, T., Landon, K., & Schwartz, A. E. (2009), *Principal turnover and academic achievement at new high schools in New York City,* NYU Wagner Research Paper No. 2011-09 (New York: NYU Institute for Education and Social Policy); and Viadero, D. (2009), Turnover in principalship: Focus of research. *Education Week, 29*(9), 1–14.

22. One example is the noncompliance of Montana governors. See Dillon, S. (2011, August 14), State challenges seen as whittling away federal education law. *New*

York Times, retrieved from http://www.nytimes.com/2011/08/15/education/15educ .html?pagewanted=all.

23. On the effectiveness of charter schools, see Lubienski, C., & Lubienski, S. T. (2006), *Charter, private, public schools and academic achievement: New evidence from NAEP mathematics data* (New York: National Center for the Study of Privatization in Education, Teachers College, Columbia University); and Zimmer, R., Gill, B., Booker, K., Lvertu, S., Sass, T. R., & Witte, J. (2009), *Charter schools in eight states: Effects on achievement, attainment, integration, and competition* (Santa Monica, CA: Rand Corporation), retrieved from http://www.rand.org/pubs/monographs/2009/RAND_MG 869.pdf.

24. Brill, S. (2011), *Class warfare: Inside the fight to fix America's schools* (New York: Simon & Schuster).

25. Reeves, D. (2011), Neutron bombs and school turnarounds. *ASCD Express,* 6(12), retrieved from http://ascd.org/ascd-express/vol6/612-reeves.aspx.

26. Fullan, M. (2011), *Choosing the wrong drivers for whole system reform,* Seminar Series 204 (East Melbourne, Australia: Centre for Strategic Education). See also Andy Hargreaves and Alma Harris's Beyond Expectations report and the section on five fallacies of educational change. The Beyond Expectations study is documented in a report for the National College for School Leadership in the United Kingdom and can be retrieved from http://www.nationalcollege.org.uk/index/leadershiplibrary/ leadingschools/school-improvement/international-perspectives-on-developing -high-quality-leadership/performance-beyond-expectations.htm.

27. Auguste et al., *Closing the talent gap.* This September 2010 report by McKinsey & Company looks at top-performing education systems in the world and reports that one reason for their "extraordinary results" is because they recruit, develop, and retain top talent as an education strategy.

28. For writing that explains Canadian success on PISA, especially in the provinces of Alberta and Ontario, see Shirley & Hargreaves, *The global fourth way;* and Hargreaves, A. (2011, January 26), Canada's culture of excellence in education, *Toronto Star,* retrieved from http://www.thestar.com/opinion/editorialopinion/article/928064 -canada-s-culture-of-excellence-in-education.

Other reports that document high-quality systems include OECD, *Strong performers and successful reformers in education;* Mourshed et al., *How the world's most improved school systems keep getting better;* and Barber & Mourshed, *How the world's best-performing school systems come out on top.*

For a case study from Alberta, refer to the review that one of us co-directed on the Alberta Initiative for School Improvement: Hargreaves et al., *The learning mosaic.*

References discussing Finland's education system and remarkable trajectory include: Hargreaves et al., The Finnish approach to system leadership; and Sahlberg, *Finnish lessons.*

CHAPTER 4: INVESTING IN CAPABILITY AND COMMITMENT

1. The classic advice on this came from Nathaniel Lees Gage, the legendary researcher on teacher effectiveness. See Gage, N. L. (1978), *The scientific basis of the art of teaching* (New York: Teachers College Press).

2. See Elmore, R. F. (2004), *School reform from the inside out: Policy, practice and performance* (Cambridge, MA: Harvard Education Press).

3. For a more detailed argument about the role of evidence in educational change and educational research, and about the misuse of evidence in improvement and reform settings, see Hargreaves, A., & Stone-Johnson, C. (2009), Evidence-informed change and the practice of teaching, *in* J. D. Bransford, D. J. Stipek, N. J. Vye, L. M. Gomez, & D. Lam (Eds.), *The role of research in educational improvement* (pp. 89–110) (Cambridge, MA: Harvard Education Press).

4. This challenge to the traditional reading of the results from District 2 is discussed in detail in chapters 3 and 4 of Ravitch, D. (2010), *The death and life of the great American school system: How testing and choice are undermining education* (New York: Basic Books). In chapter 4, Ravitch also discusses the attempts to transplant the District 2 strategies to San Diego.

5. One of us came across this phenomenon in Canada in the 1990s. We called it "recycled change." An innovative high school we had studied created a new system of student mentoring that was adopted and implemented by the government but with less flexibility and fewer resources for numbers of mentors or hours of mentoring— so the proposal became unimplementable in the school that invented it. See chapter 5 of Hargreaves, *Teaching in the knowledge society.*

6. The classic study in business of the relationship between innovation and improvement is found in Christensen, C. M. (1997), *The innovator's dilemma: When new technologies cause great firms to fail* (Boston: Harvard Business School Press). Using the example of the history of disk drives, Christensen shows how companies that once innovated become intent on making incremental improvements to their existing model and resist attempts by their own innovators to launch dramatically different products such as smaller disk drives, laptops, palmtops, tablet computers, and so on. The innovators then migrate elsewhere and develop their product, which eventually overtakes that of their original host organization. In this way, improvement of what exists or once existed can impede innovation in much-needed new practice.

7. One of the most infamous cases of systemic cheating was reported in Atlanta. See Severson, K. Systematic cheating is found in Atlanta's school system. More details of the report were discussed in Chapter 2.

8. Riehl, C. (2006), Feeling better: A comparison of medical research and education research, *Educational Researcher, 35*(5), 24–29.

9. One of us has written extensively on the phenomenon of teacher nostalgia, based on a study of the experience of different generations in teaching of educational reform from the 1970s to the present. The key finding was that all teachers who had

started their careers in the 1960s and 1970s had nostalgia for individual professional freedom and autonomy. Teachers in innovative schools regretted the loss of the innovative environments that gave them freedom to develop new practice, while secondary teachers in more traditional schools bemoaned the loss of their autonomy to teach in the traditional, highly teacher-centered, and culturally exclusionary ways they preferred. See Goodson, I., Moore, S., & Hargreaves, A. (2006), Teacher nostalgia and the sustainability of reform: The generation and degeneration of teachers' missions, memory, and meaning, *Educational Administration Quarterly, 42*(1), 42–61; and Hargreaves, A., & Fink, D. (2006), *Sustainable leadership* (San Francisco: Jossey Bass/Wiley).

10. Barber, M. (2007), *Instruction to deliver: Tony Blair, the public services and the challenge of delivery* (London: Methuen).

11. For a summary of the critiques of the implementation of the English strategy, see Hargreaves, *Teaching in the knowledge society*; Hargreaves & Shirley, *The fourth way.*

12. See Hargreaves et al., The Finnish approach to system leadership; and Hargreaves & Shirley, *The fourth way.*

For prominent international assessments of and explanations for Finland's performance and what we can learn from it, see "Finland: Slow and steady reform for consistently high results," chapter 5 *in* OECD, *Strong performers and successful reformers in education.*

For information on Finland's education system and key analyses by Finnish insider Pasi Sahlberg, see Aho et al., *Policy development and reform principles of basic and secondary education in Finland since 1968.* See also Sahlberg, *Finnish lessons.*

13. On the importance of "precision," see Fullan, M., Hill, P., & Crevola, C. (2008), *Breakthrough* (Thousand Oaks, CA: Corwin Press).

14. On the distinction between *best* and *next* practice, see Hannon, V. (2008), Should educational leadership focus on 'best practice' or 'next practice'? *Journal of Educational Change, 9*(1), 77–81; and Caldwell, B. J., & Spinks, J. M. (2008), *Raising the stakes: From improvement to transformation in the reform of schools* (Abingdon, UK: Routledge).

15. For comparison of U.S. and Finnish teachers' workload, see Sahlberg, *Finnish lessons.*

16. Hattie, *Visible learning: A synthesis.*

17. Hattie, J. (2012), *Visible learning inside: Maximizing student achievement* (London: Routledge).

18. Hattie points to this more richly contextualized meaning in six signposts in Hattie, *Visible learning: A synthesis,* pp. 238–239.

19. Hattie, *Visible learning inside.*

20. See Marzano, R. J. (2007), *The art and science of teaching: A comprehensive framework for effective instruction* (Alexandria, VA: Association for Supervision and Curriculum Development); and Marzano, R. J., Marzano, J. S., & Pickering, D. J.

(2003), *Classroom management that works: Research-based strategies for every teacher* (Alexandria, VA: Association for Supervision and Curriculum Development).

21. The definitions of "capable" and "competent" are taken from the Merriam-Webster online dictionary, retrieved from http://www.merriam-webster.com/dictionary/competent and http://www.merriam-webster.com/dictionary/capable.

22. On winning streaks, see Kanter, R. M. (2004), *Confidence: How winning streaks and losing streaks begin and end* (New York: Tree Rivers Press).

23. Mary Jean Gallagher is the author of the Ontario case, which was reported by personal communication with Michael Fullan. Katherine Ghent is the author of the Limeside case, which is part of the Performance Beyond Expectations study (2011) directed by Andy Hargreaves and Alma Harris and documented in Hargreaves, A., & Harris, A. (2011), *Performance beyond expectations* (Nottingham, UK: National College for School Leadership), retrieved from http://www.nationalcollege .org.uk/index/leadershiplibrary/leadingschools/school-improvement/international -perspectives-on-developing-high-quality-leadership/performance-beyond-expecta tions.htm.

24. See the Limeside case from the Performance Beyond Expectations study (2011), which is documented in Hargreaves & Harris, *Performance beyond expectations*.

25. For references on high performance in Finland, see note 12 for Chapter 4.

26. See research by Day, C., Stobart, G., Sammons, P., Kington, A., & Gu, Q. (2007), *Teachers matter: Connecting lives, work and effectiveness* (Berkshire, UK: Open University Press); and Day, C., & Gu, Q. (2010), *The new lives of teachers: Teacher quality and school development* (Abingdon, UK: Routledge).

27. Day et al., *Teachers matter*, p. 125.

28. Day et al., *Teachers matter*, p. 131.

29. Day et al., *Teachers matter*, p. 126.

30. Day et al., *Teachers matter*, p. 129.

31. Day et al., *Teachers matter*, p. 126.

32. Day et al., *Teachers matter*, p. 126.

33. Day et al., *Teachers matter*, p. 129.

34. Day et al., *Teachers matter*, p. 136.

35. Day et al., *Teachers matter*, p. 125.

36. Day et al., *Teachers matter*, p. 130.

37. See Shirley & Hargreaves, *The global fourth way*, for a first-hand comparison of these three countries. For other comparisons that include Ontario but not Alberta, see OECD, *Strong performers and successful reformers in education*; Mourshed et al., *How the world's most improved school systems keep getting better*; and Barber & Mourshed, *How the world's best-performing school systems come out on top*. See also Tucker, *Standing on the shoulders of giants*.

38. Day et al., *Teachers matter*, p. 233.

39. See the classic study by Ashton, P. T., & Webb, R. B. (1986), *Making a difference: Teachers' sense of efficacy and student achievement* (New York: Longman).

More recent work on teachers' self-efficacy includes Tschannen-Moran, M., Hoy, A. W., & Hoy, W. K. (1998), Teacher efficacy: Its meaning and measure. *Review of Educational Research, 68*(2), 202–248; Palardy, G. J., & Rumberger, R. W. (2008), Teacher effectiveness in first grade: The importance of background qualifications, attitudes, and instructional practices for student learning. *Educational Evaluation & Policy Analysis, 30*(2), 111–140; and Parker, K., Hannah, E., & Topping, K. J. (2006), Collective teacher efficacy, pupil attainment and socio-economic status in primary school, *Improving Schools, 9*(2), 111–129.

40. See Day et al., *Teachers matter*.

41. See Huberman, M. (1989), The professional life cycle of teachers, *Teachers College Record, 91*(1), 31–57. The work of Day et al., *Teachers matter*; and Day & Gu, Q. *The new lives of teachers*, builds on Huberman's work, for instance by introducing the six phases of teachers' careers.

42. See Hargreaves, A. (2005), Educational change takes ages: Life, career and generational factors in teachers' emotional responses to educational change, *Teaching and Teacher Education, 21*(8), 967–983.

43. Hargreaves, Educational change takes ages, p. 975.

44. Hargreaves, Educational change takes ages, p. 975.

45. See Sikes, P. (1985), The life cycle of the teacher, *in* S. Ball & I. Goodson (Eds.), *Teachers' lives and careers* (pp. 27–60) (London: Falmer).

46. Huberman, The professional life cycle of teachers.

47. See Lieberman, A., & Miller, L. (2005), *Teacher leadership* (San Francisco: John Wiley & Sons); Crowther, F., Ferguson, M., & Hann, L. (2009), *Developing teacher leaders: How teacher leadership enhances school success* (2nd ed.) (Thousand Oaks, CA: Corwin); and Harris, A. (2009), Teacher leadership and organizational development, *in* B. McGaw, P. Peterson, and E. Baker (Eds.), *The international encyclopedia of education* (3rd ed., pp. 40–44) (Oxford, UK: Elsevier).

48. A summary of the attrition rates of teachers in the United States is provided by Papay, J. (2007), *Aspen Institute datasheet: The teaching workforce* (Washington, DC: The Aspen Institute), retrieved from http://www.aspeninstitute.org/atf/cf/%7BDEB6 F227-659B-4EC8-8F84-8DF23CA704F5%7D/Ed_AspenTeacherWorkforceDatasheet .pdf.

See also Loeb, S., & Reininger, M. (2004), *Public policy and teacher labor markets: What we know and why it matters* (East Lansing: The Education Policy Center at Michigan State University), retrieved from http://www.eric.ed.gov/PDFS/ED485592 .pdf.

49. See Auguste et al., *Closing the talent gap*.

50. See Cochran-Smith, M., McQuillan, P. J., Barnatt, J., D'Souza, L., Jong, C., Shakman, K., Terrell, D., Lam, K., Gleeson, A. M., & Mitchell, K. (in press), Teaching practice and early career decisions: Findings from a longitudinal cross-case study, *American Educational Research Journal*.

51. Becker, H. S. (1952), The career of the Chicago Public School teacher, *American Journal of Sociology, 57*(5), 470–477.

52. Johnson, S. M., & The Project on the Next Generation of Teachers (2004), *Finders and keepers: Helping new teachers survive and thrive in our schools* (San Francisco: Jossey-Bass).

53. Stone-Johnson, C. (2011), Talkin' 'bout my generation: Boomers, Xers, and educational change. *Journal of Educational Change, 12*(2), 221–239.

54. On "new professionals," see Troman, G., & Woods, P. (2000), Careers under stress: Teacher adaptations at a time of intensive reform. *Journal of Educational Change, 1*(3), 253–275. On "constrained professionalism," see Wills, J. S., & Sandholtz, J. H. (2009), Constrained professionalism: Dilemmas of teaching in the face of test-based accountability, *Teachers College Record, 111*(4), 1065–1114.

55. Stone-Johnson, Talkin' 'bout my generation, p. 236.

56. Hargreaves, Educational change takes ages, all quotes from p. 979.

57. See Drake, C. (2002), Experience counts: Career stage and teachers' response to mathematics education reform, *Educational Policy, 16*(2), 311–337.

58. Both quoted passages are from Drake, Experience counts, p. 320.

59. See Barber, Instruction to deliver.

60. Drake, Experience counts, p. 333.

CHAPTER 5: PROFESSIONAL CAPITAL

1. This opening discussion of professionalism draws on an argument first set out in Goodson, I. F., & Hargreaves, A. (Eds.) (1996), *Teachers' professional lives* (Abingdon, UK: RoutledgeFalmer).

2. The classic discussion of the defining characteristics of professions is to be found in Etzioni, A. (1969), *Semiprofessionals and their organization: Teachers, nurses, social workers* (New York: Free Press).

3. See Hargreaves et al., The Finnish approach to system leadership, p. 81.

4. Sahlberg, *Finnish lessons.*

5. The two quotations are taken from Sahlberg, *Finnish lessons,* p. 76.

6. The argument regarding the different stages through which teacher training and teacher professionalism have progressed was first set out in Hargreaves, A. (2000), Four ages of professionalism and professional learning, *Teachers and Teaching: History and Practice, 6*(2), 151–182.

7. See, for instance, Otterman, Ed schools' pedagogical puzzle.

8. Goodson & Hargreaves, *Teachers' professional lives.*

9. OCED (2011), *Reviews of national policies for education: Improving lower secondary schools in Norway 2011* (Paris: OECD).

10. Office for Standards in Education (2008), *Rising to the challenge: A review of the Teach First initial teacher training programme* (London: Author), p. 5, retrieved from http://www.ofsted.gov.uk/resources/rising-challenge-review-of-teach-first-initial-teacher-training-programme.

11. National Council for Accreditation for Teacher Education (NCATE) (2010, November), *Report of the blue ribbon panel on clinical preparation and partnerships for improved student learning,* retrieved from http://www.ncate.org/LinkClick.aspx?fileticket=zzeiB1OoqPk%3d&tabid=715.

12. Shaw, G. B. (1988, first published 1906), *The doctor's dilemma: A tragedy* (Harmondsworth, UK: Penguin).

13. Hargreaves, A. (2001), The emotional geographies of teaching. *Teachers College Record, 103*(6), 1056–1080, quote from p. 1070.

14. See Mourshed et al., *How the world's most improved school systems keep getting better;* and Auguste et al., *Closing the talent gap.*

15. After developing the concept of *professional capital,* we undertook an extensive search to determine whether the expression or concept already existed in the literature. There is no major or widely known use of the concept in the social and public sector, but it has been raised, in a different way, in doctoral-level or other exploratory studies of professionalism in health and social work in Australia. See Gobbi, M. (2010), Learning nursing in the workplace community: The generation of professional capital in C. Blackmore (Ed.), *Social learning systems and communities of practice* (pp. 145–162) (Milton Keynes, UK: Open University Press); and Brodie, P. (2003), *The invisibility of midwifery: Will developing professional capital make a difference?* The Brodie research was submitted for the Doctor of Midwifery, University of Technology, Sydney.

More commonly, professional capital has been discussed in business and finance. An early reference comes from Perkin (1990), who argues that professional capital is more tangible than stocks or shares. See Perkin, H. (1990), *The rise of professional society: England since 1880* (London: Routledge). In another business/economics example, Manigart & Strufy (1997) discuss the modest numbers of private investors in the start-up phase of new investments as compared to professional capital providers. See Manigart, S., & Strufy, C. (1997), Financing high technology startups in Belgium: An explorative study, *Small Business Economics, 9*(2), 125–135, retrieved from http://metaquest.bc.edu:4000/sfx_local?sid=google&auinit=S&aulast=Manigart&atitle=Financing+high+technology+startups+in+Belgium:+An+explorative+study&title=Small+business+economics&volume=9&issue=2&date=1997&spage=125&issn=0921-898X. A more recent study in Russia by Elena Avraamova (2002) includes professional capital as one variable of educational capital. She calculates professional capital as an index based on self-appraisal of professionalism. See Avraamova, E. (2002), Capacity of the Russian population for adaptation to the market environment, *Russian Economic Trends, 11*(3), 54–59.

In the only other educational reference to professional capital we could locate, Thomas Sergiovanni (1999) looks at the role of capital in educational leadership. He defines how "capital" refers to "the value of something that when properly invested produces more of that thing which then increases overall value. This emphasis on capital development provides the conditions necessary to improve the level of student learning and development. Capital expansion is, therefore, the key mediating variable that stands between pedagogical leadership and school results" (p. 38). He then discusses the role of several kinds of capital—human, academic, intellectual, and social. There is a short section on professional capital. Sergiovanni covers part of our terrain in treating professional capital as the exercise of social capital in the professional workplace to examine shared practice—but his delineation of professional capital does not incorporate the kinds of capital that develop professional judgment. Thus: "Good schools take collegiality seriously—so seriously that they strive to create a single practice of teaching in the school that is shared by many. They cultivate communities of practice as a way to generate professional capital. One hallmark of an established profession is the willingness of its members to be concerned not only with their own practices but with the practice itself. Professional capital is created as a fabric of reciprocal responsibilities, and support is woven among the faculty that adds value to teachers and students alike" (p. 40). See Sergiovanni, T. J. (1999), Leadership as pedagogy, capital development and school effectiveness, *International Journal of Leadership in Education*, *1*(1), 37–56.

16. The concept of "human capital" was perhaps first used by Adam Smith, who referred to it as "the acquired and useful abilities of all the inhabitants or members of the society. The acquisition of such talents, by the maintenance of the acquirer during his education, study, or apprenticeship, always costs a real expense, which is a capital fixed and realized, as it were, in his person. Those talents, as they make a part of his fortune, so do they likewise that of the society to which he belongs. The improved dexterity of a workman may be considered in the same light as a machine or instrument of trade which facilitates and abridges labor, and which, though it costs a certain expense, repays that expense with a profit." See Smith, A. (1776), *An inquiry into the nature and causes of the wealth of nations, Book II: Of the nature, accumulation, and employment of stock*. The quotation is taken from Smith, A. (1776/2009), *The wealth of nations: Books I–III complete and unabridged* (New York: Classic House Books), p. 202.

A discussion of Adam Smith's conception of human capital is found in Spengler, J. J. (1977), The invisible hand and other matters: Adam Smith on human capital, *The American Economic Review*, *67*(1), 32–36.

17. See the seminal text by Loury, G. C. (1977), A dynamic theory of racial income differences, *in* P. A. Wallace and A. LeMund (Eds.), *Women, minorities, and employment discrimination* (pp. 153–188) (Lexington, MA: Lexington Books); and Loury, G. C. (1987), Why should we care about group inequality? *Social Philosophy and Policy*, *5*(1), 249–271.

18. See Coleman, J. S. (1986), Social theory, social research and a theory of action. *American Journal of Sociology*, *91*(6), 1309–1335; and Coleman, J. S. (1988), Social capital in the creation of human capital. *American Journal of Sociology*, *94*(Supplement: *Organizations and Institutions: Sociological and Economic Approaches to the Analysis of Social Structure*), S95–S120, retrieved from http://onemvweb.com/sources/sources/social_capital.pdf.

19. Coleman, Social capital in the creation of human capital, p. S101.

20. See Coleman, Social capital in the creation of human capital, p. S111.

21. Putnam, R. D. (2001), *Bowling alone: The collapse and revival of American community* (New York: Simon & Schuster).

22. Pickett, K., & Wilkinson, R. (2011), *The spirit level: Why greater equality makes societies stronger* (New York: Bloomsbury Press).

23. Bryk, A., & Schneider, B. (2002), *Trust in schools: A core resource for improvement* (New York: Russell Sage Foundation).

24. Odden, *The strategic management of human capital in education.*

25. There is rich academic discourse on social capital and inequality. Classic works on social capital are from Bourdieu, P. (1983/1986), The forms of capital (R. Nice, Trans.), *in* J. G. Richardson (Eds.), *Handbook of theory and research for the sociology of education* (pp. 241–258) (Westport, CT: Greenwood Press); and Coleman, J. S., Campbell, E. Q., Hobson, C. J., McPartland, J., Mood, A. M., Weinfeld, F. D., & York, R. L. (1966), *Equality of educational opportunity* (Washington, DC: U.S. Department of Health, Education, and Welfare).

For work that discusses social capital in the context of education, see Monkman, K., Ronald, M., & Théramène, F. D. (2005), Social and cultural capital in an urban Latino school community, *Urban Education, 40*(1), 4–33; Gonzales, R. G. (2010), On the wrong side of the tracks: Understanding the effects of school structure and social capital in the educational pursuits of undocumented immigrant students, *Peabody Journal of Education, 85*(4), 469–485; Perna, L. W. (2000), Racial and ethnic group differences in college enrollment decisions, *New Directions for Institutional Research, 27*(3), 65–83; and Coleman, Social capital in the creation of human capital.

26. Leana, The missing link in school reform, pp. 29–35.

27. See Garet, M. S., Cronen, S., Eaton, M., Kurki, A., Ludwig, M., Jones, W., Uekawa, K., Falk, A., Bloom, H. S., Doolittle, F., Zhu, P., & Sztejnberg, L. (2008, September), *The impact of two professional development interventions on early reading instruction and achievement,* NCEE 2008-4030 (Washington, DC: National Center for Education Evaluation and Regional Assistance, Institute of Education Sciences); and Garet, M. S., Wayne, A. J., Stancavage, F., Taylor, J., Walters, K., Song, M. L., Brown, S., Hurlburt, S., Zhu, P., Sepanik, S., & Doolittle, F. (2010, April), *Middle school mathematics professional development impact study: Findings after the first year of implementation,* NCEE 2010-4009 (Washington, DC: National Center for Education Evaluation and Regional Assistance, Institute of Education Sciences).

28. A search on "decisional law" in Westlaw, a search engine frequently used by lawyers, indicates that decisional law is like case law. Westlaw defines "case law" as legal principles enunciated and embodied in judicial decisions or cases. In the United States and Canada, this is also similar to common law or laws set on court decisions. Here is an example using Florida's rules of criminal procedure: "New decisional law which announces new procedural principles applicable to the trial or appeal of criminal cases and which is not 'prospective only' will also generally not

apply in criminal cases that are already final when the new decision is handed down"
[22 Fla. Prac., Criminal Procedure § 1:13 (2011)]. Our use of *decisional capital*
diverges slightly from the juridical definition of decisional law in that we define decisional capital as an informal as well as a formal process of developing the capacity for
expert judgment over time.

29. Shulman, J. H., & Colbert, J. A. (Eds.) (1987), *The mentor teacher casebook*
(San Francisco: Far West Laboratory for Educational Research and Development).

30. City, E. A., Elmore, R. F., Fiarman, S. E., & Teitel, L. (2009), *Instructional
rounds in education: A network approach to improving teaching and learning* (Cambridge, MA: Harvard Education Press).

31. Gladwell, M. (2008), *Outliers: The story of success* (New York: Little, Brown),
p. 39. The study Gladwell refers to in this passage was conducted in the 1990s by
K. Anders Ericsson and two colleagues. The original report of that work is Ericsson,
K. A., Krampe, R. T., & Tesch-Römer, C. (1993), The role of deliberate practice in the
acquisition of expert performance. *Psychological Review, 100*(3), 363–406.

32. Daniel J. Levitin, quoted in Gladwell, *Outliers,* p. 40. Levitin's comments
originally appeared in Levitin, D. J. (2006), *This is your brain on music: The science of
a human obsession* (New York: Dutton), p. 197.

33. Gladwell, *Outliers,* p. 42.

34. Gawande, A. (2002), *Complications: A surgeon's notes on an imperfect science*
(New York: Metropolitan Books), p. 236.

35. Gawande, *Complications,* p. 249.

36. Schön, D. A. (1983), *The reflective practitioner: How professionals think in
action* (New York: Basic Books); and Schön, D. A. (1987), *Educating the reflective
practitioner: Toward a new design for teaching and learning and learning in the professions* (San Francisco: Jossey-Bass).

37. MacDonald, E., & Shirley, D. (2009), *The mindful teacher* (New York: Teachers College Press).

38. Hargreaves, A., & Fullan, M. (1998), *What's worth fighting for out there?*
(New York: Teachers College Press).

39. Lewin, K. (1946), Action research and minority problems. *Journal of Social
Issues, 2*(4), 34–46, quote from p. 35.

40. Gallagher, M. J. (2010), Ontario Literacy and Numeracy Secretariat, personal communication.

41. Cochran-Smith, M., & Lytle, S. L. (2009), *Inquiry as stance: Practitioner
research in the next generation* (New York: Teachers College Press).

42. See Pascal, C. E. (2009), *With our best future in mind: Implementing early
learning in Ontario,* Report to the Premier of Ontario (Toronto: Government of
Ontario).

CHAPTER 6: PROFESSIONAL CULTURE AND COMMUNITIES

1. This example is drawn from data collected in the Essential for Some, Good for All study (2009–2012) directed by Andy Hargreaves and Henry Braun in partnership with the Council of Ontario Directors of Education (CODE), Oakville, Ontario.

2. This provincial philosophy was published in 2009 by the Ontario Ministry of Education as a report entitled *Learning for All K–12,* retrieved from http://www .ontariodirectors.ca/L4All/L4A_en_downloads/LearningforAll%20K-12%20 draft%20J.pdf.

3. Hargreaves, A. (1994), *Changing teachers, changing times: Teachers' work and culture in the postmodern age* (London: Cassell); and Fullan, M. (1999), *Change forces: The sequel* (London: Falmer Press).

4. Rudduck, J. (1991), *Innovation and change* (Milton Keynes, UK: Open University Press), p. 31.

5. Rosenholtz, S. J. (1991), *Teacher's workplace: The social organization of schools* (Harlow, UK: Longman Group).

6. Rosenholtz, *Teachers' workplace,* p. 37.

7. Rosenholtz, *Teachers' workplace,* p. 83.

8. Lortie, D. (1975), *Schoolteacher: A sociological study* (Chicago: University of Chicago Press).

9. Lortie, *Schoolteacher,* p. 210.

10. Hargreaves, A., & Tucker, E. (1991), Teaching and guilt: Exploring the feelings of teaching. *Teaching & Teacher Education, 7*(5/6), 491–505.

11. Hargreaves, *Teaching in the knowledge society,* p. 142.

12. Abrahamson, E. (2004), *Change without pain* (Boston: Harvard Business School Publishing).

13. Rosenholtz, *Teachers' workplace,* p. 73.

14. Newmann, F. M., & Wehlage, G. (1995), *Successful school restructuring* (Madison, WI: Center on Organization and Restructuring of Schools), retrieved from http://www.wcer.wisc.edu/archive/cors/Successful_School_Restruct.html; and McLaughlin, M., & Talbert, J. (2001), *Professional communities and the work of high school teaching* (Chicago: University of Chicago Press).

15. Little, J. W. (1990), The persistence of privacy: Autonomy and initiative in teachers' professional relations. *Teachers College Record, 91*(4), 509–536.

16. Nias, J. (1989), *Primary teachers talking: A study of teaching as work* (London: Routledge).

17. Fullan, M., & Hargreaves, A. (1991), *What's worth fighting for: Working together for your school* (Toronto: Ontario Public Schools Teachers' Federation); and Hargreaves, A., & Macmillan, R. (1995), The balkanization of teaching, *in* J. W. Little & L. S. Siskin (Eds.), *Subjects in question: Departmental organization and the high school* (pp. 141–171) (New York: Teachers College Press).

In the light of recent global conflicts, the term "balkanization" might be regarded as sensitive and controversial by some. However, the word first came into usage in 1919 at the time of the original Balkan wars, and now has widespread application outside politics. The Merriam-Webster dictionary defines the term "balkanized" as meaning "to break up (as a region or group) into smaller and often hostile units." The term has references that stretch from structural and political divisions within organizations to the development of different niches in pop music. Because of its sensitivity, we sought other terms such as "silos," "compartmentalization," and so on, but none of them capture the structural, cultural, and political aspects of division and divisiveness in the way that "balkanization" does.

18. Fink, D. (2000), *Good schools/real schools: Why school reform doesn't last* (New York: Teachers College Press).

19. Hargreaves, A. (1991), Contrived collegiality: The micropolitics of teacher collaboration, *in* J. Blasé (Ed.), *The politics of life in schools: Power, conflict and cooperation* (pp. 46–72) (London: Sage Publications).

20. Klette, K. (1997), Teacher individuality, teacher collaboration and repertoire building: Some principal dilemmas. *Teachers and Teaching, (3)*2, 243–256.

21. Hargreaves, A., & Skelton, J. (2011), Politics and systems of coaching and mentoring, *in* S. Fletcher & C. Mullen (Eds.), *The Sage handbook of mentoring and coaching in education* (Los Angeles: Sage).

22. Mourshed et al., *How the world's most improved school systems keep getting better*, p. 75.

23. The original work came from a study of teachers' uses of preparation time, much of which was reported in Hargreaves, *Changing teachers, changing times.*

24. Dufour, R. (1992), Work together: But only if you want to. *Phi Delta Kappan, 92*(5), 57–61.

25. Datnow, A. (2011), Collaboration and contrived collegiality: Revisiting Hargreaves in an age of accountability. *Journal of Educational Change, 12*(2), 147–158.

26. Datnow, Collaboration and contrived collegiality, p. 156.

27. Datnow, Collaboration and contrived collegiality, p. 156.

28. Hord, S. M. (1997), *Professional learning communities: Communities of continuous inquiry and improvement* (Austin, TX: Southwest Education Development Laboratory).

29. Dufour, R., Dufour, R., Eaker, R., & Karhanek, G. (2010), *Raising the bar and closing the gap: Whatever it takes* (Bloomington, IN: Solution Tree Press); and Eaker, R., & Keating, J. (2012), *Every school, every team, every classroom* (Bloomington, IN: Solution Tree Press).

30. Merton, R. K. (1949), *Social theory and social structure* (New York: The Free Press).

31. Sumara, D., & Davis, B. (2009), Using complexity science to study the impact of AISI on cultures of education in Alberta, *in* Hargreaves et al., *The learning mosaic*, pp. 34–50.

32. Wood, D. (2007), Teachers' learning communities: Catalyst for change or a new infrastructure for the status quo? *Teachers College Record, 109*(3), 699–739.

33. Naylor, C. (2005), *A teacher union's collaborative research agenda and strategies: One way forward for Canadian teacher unions in supporting teachers' professional development* (Vancouver: British Columbia Teachers Federation).

34. For a more extended discussion of the work of the California Teachers' Association in this educational reform, see Shirley & Hargreaves, *The global fourth way.*

35. See Hargreaves & Harris, *Performance beyond expectations.*

36. Hargreaves & Harris, *Performance beyond expectations.*

37. Taylor, R. H., & Sunstein, C. R. (2008), *Nudge: Improving decisions about health, wealth, and happiness* (New Haven, CT: Yale University Press).

38. Schwartz, B. (2004), *The paradox of choice: Why more is less* (New York: HarperCollins).

39. This example is drawn from data collected in the Essential for Some, Good for All study (2009–2012).

40. See Datnow, A., Borman, G., Stringfield, S., Rachuba, L., & Castellano, M. (2003), Comprehensive school reform in culturally and linguistically diverse contexts: Implementation and outcomes from a four-year study. *Educational Evaluation and Policy Analysis, 25*(2), 25–54.

41. See Hargreaves, A., Shirley, D., Evans, M. P., Stone-Johnson, C., & Riseman, D. (2007), *The long and short of school improvement: Summary of the evaluation report of the Raising Achievement Transforming Learning project of the Specialist Schools and Academies Trust* (London: Specialist Schools and Academies Trust).

42. See the website of the National College for School Leadership, http://www.nationalcollege.org.uk/.

43. See the websites of the National Teaching Schools, http://www.nationalcollege.org.uk/index/professional-development/teachingschools.htm; and the National Conference of State Legislatures (NCSL), http://www.ncsl.org/.

44. Hargreaves et al., *The long and short of school improvement.*

45. Hill, R. (2010), *Chain reactions: A thinkpiece on the development of chains of schools in the English school system* (Nottingham, UK: National College for School Leadership).

46. Lindsay, G., Muijs, D., Arweck, E., Harris, A., Chapman C., & Goodall, J. (2007), *Evaluation of the federations policy,* Evaluation of Federations Programme DCSF 2003171 (London: Department for Children's Services and Families).

47. Fullan, *The moral imperative realized.*

48. On collaborative competition, see Fullan, *All systems go.* On friendly rivalry and co-opetition, see Hargreaves & Harris, *Performance beyond expectations*; and Hargreaves, A., Shirley, D., Harris, A., & Boyle, A., (2010), The collaborative edge: How helping others helps you. *Principal, 89*(4), 16–21.

49. Leana, The missing link in school reform, pp. 29–35.

50. Robinson, V. (2011), *Student-centered leadership* (San Francisco: Jossey-Bass).

51. Leithwood, K. (2011), *Characteristics of high performing school systems,* Final Report (Toronto: Institute for Education Leadership).

CHAPTER 7: ENACTING CHANGE

1. Hunt, M. L. (1950), *Better known as Johnny Appleseed* (Philadelphia: Lippincott Williams & Wilkins).

2. Rosenberg, *Join the club,* p. xix.

3. Fullan, M. (2011), *Change leader: Learning to do what matters most* (San Francisco: Jossey-Bass).

4. Briskin et al., *The power of collective wisdom,* p. 4.

5. Follett, *The new state,* p. 230.

6. For more details on "simplexity" see Fullan, M. (2010), *Motion leadership* (Thousand Oaks, CA: Corwin Press).

7. Hunt, D. E. (1987), *Beginning with ourselves: In practice, theory, and human affairs* (Cambridge, MA: Brookline Books).

8. Hargreaves, A., & Shirley, D. (2009), The persistence of presentism. *Teachers College Record, 111*(11), 2505–2534.

9. Jackson, P. W. (1968), *Life in classrooms* (New York: Holt, Rinehart & Winston).

10. The expression "tyranny of the blank page" is widely attributed to William Faulkner, but we have been unable to locate a specific source.

11. McDonald & Shirley, *The mindful teacher.*

12. Bryk & Schneider, *Trust in schools.*

13. Morrell, M., Capparell, S., & Shackleton, A. (2002), *Shackleton's way: Leadership lessons from the great Antarctic explorer* (New York: Penguin).

14. Tower Hamlets is one of the cases in the Performance Beyond Expectations study (2011), which is documented in Hargreaves & Harris, *Performance beyond expectations.*

15. See the website of the School Administration Manager (SAM) Project, http://www.education.ky.gov/kde/administrative+resources/school+improvement/leadership+and+evaluation/kentucky+cohesive+leadership+system+%28kycls%29/school+administration+manager+project.htm.

16. Mourshed et al., *How the world's most improved school systems keep getting better,* p. 4.

17. Cabot Academy is one of the cases in the Performance Beyond Expectations study (2011), which is documented in Hargreaves & Harris, *Performance beyond expectations.*

18. Johnson, S. (2010), *Where good ideas come from: The natural history of innovation* (New York: Riverhead Books).

19. Sharratt, L., & Fullan, M. (2012), *Putting the FACES on data* (Thousand Oaks, CA: Corwin Press).

20. Office for Standards in Education (2008), *Using data, improving schools*, Foreword by Christine Gilbert (Manchester, UK: Author), retrieved from http://www.ofsted.gov.uk/resources/using-data-improving-schools.

21. Hargreaves, A., Halász, G., & Pont, B. (2007), *School leadership for systemic improvement in Finland: A case study report for the OECD activity Improving School Leadership* (Paris: OECD), p. 86, retrieved from http://www.oecd.org/officialdocuments/publicdisplaydocumentpdf/?cote=EDU/EDPC%282008%298&docLanguage=En.

22. Levin, B. (2008), *How to change 5000 schools* (Cambridge, MA: Harvard Education Press); and Fullan, *All systems go*.

23. OECD (2011, March 16–17), *Building a high-quality teaching profession: Lessons from around the world* (Paris: OECD), retrieved from http://www2.ed.gov/about/inits/ed/internationaled/background.pdf.

24. Rubinstein & McCarthy, *Reforming public school systems through sustained union–management collaboration*.

25. See *New York Times* (2011, September 25), New Haven's teacher improvement plan [editorial], retrieved from http://www.nytimes.com/2011/09/26/opinion/new-havens-teacher-improvement-plan.html?_r=1.

26. Commission on Effective Teachers and Teaching (2011), *Transforming teaching: Connecting professional responsibility with student learning* (Washington, DC: National Education Association).

27. See Permanent Delegation of Canada to the OECD (2009, March–April), *Canada OECD info* (Ottawa: Canada International), retrieved from http://www.canadainternational.gc.ca/oecd-ocde/marchapril2009-marsavril2009.aspx?view=da.

28. See UNICEF (2007), *Child poverty in perspective: An overview of child well-being in rich countries,* Innocenti Report Card 7 (Florence, Italy: UNICEF Innocenti Research Centre), retrieved from http://www.unicef.org/media/files/ChildPovertyReport.pdf.

29. Sweet, R., & Meates, A. (2010), *ICT and low achievers: What does PISA tell us?* (Paris: OECD), retrieved from http://www.oecd.org/dataoecd/29/29/33680762.pdf.

30. Mandela, N. (1995, May 8), Speech by President Nelson Mandela at the launch of the Nelson Mandela Children's Fund, Mahlamba'ndlopfu, Pretoria, South Africa.

Index

Accountability, 11, 22–23, 35–36
Achievement
  collaborative cultures and, 111–112
  overview, 191n5, 195n27
  professional capital and, 4
  quality of the teacher and, 15–16, 16–18, 42–44
  school-to-school collaboration and, 137–140
  stereotypes of teaching and, 26–27
  teaching and, 10–13, 22
  wrong strategies to obtain, 5–7
Action agenda, 7–9
Action guidelines for change
  overview, 152–154. *See also* Change
  schools and district leaders, 163–173
  state, national, and international organizations, 173–185
  teachers and, 154–163
Action research, 99. *See also* Reflective practice
Administrators. *See also* Principals
  action guidelines for, 162–163, 163–173, 165–167
  clusters, networks, and federations and, 142
  collaborative cultures and, 113–114
  contrived collegiality and, 117–126, 168–169
  failed solutions, 40
  individualism and, 108
  problems and dilemmas with teaching today, 35–36
  professional culture and, 144–146
  professional learning communities and, 133–136
  SAM Schools Project, 165–167
Advantaged social backgrounds, 13–14, 17
Alberta. *See* Canada
Alberta Initiative for School Improvement, 189n7
Alliances of schools, 138–140. *See also* Clusters, networks, and federations

American Federation of Teachers (AFT), 181–182
Appleseed, Johnny, 148–149
Architecture of buildings and classrooms, 108
Arranged collegiality, 118–119, 125. *See also* Contrived collegiality
Art of teaching, 27
Ashton, Pat, 62
Assistive technologies, 54. *See also* Technology
Attrition rates, 188n5, 192n10, 194n20. *See also* Retention rates
Australia
  action guidelines for change and, 170, 178, 179
  clusters, networks, and federations and, 170
  contrived collegiality and, 117–118
  professional capital and, 78
  quality of the teacher and, 18
  teacher bashing and, 37
Authenticity, 157
Autonomy
  change and, 149–150
  professional culture and, 144
  professionalism and, 80, 82

Balkanization, 106, 115–117, 206n17. *See also* Collaborative cultures; Culture
Becker, Howard, 69
Beginning with Ourselves (Hunt), 155
Best practice, 50–54
Beyond Expectations study, 130–131
Blair, Tony, 49–50
Blase, Jo, 8
Blase, Joe, 8
Boomer generation of teachers
  action guidelines for change and, 178
  career and, 70–72
  change and, 150
  overview, 76–77
Boyle, Alan, 138–140, 164–165
Braun, Henry, 132

About the Authors

ANDY HARGREAVES is the Thomas More Brennan Chair in the Lynch School of Education at Boston College. Before this, he taught primary school and lectured in several English universities, including Oxford. Prior to coming to Boston College, he was co-founder and director of the International Centre for Educational Change at the Ontario Institute for Studies in Education in Toronto. He was the founding Editor-in-Chief of the *Journal of Educational Change,* is the leading editor of the first and second *International Handbooks of Educational Change,* and created the Educational Change Special Interest Group within the American Educational Research Association. He presents to and consults widely with governments, foundations, teacher unions, administrator associations, and other groups across the world.

Professor Hargreaves has an Honorary Doctorate from Scandinavia's oldest university, Uppsala, in Sweden. He has received the Whitworth Award for outstanding contributions to educational research in Canada. His books have achieved outstanding writing awards from the American Educational Research Association, the American Libraries Association, the American Association of Colleges for Teacher Education, and the National Staff Development Council. His most recent books are *Sustainable Leadership* (with Dean Fink) and *The Fourth Way* (with Dennis Shirley). His books have been translated into many languages. His website is www.andyhargreaves.com.

MICHAEL FULLAN is Professor Emeritus at Ontario Institute for Studies in Education, University of Toronto, and Special Adviser on Education to the Premier of Ontario, Dalton McGuinty. He consults widely on system reform in countries around the world and conducts workshops on leadership for change.

Professor Fullan has written a number of award-winning books that have been published in many languages. His latest books are *Change Leader, Putting the FACES on Data* (with Lyn Sharratt) and the forthcoming *Stratosphere: Integrating Technology, Pedagogy, and Change Knowledge.* His website is www .michaelfullan.ca.